"What always amazes me about Dave Aaker is his uncanny ability to see through the fog and mist and discern a new and fundamental truth that in retrospect seems so perfectly obvious as to seem simplistic. It is just that no one else sees what Dave does. That is exactly the case with *Brand Relevance*. Aaker perceives that it is no longer brand preference that is pivotal but rather brand relevance has now become key. Brand relevance that yields sustainable differentiation resulting in new categories or subcategories of products or services where competitors are less or even non-relevant. Forget your line extensions and white space analyses, get on the brand relevance bandwagon."

—**Peter Sealey,** former chief marketing officer,
Coca-Cola and Columbia Pictures
and author, *Simplicity Marketing*

"Aaker offers a fresh approach to brand strategy by observing that most marketers spend their time trying to build or maintain brand preference when they should focus on building brand relevance wins through inventing new categories and subcategories to meet consumers' changing needs."

—**Philip Kotler,** S.C. Johnson & Son Distinguished
Professor of International Marketing at the
Northwestern University and management guru

"Dave has done it again! Students of brand management from the classroom to the boardroom will appreciate the insights, challenges, and practical perspectives of *Brand Relevance*. Like many of Dave's works, this will have a prominent place on my shelf of well-read, frequently-referenced business books."

—**Denice Torres,** president, North America
CNS Ortho-McNeil-Janssen Pharmaceuticals, Inc

"Dave Aaker has become the foremost authority on branding because of his knack for providing insightful, practical advice to marketers. *Brand Relevance* is Aaker at his best: Tackling a challenging problem with fresh ideas and compelling examples. He convincingly shows how brands can mean the most to consumers."

—**Kevin Lane Keller,** E. B. Osborn Professor of Marketing
at the Tuck School of Business at Dartmouth,
and author, *Strategic Brand Management*

"Aaker's concept of brand relevance provides an innovation-based path to win in the face of market dynamics."

—**David Stachon,** chief marketing officer,
ERGO Insurance Group

"Dave Aaker has taught me a lot over the years. Here he goes again. Always redefining. Clarity jumps off the first pages—it's less about the brand-preference battle than the brand-relevance war. We work hard at business schools to build students' capacity for clear problem statements. By bringing clarity to the real problem, he delivers great opportunity. I especially appreciate his focus on establishing relevance through disciplined process. I also appreciate his links to innovation and how to make it pay."

—**Richard K. Lyons,** dean, Haas School of Business, University of California, Berkeley

"Aaker has hit the nail on the head with *Brand Relevance*, perhaps the biggest challenge 21st century brands face is to risk innovating and—even more terrifying—transforming oneself. You've gotta take the leap or risk getting left behind."

—**Ann Lewnes,** chief marketing officer, Adobe

"David Aaker's *Brand Relevance* brings branded insight to the process of innovation. Loaded with powerful examples, his definition of 'sub-categories' provides a contextual sweet spot between close-in product improvements and highly elusive "transformational" innovations. David's strategic model brings a potent and practical question for business leaders to ask: 'Does this innovation create a new sub-category to which competitors are no longer relevant?' The numerous examples really help bring it to life"

—**Ian R. Friendly,** executive vice president, General Mills

"David Aaker's latest book is a downright challenge to marketers and strategists—stay the course with familiar approaches to building brand preference and risk the likelihood of being made irrelevant by those who jump right on Aaker's lessons. Despite the challenges involved with brand relevance, it's clearly a path to potential substantial growth."

—**Meredith Callanan,** vice president corporate marketing and communication, T. Rowe Price

"For an established brand like Allianz, Aaker's insights are a "wake up call" because a market leader like us can lose our position if new brands leverage innovation and technology to redefine insurance. We have a lot to lose if we lose the relevance game."

—**Joseph K. Gross,** executive vice president, Allianz SE

Brand Relevance

Brand Relevance

Making Competitors Irrelevant

David A. Aaker

JOSSEY-BASS
A Wiley Imprint
www.josseybass.com

Published by Jossey-Bass
A Wiley Imprint
989 Market Street, San Francisco, CA 94103-1741—www.josseybass.com

Readers should be aware that Internet Web sites offered as citations and/or sources for further
information may have changed or disappeared between the time this was written and when
it is read.

Limit of Liability/Disclaimer of Warranty: While the publisher and author have used their best
efforts in preparing this book, they make no representations or warranties with respect to the
accuracy or completeness of the contents of this book and specifically disclaim any implied
warranties of merchantability or fitness for a particular purpose. No warranty may be created or
extended by sales representatives or written sales materials. The advice and strategies contained
herein may not be suitable for your situation. You should consult with a professional where
appropriate. Neither the publisher nor author shall be liable for any loss of profit or any other
commercial damages, including but not limited to special, incidental, consequential, or other
damages.

Jossey-Bass books and products are available through most bookstores. To contact Jossey-Bass
directly call our Customer Care Department within the U.S. at 800-956-7739, outside the U.S.
at 317-572-3986, or fax 317-572-4002.

Jossey-Bass also publishes its books in a variety of electronic formats. Some content that appears
in print may not be available in electronic books.

Library of Congress Cataloging-in-Publication Data

Aaker, David A.
    Brand relevance : making competitors irrelevant / David A. Aaker. — 1st ed.
        p.   cm. — (The Jossey-Bass business and management series)
    Includes bibliographical references and index.
    ISBN 978-0-470-61358-0 (cloth)
    ISBN 978-0-470-92259-0 (ebk)
    ISBN 978-0-470-92260-6 (ebk)
    ISBN 978-0-470-92261-3 (ebk)
        1. Brand name products.   2. Branding (Marketing)   3. Technological innovations.
    I. Title.
    HD69.B7A21535 2011
    658.8'27—dc22

                                                                      2010036007

Printed in the United States of America
FIRST EDITION
HB Printing   10 9 8 7 6 5 4 3 2 1

The Jossey-Bass Business & Management Series

Contents

To my wife Kay and my daughters Jennifer, Jan, and Jolyn who inspire with their support, vitality, compassion, love, and friendship.

Preface

During the last ten years, I have been struck by how the concept of brand relevance could explain so much about strategic successes, market dynamics, and even brand declines. A brand could develop great marketing supported by large budgets but not make a dent in the market unless it drove a new category or subcategory of products or services, unless a new competitive arena in which the competitors were no longer relevant emerged. Then success could be dramatic in terms of sales, profits, and market position. It seems clear that success is about winning not the brand preference battle but, rather, the brand relevance war with an innovative offering that achieves sustainable differentiation by creating a new category or subcategory.

When you start looking, it is amazing how many examples of new categories and especially subcategories that appear in virtually all industries. It is clear, however, that achieving that result is not easy or without risks. There are many failures and disappointments, few of which are visible. Success requires timing— the market, the technology, and the firm all have to be ready. Further, the offering concept that will drive the new category or subcategory needs to be generated and evaluated, the new category or subcategory needs to be actively managed, and barriers against competitors have to be created. All of these tasks are difficult and require support from an organization that may have conflicting priorities and resource constraints.

I also observed that often brands were in decline not because they had lost their ability to deliver or the loyalty of their users was fading, but because they had became less relevant. What declining brands were selling was no longer what customers were buying, because customers were attracted by a new category or subcategory. Or the declining brands might have slipped out of the consideration set because they simply lost energy and visibility. In that case, the failure of brand management to understand the real problem meant that marketing programs were ineffective and resources were wasted or misdirected.

At the same time, my ongoing research and writing on business strategy, as reflected in my book Strategy Market Management, currently in its ninth edition, made me see that virtually all markets are now buffeted by change, not only in high tech but also in durables, business-to-business, services, and packaged goods. Change, driven by technology, market trends, and innovation of every type, is accelerated by our "instant media." The processes and constructs supporting the development of business strategies clearly need to be adapted and refined. To me the key is brand relevance. The way for a firm to get on top of its strategies in a time of change is to understand brand relevance, to learn how a firm can drive change through innovations that will create new categories and subcategories—making competitors less relevant—and how other firms can recognize the emergence of these new categories and subcategories and adapt to them.

The goal of this book is to show the way toward winning the brand relevance battle by creating categories or subcategories for which competitors are less relevant or not relevant at all, managing the perceptions of the categories or subcategories, and creating barriers protecting them. The book also looks at how brands can maintain their relevance in the face of market dynamics. Over twenty-five case studies provide insight into the challenges and risks of fighting brand relevance battles.

There are dozens of other strategy books that in one way or another talk about growth strategies based on innovations. They have made a significant contribution to strategic thought and practice. However, this book has several distinctive thrusts and features that are missing in much of this library. First, this book emphasizes branding and branding methods. In particular, it highlights the importance of defining, positioning, and actively managing the perceptions of the new category or subcategory. Second, it emphasizes the need to create barriers to entry so that the time in which competitors are irrelevant is extended. Third, it explicitly includes substantial innovation as well as transformational innovation as routes to new categories or subcategories. Finally, it also explicitly suggests that subcategories can be created as well as categories. For every opportunity of creating a new category or employing transformational innovation, there are many chances to create subcategories and use substantial innovation.

One objective of the book is to provide a process by which a firm can create new categories or subcategories and make competitors irrelevant. It involves four tasks, each of which is covered in a chapter: concept generation, evaluation, defining the category or subcategory, and creating barriers to competitors.

A second objective is to define the brand relevance concept and show its power as a way to drive and understand dynamic markets. Toward that end academic research is used to provide insights, and over two dozen case studies are presented that illustrate the challenges, risks, uncertainties, and payoffs of creating new categories or subcategories.

A third objective is to consider the threat of losing brand relevance, how it happens, and how it can be avoided. Although relevance dynamics represents an opportunity to create new markets, it also represents a risk for those brands who ignore market dynamics because they are unaware of the changes in their markets or because they are focused on a strategy that has worked in the past.

A final objective is to profile what characteristics an organization needs to have to support substantial or transformational innovation that will lead to new categories or subcategories.

I owe a debt to many for this book. The stimulating work of strategy and brand thinkers that preceded this effort helped me refine some ideas. Michael Kelly of Techtel, in many discussions over biking, helped spark my interest in relevance. My colleagues at Dentsu helped me refine and extend my ideas. The Prophet team is an inspiration with its incredible work. I especially thank Michael Dunn, a gifted CEO, who provided me with the bandwidth and support to write the book; Karen Woon, who was a sounding board throughout; and Andy Flynn, Agustina Sacerdote, Erik Long, and Scott Davis, who offered suggestions that made a difference. I also thank my friends Katy Choi and Jerry Lee, who are making the book happen in Korea with a huge event as well. The design team at Prophet, Stephanie Kim Simons, Marissa Haro, and Kelli Adams were instrumental in creating the cover. I would like to thank Kathe Sweeney and her colleagues at Jossey-Bass for having confidence in the book. I also would like to thank the production editor Justin Frahm and the copy editor Francie Jones who moved the process along and, more important, challenged me to improve the manuscript in both small and large ways. Finally I would like to thank my daughter, friend, and colleague Jennifer Aaker and her husband and coauthor Andy Smith who supported my efforts in so many ways.

You do not merely want to be considered just
the best of the best. You want to be considered the
only ones who do what you do.

—*Jerry Garcia, The Grateful Dead*

1

WINNING THE BRAND RELEVANCE BATTLE

First they ignore you. Then they ridicule you. Then
they fight you. Then you win.
                    —*Mahatma Gandhi*

Don't manage, lead.
                    —*Jack Welch, former GE CEO*
                    and management guru

Brand relevance has the potential to both drive and explain
market dynamics, the emergence and fading of categories and
subcategories and the associated fortunes of brands connected to
them. Brands that can create and manage new categories or subcategories making competitors irrelevant will prosper while others will be mired in debilitating marketplace battles or will be
losing relevance and market position. The story of the Japanese
beer industry and the U.S. computer industry illustrate.

The Japanese Beer Industry

For three and a half decades the Japanese beer market was
hypercompetitive, with endless entries of new products (on the
order of four to ten per year) and aggressive advertising, packaging innovations, and promotions. Yet the market share trajectory of the two major competitors during these thirty-five years
changed only four times—three instigated by the introduction of new subcategories and the fourth by the repositioning
of a subcategory. Brands driving the emergence or repositioning of the subcategories gained relevance and market position,

whereas the other brands not relevant to the new subcategories lost position—a remarkable commentary on what drives market dynamics.

Kirin and Asahi were the main players during this time. Kirin, the dominant brand from 1970 to 1986 with an unshakable 60 percent share, was the "beer of beer lovers" and closely associated with the rich, somewhat bitter taste of pasteurized lager beer. A remarkable run. There were no offerings that spawned new subcategories to disturb.

Asahi Super Dry Appears

Asahi, which in 1986 had a declining share that had sunk below 10 percent, introduced in early 1987 Asahi Super Dry, a sharper, more refreshing beer with less aftertaste. The new product, which contained more alcohol and less sugar than lager beers and had special yeast, appealed to a new, younger generation of beer drinkers. Its appeal was due in part to a carefully crafted Western image supported by its label (see Figure 1.1), endorsers, and advertising. Both the product and the image were in sharp contrast to Kirin.

In just a few years, dry beer captured over 25 percent of the market. In contrast, it took light beer eighteen years to gain 25 percent of the U.S. market. It was a phenomenon of which Asahi Super Dry, perceived to be the authentic dry beer, was the beneficiary. In 1988 Asahi's share doubled to over 20 percent and Kirin's fell to 50 percent. During the ensuing twelve years Asahi continued to build on its position in the dry beer category, and in 2001 it passed Kirin and became the number-one brand in Japan with a 37 percent share, a remarkable result. Think of Coors passing Anheuser-Busch, a firm with a long-term market dominance similar to the one Kirin enjoyed.

It is no accident that Asahi was the firm that upset the market. In 1985 Asahi had an aggressive CEO who above all wanted to change the status quo, both internally and externally. Toward that end he changed the organizational structure and culture to encourage innovation. Of course, he was "blessed" with financial and market crises. Kirin, however, had an organization entirely focused on maintaining the current momentum and on doing exactly what they had always done.

Kirin responded in 1988 with Kirin Draft Dry beer but, after having touted Kirin lager beer for decades, lacked credibility in the new space. Further, the ensuing "dry wars," in which Asahi forced Kirin to make changes to its packaging to reduce the similarity of Kirin Draft Dry to the Asahi product, reinforced the fact that Asahi was the authentic dry beer. Kirin, whose heart was never in making a beer that would compete with its golden goose with its rich tradition and many loyal buyers, was perceived by many as the bully trying to squash the feisty upstart. Over the ensuing years, a bewildering number of efforts by Kirin and the other beer firms to put a dent in the Asahi advance were unsuccessful.

Kirin Ichiban Arrives

The one exception to efforts to create new subcategories with new beer variants was Kirin Ichiban, introduced in 1990, made from a new and expensive process involving more malt; filtering at low temperature; and, most important, using only the "first press" product. Its taste was milder and smoother than Kirin Lager's, with no bitter aftertaste. Competitors were stymied by the cost of the process, the power of the Kirin Ichiban brand, and the distribution clout of Kirin. Kirin Ichiban caused a pause in the decline of the Kirin market share that lasted from 1990 to 1995. Its role in the Kirin portfolio steadily grew until, in 2005, it actually sold more than Kirin Lager—although the combination of the two was then far behind Asahi Super Dry.

Dry Subcategory is Reenergized

In 1994 Asahi, by this time the only dry beer brand, developed a powerful subcategory positioning strategy around both freshness and being the number-one draft beer with a global presence. While Asahi was enhancing the dry subcategory, Kirin was simultaneously damaging the lager subcategory. Perhaps irritated by Asahi's number-one-draft-beer claim, Kirin converted to a draft beer making process and changed Kirin Lager to Kirin Lager Draft (the original still was on the market as Kirin Lager Classic but was relegated to a small niche). Kirin tried to make Kirin Lager Draft more appealing to a younger audience, but instead its image became confused, and its core customer base was disaffected. As a result, from 1995 to 1998 the subcategory battle between dry and lager resulted in Asahi Super Dry extending its market share eight points to just over 35 percent, while Kirin was falling nine points to around 39 percent.

Happoshu Enters

In 1998 a new subcategory labeled *happoshu*, a "beer" that contained a low level of malt and thus qualified for a significantly lower tax rate, got traction when Kirin entered with its Kirin Tanrei brand (Suntory introduced the first happoshu beer in 1996 but lost its position to Tanrei). By early 2001, after this new subcategory had garnered around 18 percent of the beer market, Asahi finally entered, but could not dislodge Kirin. The Asahi entry had a decided taste disadvantage, in large part because Kirin Tanrei had a sharper taste that was reminiscent of Asahi Super Dry. Asahi wanted no such similarity for its happoshu entry because of the resulting potential damage to Asahi Super Dry.

By 2005 Kirin had taken leadership in both the happoshu subcategory and in another subcategory, a no-malt beverage termed "the third beer," which had an even greater tax advantage. From 2005 on, these two new subcategories captured over 40 percent of the Japanese beer market. In 2009 the two Kirin entries did well, with over three times the sales of the Asahi entries, and actually outsold the sum of Kirin Lager and Kirin Ichiban sales by 50 percent. As a result, Kirin recaptured market share leadership in the total beer category including happoshu and the third beer, albeit by a small amount, despite the fact that Asahi had nearly a two-to-one lead in the conventional beer category.

The changes in what people buy and in category and subcategory dynamics are often what drive markets. Figure 1.2 clearly shows the four times the market share trajectory in the Japanese beer market changed—all driven by subcategory dynamics. Brands that are relevant to the new or redefined category or subcategory, such as Asahi Super Dry in 1986 or Kirin Ichiban in 1990 or Kirin Tanrei in 1998, will be the winners. And brands that lose relevance because they lack some value proposition or are simply focused on the wrong subcategory will lose. That can happen insidiously to the dominant, successful brands, as with Kirin Lager in the mid-1980s and Asahi in the late 1990s.

Figure 1.1 Asahi Super Dry Can

Note the English terms.

Figure 1.2 The Asahi-Kirin Beer War

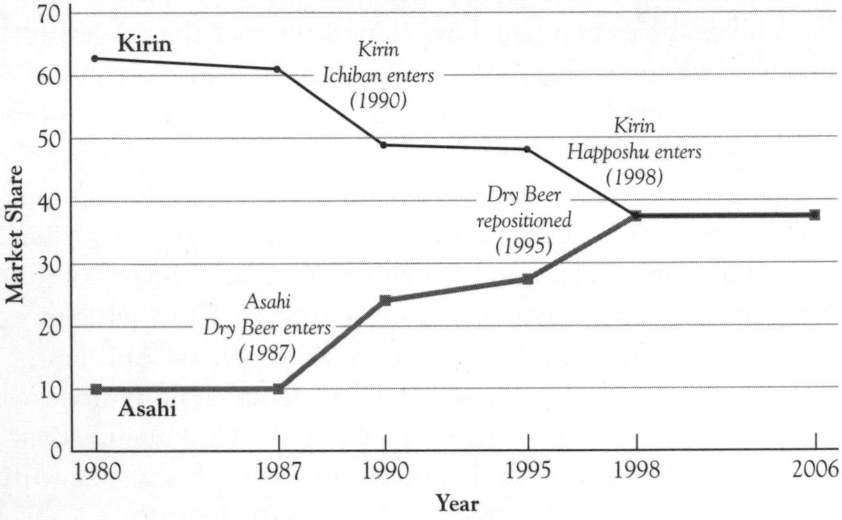

Note the importance of brands in the ability of firms to affect category and subcategory position. Kirin Lager captured the essence of lager and the Kirin heritage. Asahi Super Dry defined and represented the new dry subcategory, even when Kirin Draft Dry was introduced. Kirin Tanrei was the prime representative of the happoshu category. And the repositioning of Asahi Super Dry really repositioned the dry subcategory, because at that point Asahi was the only viable entry.

The U.S. Computer Industry

Consider also the dynamics of the U.S. computer industry during the last half century and how these dynamics affected the winners and losers in the marketplace. The story starts in the 1960s when seven manufacturers, all backed by big firms, competed for a place in the mainframe space. However, as "computers as hardware" suppliers they became irrelevant in the face of IBM, who defined its offering as a problem-relevant systems solution supplier and thus created a subcategory. Then came the minicomputer subcategory in the early 1970s, led by Digital Equipment Corporation (DEC), Data General, and HP, in which a computer served a set of terminals and in which the mainframe brands were not relevant.

The minicomputer business itself became irrelevant with the advent of servers and personal computers as hardware, and Data General and DEC faded while HP adapted by moving into other subcategories. Ken Olsen, the DEC founder and CEO, has famously been quoted as saying in 1977, "There is no reason why any individual would want a computer in his home." Although the quote was taken out of context, the point that emerging subcategories, in this case the personal computer (PC) subcategory, are often underestimated is a good one.[1]

The PC subcategory itself fragmented into several new subcategories driven by very different firms. IBM was the early dominant brand in the PC subcategory, bringing trust and reliability. Dell defined and led a subcategory based on building to order with up-to-date technology and direct-to-customer sales and service. A portable or luggable niche was carved out of the personal computer segment, initially by Osborne in 1981 with a twenty-four-pound monster and ultimately in 1983 by Compaq, who became the early market leader. Then came the laptop, which was truly portable. Toshiba led this subcategory at first, until the IBM ThinkPad took over the leadership position with an attractive design and clever features.

Sun Microsystems led in the network workstation market, and SGI (Silican Graphics) led in the graphic workstation market, both involving heavy-duty, single-user computers. The workstation market evolved into the server subcategory. Sun was a dominant server brand in the late 1990s for Internet applications, but fell back as the Internet bubble burst.

In 1984 Apple launched the Macintosh (Mac), creating a new subcategory of computers. It was revolutionary because it changed the interaction of a user with a computer by introducing new tools, a new vocabulary, and a graphical user interface. There was a "desktop" with intuitive icons, a mouse that changed communication with a computer, a toolbox, windows to keep track of applications, a drawing program, a font manager, and on and on. And it was in a distinctively designed cabinet under the Apple brand. In the words of the Mac's father, Steve Jobs, it was "insanely great."[2] The 1984 ad in which a young women in bright red shorts flings a sledgehammer into a screen where "big brother" (representing of course IBM) spouts out an ideology of sameness was one of the most notable ads of modern times. For the next decade and more there were core Mac users, especially among the creative community, who were passionately loyal to the Mac and enjoyed visible, self-expressive benefits from buying and using the brand. It took six years for Microsoft to come up with anything comparable.

In 1997 Steve Jobs, returning from a forced twelve-year exile from Apple, was the driving force behind the iMac ("i" initially represented "Internet enabled" but came to mean simply "Apple"). The iMac provided a new chapter to the Mac saga and became a new—or at least a revised—subcategory. The best-selling computer ever, its design and coloring were eye-catching. Incorporating the then-novel use of the USB port, Apple made the remarkable decision to omit a floppy disk. Instead of dooming the product as many predicted, this made the product appear advanced—made for an age in which people would share files over the Internet instead of via disks.

Another computer revolution is under way. Products such as smart phones and tablets like iPad are replacing laptop and even desktop computers for many applications. The new winners are firms such as Apple, Google with its Android software, the communication firms AT&T and Verizon, server farms, and application entrepreneurs. The losers will be the conventional computer hardware and software businesses.

As in the case of Japanese beer, it was the emergence of new subcategories such as solutions-focused mainframes, minicomputers, workstations, servers, PCs, Macintosh, portables, laptops, notebooks, and tablets that create the market dynamics that changed the fortunes of the participates. Again and again competitors fell back or disappeared, and new ones emerged as new subcategories were formed. The ongoing marketing efforts involving advertising, trade shows, and promotions had little impact on the market dynamics. A similar analysis could be made concerning most industries.

■ ■ ■

Brand relevance is a powerful concept. Understanding and managing relevance can be the difference between winning by becoming isolated from competitors or being mired in a difficult market environment where differentiation is hard to achieve and often short-lived. It is not easy, however, but requires a new mind-set that is sensitive to market signals, is forward looking, and values innovation.

This chapter starts by defining and comparing the two perspectives of the marketplace, the brand preference model and the brand relevance model. It then describes the central concept of creating a new category or subcategory and the role of substantial and transformational innovation in that process. The next section describes the new management task, to influence and manage the perceptions and position of the new category and subcategory. The chapter then turns to the potential power of the first mover advantage and the value of being a trend driver. The payoff of creating new categories and subcategories is then detailed and followed by a description of the four tasks that are necessary to create a new category or subcategory. Finally, the brand relevance concept is contrasted with approaches put forth by other authors toward a similar objective and the rest of the book is outlined.

Gaining Brand Preference

There are two ways to compete in existing markets—gaining brand preference and making competitors irrelevant.

The first and most commonly used route to winning customers and sales focuses on generating brand preference among the brand choices considered by customers, on beating the competition. Most marketing strategists perceive themselves to be engaged in a brand preference battle. A consumer decides to buy an established product category or subcategory, such as SUVs. Several brands have the visibility and credibility to be considered—perhaps Lexus, BMW, and Cadillac. A brand, perhaps Cadillac, is then selected. Winning involves making sure the customer prefers Cadillac to Lexus and BMW. This means that Cadillac has to be more visible, credible, and attractive in the SUV space than are Lexus and BMW.

The brand preference model dictates the objectives and strategy of the firm. Create offerings and marketing programs that will earn the approval and loyalty of customers who are buying the established category or subcategory, such as SUVs. Be preferred over the competitors' brands that are in that category or subcategory, which in turn means being superior in at least one of the dimensions defining the category or subcategory and being at least as good as competitors in the rest. The relevant market consists of those who will buy the established category or subcategory, and market share with respect to that target market is a primary measure of success.

The strategy is to engage in incremental innovation to make the brand ever more attractive or reliable, the offering less costly, or the marketing program more effective or efficient. It is all about continuous improvement—faster, cheaper, better—which has its roots in Fredrick Taylor's scientific management with his time and motion studies a century ago and continues with such approaches as Kaisan (the Japanese continuous improvement programs), Six Sigma, reengineering, and downsizing.

This classic brand preference model is an increasingly difficult path to success in today's dynamic market because customers are not inclined or motivated to change brand loyalties. Brands are perceived to be similar at least with respect to the delivery of functional benefits, and often these perceptions are accurate. Why rethink a product and brand decision that has worked when alternatives are similar? Why go to the trouble to even locate alternatives? Seeking alternatives is a mental and behavioral effort with little perceived payoff. Further, people prefer the familiar, whether in regard to a route to work, music, people, nonsense words, or brands.

It is inordinately difficult to create an innovation that will significantly alter market momentum. When there is an enhanced offering that should stimulate switching behavior, competitors usually respond with such speed and vigor that any advantage is often short-lived. Further, marketing programs that upset the market are rare because brilliance is hard to come by and resources for implementation are scarce.

As a result of the difficulty of changing customer momentum and the fact that there are diminishing returns to cost-reduction programs, preserving margins in the face of capable and well-funded competitors is challenging. A market with competitors engaging in brand preference strategies is usually a recipe for unsatisfactory profitability.

Such Japanese beer companies as Asahi and also Suntory and Sapporo pursued brand preference strategies from 1960 to 1986 without making a dent in the Kirin position. The heritage and appeal of Kirin's lager beer, its loyal buyer base, and the associated distribution clout made Kirin able to resist all types of product and marketing initiatives of competitors, aggressive and clever though they were.

Brand preference strategies, the focus of most firms, are particularly risky in dynamic markets because incremental innovation will often be made inconsequential by marketplace dynamics. Bob McDonald, the CEO of P&G, introduced the acronym VUCA to describe today's world—volatile, uncertain, complex, and ambiguous.[3] Product categories and subcategories are no longer stable but rather emerging, fading, and evolving. Products are proliferating at a faster and faster rate.

There are a host of forceful trends that provide impetus for new categories and subcategories. For a flavor of the trends out there, consider the following:

- The emergence of Web sites as knowledge centers has allowed brands to become go-to authorities. Pampers, for example, redefined its business from selling diapers to providing innovation on baby care and a hub for social interaction around babies.
- The green movement and sustainability objectives have affected brand choice. Firms from autos to stores to packaged goods, and on and on have adjusted their operations and offerings to be responsive.
- The growing popularity of Asian cuisine has created subcategories in restaurants and in packaged goods.
- The projected growth of the over-sixty-five population from just under forty million in 2010 to over seventy million in 2030 creates opportunities to develop subcategories from gift stores to cruises to cars.
- People taking control of their personal health suggests opportunities for a host of medical support categories to emerge, ranging from weight control to physical therapy to mental stimulation.

Change is in the air everywhere, and change affects what people buy and what brands are relevant. Marketing strategies need to keep up. A winning strategy today may not prevail tomorrow. It might not even be relevant tomorrow. Success becomes a moving target, and the same management styles that worked in the past may be losing their ability to generate ongoing wins. Blindly following a strategy that advocates a firm to "stick to your knitting," "keep your focus," "avoid diluting your energies," and so on may still be optimal but is more risky than ever.

The Brand Relevance Model

The second route to competitive success is to change what people buy by creating new categories or subcategories that alter the ways they look at the purchase decision and user experience. The goal is thus not to simply beat competitors; it is rather to make them irrelevant by enticing customers to buy a category or subcategory for which most or all alternative brands are not considered relevant because they lack context visibility or credibility. The result can be a market in which there is no competition at all for an extended time or one in which the competition is reduced or weakened, the ticket to ongoing financial success.

Defining Relevance

To better understand relevance, consider a simple model of brand-customer interaction in which brand choice involves four steps organized into two distinct phases, brand relevance and brand preference, as shown in Figure 1.3.

Step One: The person (customer or potential customer) needs to decide which category or subcategory to buy and use. Too often a brand is not selected or even considered because the person fails to select the right category or subcategory rather than because he or she preferred one brand over another. If a person decides to buy a minivan rather than a sedan or an SUV, for example, he or she will exclude a large set of brands that are not credible in the minivan space.

One challenge is to create the category or subcategory by conceiving and executing an innovative offering. Another challenge is to manage the resulting category or subcategory and to influence its visibility, perceptions, and people's loyalty to it. The goal is to encourage people to think of and select the category or subcategory.

The fact that the person selects the category or subcategory, perhaps a compact hybrid, makes the starting place very

Figure 1.3 Brand Preference Versus Brand Relevance

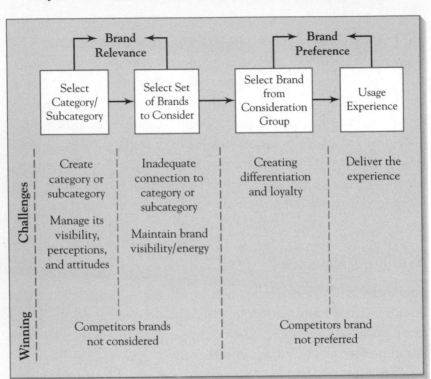

different than under the brand preference context in which the category or subcategory is assumed to be given. Instead of encompassing only those buying an established category or subcategory, the target market is much broader, consisting of anyone who might benefit from the new category or subcategory. The selection of the category or subcategory is now a crucial step that will influence what brands get considered and thus are relevant.

Step Two: The person needs to determine which brands to consider. This is a screening step to exclude brands that are unacceptable for some reason. A brand is not relevant unless it appears in the person's consideration set. There are two principle relevance challenges: category or subcategory relevance and visibility and energy relevance (these will be elaborated in Chapter Ten).

Category or Subcategory Relevance: The firm as represented by a brand needs to be perceived as making what the people are buying and have credibility with respect to its offering. There can't be a perception within the selected category or subcategory that the brand lacks the capability or interest to be a player, or that the brand lacks a key characteristic of the category or subcategory.

Visibility and Energy Relevance: The brand, particularly when establishing or entering a new category or subcategory, needs to have visibility—it needs to come to mind when the product category or subcategory is selected. In addition, the brand needs to create and maintain enough energy so that it does not fade into the background. Brands that are tired, lack personalities, are not associated with innovation, and are simply uninteresting may not make the consideration set even though they are known and credible.

Step Three: Perhaps after some evaluation, the person picks one brand. That brand is preferred over others, perhaps because of a logical reason, due to some emotional or self-expressive benefit, or perhaps simply because of convenience or habit. The challenge is to create differentiation and bases of loyalty so that the brand is preferred.

Step Four: The person uses the product or service, and a user experience results. The use evaluation will depend not only on his or her expectations of the brand but also according to expectations of the product category or subcategory as conceptualized in the first step. The user experience can influence the next cycle of brand-person interaction.

Brand relevance involves the first two steps. A brand will be relevant if it is included in the consideration set for a target category or subcategory and if that category or subcategory precipitates the decision. Both conditions are needed. If either is missing, the brand lacks relevance and no amount of differentiation, positive attitudes, or brand-customer relation-ships will help.

More formally we define brand relevance as occurring when two conditions are met:

- *The target category or subcategory is selected.* There is a per-ceived need or desire on the part of a customer for the targeted category or subcategory, which is defined by some combination of attributes, applications, user groups, or other distinguishing characteristics.
- *The brand is in the consideration set.* The customer consid-ers the brand when he or she is making a decision to buy or use that target category or subcategory. In other words, the brand passes the screening test.

Steps three and four define brand preference. One brand is preferred within a set of brands being considered. In static mar-kets, brand preference is the primary goal of competition and marketing but, as already noted, this type of competition is dif-ficult and frustrating and markets are increasingly dynamic, which makes brand preference strategies futile.

Winning under the brand relevance model is now qualita-tively different than under brand preference competition. Under the brand preference model, the winning brand is preferred to others in the established category or subcategory. Under brand relevance, in contrast, winning occurs when other brands are not considered given the selection of the category or subcate-gory. Some or all competitor brands are not visible and credible with respect to the new category or subcategory, even though in other established categories they might not only be visible and credible but even have the highest reputation and customer loy-alty. When competitors' brands are not considered, the only rel-evant brand wins by default.

Relevance and preference are interrelated. In particular, rele-vance affects both components of brand preference. Defining and framing the category or subcategory will affect brand perceptions and thus brand preference. For example, if the category or subcategory is redefined to elevate the importance of a benefit, such as safety in automobiles, that benefit will play a larger role in the brand preference decision. Further, because relevance can affect the consideration set such that brands are excluded, the preference challenge may be reduced. At the extreme, if the consideration set is reduced to one, the preference decision is dictated by relevance.

Brand preference can also affect brand relevance. If a brand is preferred because of a compelling brand proposition, a strong personality, a satisfying user experience, and a positive customer relationship, then it will affect the consideration set and may well influence or drive attitudes toward the category or subcategory. Further, if the brand's user experience exceeds expectations, the brand should become more prominent in a person's mind. So if a Prius succeeds in generating interest, energy, and admiration, it will be firmly in the consideration set and should also reinforce the category or subcategory selection decision. Similarly, if the in-store experience at Nordstrom is positive, then this will reinforce the attitude toward a high-touch retail experience and the inclusions of Nordstrom in the consideration set.

Creating New Categories or Subcategories

The brand relevance strategy is to create offerings so innovative that new categories and subcategories will be formed. The idea is to create a competitive arena in which your competitors are at a decided disadvantage and avoid others in which that condition is missing. Sun Tzu, the military strategist, said over two thousand years ago that "the way is to avoid what is strong and to strike at what is weak."[4]

The opportunity is to redefine the market in such a way that the competitor is irrelevant or less relevant, possibly by making the competitor's strengths actually become weaknesses. For example, when Asahi introduced dry beer, the strength of Kirin, namely its heritage and reputation as a superior lager beer that our fathers drank, became a significant weakness in an emerging market that connected with young, cool, and Western.

A new category or subcategory will be characterized by having a new:

- *Competitor set* that will be empty or be occupied with brands that are few in number and weak
- *Definition of the category or subcategory*, with a clear point of differentiation from other categories or subcategories
- *Value proposition* changing or augmenting the basis for a relationship with a brand or creating a new one
- *Loyal customer base* that is economically worthwhile
- *Set of barriers to competitors* based on strategic assets or competencies

Gaining brand preference, of course, will also attempt to achieve clear points of differentiation, a strong value proposition, and a loyal customer base. So what is the difference between seeking brand preference and creating a new category or subcategory? The difference can be difficult to discern. It depends in part on the degree of differentiation, the strength of the new value proposition, and the size and intensity of the loyalty engendered. It also depends on the length of time these brand advantages will be projected to last. If the advantage is short-lived, such as a blockbuster promotion, then it will largely be a brand preference action, even if its impact is large.

The difference from brand preference is clear when the change in the offering is qualitatively different as opposed to having enhanced features or performance. A hybrid is a different kind of car and a laptop computer is a different computer concept. Of course, each of these has associated benefits, but the category or subcategory is not thought of at that level. You are now in the market for a hybrid and not a car that gets superior gas mileage, or you are seeking a laptop rather than one with a small footprint.

The difference is more subtle when the change in the offering represents a substantial enhancement of the offering's ability to deliver value, differentiation, and loyalty rather than a different type of offering. For example, the brand might perform noticeably better, like a Lexus 460, or it could have an added, meaningful feature in the packaging, such as the one that allows ketchup to be stored so that it is ready to serve. If that change is minor, it will be an aid to the brand preference battle. However, if the change is significant and meaningful to customers, there is a higher potential to form a new category or subcategory. Customers will have a reason to exclude other brands rather than to simply not prefer them.

Another difference is that in the brand relevance model the differentiation will be sustainable. Differentiation in the brand preference model is often marginal and temporary as competitors quickly copy. The key to forming a new category or subcategory is for the differentiation to be sustainable enough to provide a significant window to leverage the new category or subcategory before competitors become relevant. That means there are barriers to the new category or subcategory in the form of strategic assets or competencies that are substantial and inhibit competitors. A *strategic asset* is a resource, such as a brand's equity or installed customer base. A *strategic competency* is what a business unit does exceptionally well—such as managing a customer relationship program.

There are a host of sources of barriers that can turn a short-term point of differentiation into one that sustains (to be described in Chapter Nine). Among these barrier sources are protected technology, such as the Kirin Ichiban happoshu beer-making capability; a size or scale effect, such as that which Amazon and eBay have enjoyed; an operations advantage like the one UPS has developed; a design breakthrough like Chrysler had in its minivan innovation in the early 1980s; brand equity; or the loyalty of a customer base. Customer loyalty (with its associated brand strength) is often the most important barrier or at least plays a key supporting role. Whether the loyalty is based on habit and convenience or intense emotional or self-expressive benefits, it can be costly for competitor to overcome.

The Innovation Continuum

There is an innovation continuum, summarized in Figure 1.4, that spans incremental to substantial to transformational that reflects the extent to which the offering enhancement affects the marketplace. In a healthy business context a firm will make an effort to improve their product or service. The question is, What is the impact of that offering improvement and how long will that impact last? When does it create a new category or subcategory?

Incremental innovation will provide modest improvement that will affect brand preference. The level of differentiation will therefore be minor. In some cases the improvement will be so modest or so under the radar or so unappreciated by customers that its impact will not be noticeable, although an accumulation of such enhancements might have an effect. In others, the incremental innovation will provide a measurable increase

Figure 1.4 Innovation Continuum

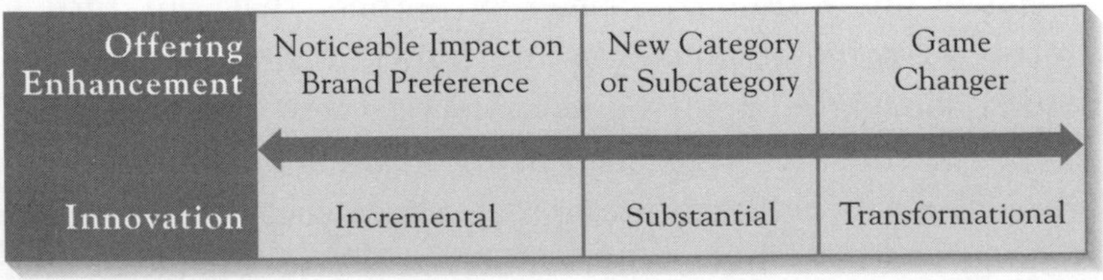

Offering Enhancement	Noticeable Impact on Brand Preference	New Category or Subcategory	Game Changer
Innovation	Incremental	Substantial	Transformational

in brand health and loyalty. But in either case it is a brand preference play.

When the innovation is substantial, there is an offering enhancement that is so noteworthy that a group of customers will not consider a brand that is not comparable. The offering might be a new feature like the Heavenly Bed at Westin. Or there might be a performance improvement that is significant, such as superior safety, economy, or design. With a substantial innovation the basic offering and competitive go-to-market strategies may be the same or have only minor differences, but the improvement in the offering will be so substantial that it defines a new category or subcategory. The resulting differentiation will be major, noticeable, and even "newsworthy" in the buying context. The iMac, with its novel design, was one such substantial innovation, as was Asahi Super Dry beer. The offering in each case was very similar to other subcategories, but a new set of dimensions was created that provided the basis for a new subcategory definition. The result was a change so substantial that customers were motivated to rethink their loyalties and perceptions of the category or subcategory. If the new dimension was missing from a competitive brand, that brand would not be considered.

The distinction between incremental and substantial is at the heart of the matter. A judgment by the involved managers that is needed is made difficult by the bias that exists. Most managers are inclined to view many incremental innovations as substantial because they are substantial in their minds. So the decision as to whether an innovation is incremental or substantial needs to be made based on more objective thinking and data. Chapter Eight will address such evaluation more fully.

When the innovation is transformational, the basic offering has changed qualitatively to the extent that existing offerings and ways of doing business are obsolete for a target segment or application, and existing competitors are simply not relevant. It will involve a new technology, a reconfiguration of the product, a different approach to operations or distribution, or a radical change to some other strategic lever that will qualitatively change the value proposition, the bases for loyalty, the way the offering is perceived, and the assets and competencies needed to deliver it. The resulting difference is dramatic, creating a marketplace game changer. The new category or subcategory will be easy to identify.

Transformational innovation is also termed *disruptive innovation*—it disrupts the competitive landscape. Tide (Ariel outside the United States) introduced a synthetic detergent technology that made soap powders obsolete. Southwest Airlines introduced a fun, up-beat personality and point-to-point journeys that changed air travel. Dell Computers, mini steel mills, and Gillette razors represent innovations that changed their respective industries. In the grocery store, Odwalla's new way of delivering fresh fruit drinks made frozen orange juice obsolete for some.

The distinction between a substantial and a transformational innovation is not always clear-cut. However, in either case, a new category or subcategory is formed. For example, a technology that enabled the introduction of baby carrots created a new subcategory, resulting in a sharp reduction in the sales of carrots presented in a conventional manner. Whether that is a substantial or a transformational innovation could be debated. Similarly, Cisco introduced a new-generation videoconference technology called Telepresence that uses massive amounts of bandwidth to provide a high-fidelity experience, making it a viable alternative for in-person meetings for firms with far-flung operations. It too could be classified either way.

The distinction between transformational, substantial, and incremental need not be based on the magnitude of a technological breakthrough. It is rather based on how much the market is affected and on whether a new category or subcategory is formed. Enterprise Rent-A-Car, who provided rental cars to people whose cars were in repair, was a transformational innovation because it represented such a different value proposition, target segment, set of assets and competencies, and business model. But the innovation that supported the company was minor, mainly in process. When Westin introduced a better bed in 1999, called the Heavenly Bed, it was not an R&D breakthrough that was involved. The bed simply used existing technology and featured upgraded quality, but it could be considered transformational because it changed the way hotels are perceived and evaluated.

Sometimes a group of incremental innovations can combine to create a substantial or even transformational innovation. Some breakout retailers, such as Whole Foods Market, have a host of incremental innovations. By themselves each of these incremental enhancements would not be noteworthy, but together they can be category or subcategory creators and even game changers.

A substantial or transformational innovation may not even involve a change in the offering. It can be driven by a reframing of the category or subcategory. DeBeers reframed their target category from jewelry to expressions of love. Thus the "Diamonds are forever" line, plus the associations with marriage and weddings, recast the category without any changes in its offering. DeBeers was no long competing with other firms selling gems or jewelry.

Identifying whether an innovation is incremental is crucial because this affects the management and investment behind that innovation. If it is incremental then there is no opportunity to create a new subcategory, and the management challenges and investment that go along with forming a new subcategory can be avoided. However, if the innovation is substantial and offers an opportunity to create a new category or subcategory, it is vital that the innovation be so labeled so that the necessary programs are developed and investments made. Of course, making the distinction between incremental and substantial is not always easy. As already noted, what brand champions think is substantial is often regarded by consumers, who live in a cluttered and dynamic media environment, to be incremental.

A major risk is that an opportunity will be lost because an innovation that had the potential to create a new category or subcategory was underestimated, because the organization was not set up to consider or pursue such options or because resources were absorbed elsewhere. This risk is particularly insidious because it has no visible impact on the financials, and yet a major missed opportunity can materially affect the strategies and fortunes of a organization going forward. Where would the Virgin brand and firm be today had it turned its back on the airline opportunity?

The other risk, more visible, is that incremental change will be misconstrued as a major one and an effort to create a new category or subcategory failed and absorbed precious resources and risk capital. Certainly there were a host of new products in the Japanese beer market that flamed out despite substantial investments and high expectations.

When evaluating the position of an innovation on the continuum, the extent to which the five characteristics of a new category or subcategory are achieved should form the basis of the analysis. Will the potential cast of characters among competitors change? Will what is being bought be different and new making the existing offerings irrelevant? Is there a qualitatively new value proposition? Is there a new base of loyal customers that will emerge? In addition, will competitor barriers be formed so that the innovation will have legs, will not be a short-term success?

Ultimately, it is the marketplace that will decide where the changed offering is on the continuum. Often an innovation or offering enhancement will be perceived by the firm as capable of changing the marketplace. In reality, however, it may be viewed by the market as another enhancement in a blur of competing claims. A package with the words "new and improved" on it is unlikely to change fundamental choice processes.

Most organizations lack a healthy mix of transformational, substantial, and incremental innovations. One study concluded that the percentage of major innovations in development portfolios dropped from 20.2 to 11.5 from 1990 to 2004. And from the mid-1990s to 2004 the percentage of total sales attributed to transformational innovation fell from 32.6 to 28.0 in 2004. There is a bias toward incremental, "little i" innovations. It is caused in part by the fact that incremental innovations for the existing core businesses tend to have the support of executives who are generating the bulk of the firm sales and profits, and in part because the payoff seems more certain and quantifiable. More on this bias and how it can be neutralized in Chapter Eleven.

Levels of Relevance

A brand is not necessarily relevant or irrelevant. In some cases, there will be a spectrum of relevance. The fuzziness or uncertainty can occur because the new category or subcategory is not yet the clear best choice for a customer. There may be a probability that it will be selected but one that is not near either certainty or zero probability.

Relevance fuzziness can also occur because of uncertainty as to whether a brand has visibility and credibility in the new space. Some brands will be coded by customers as being in the consideration set of a category or subcategory with confidence all the time. Others will never make the cut, and they are irrelevant. However, there will be others that may be relevant some of the time. In any case a fuzzy boundary can exist that separates the relevant brands from the irrelevant.

The uncertainty as to which brands are relevant will depend on the clarity of the definition of the category or subcategory. If the definition has some uncertainty, ambiguity, or fuzziness, the composition of the set of relevant brands may change depending on circumstances, the application, the brand's availability and price, the competitor price, and so on. Nothing is simple.

The New Brand Challenge

Creating a new product category or subcategory requires a new brand and marketing perspective. It is not enough to manage the brand; it is necessary also to manage the perception of the category or subcategory and to influence what category or subcategory people will buy as opposed to what brand they prefer. Asahi was able to fight off a much bigger and more resourced competitor precisely because they managed the dry beer subcategory brand from the outset while simultaneously growing its sales. And in the mid-1990s they repositioned the subcategory to regain a healthy market share growth rate.

Defining and managing the category or subcategory are new and foreign to brand and marketing strategists. The familiar challenge, in addition to differentiating the brand from competitors, is to position a brand as being relevant to an existing category or subcategory. IBM is in the service business, for example, or HP makes routers. However, when the challenge is to define and manage the category or subcategory and differentiate it from other categories or subcategories, the task is much different. The focus is not on alternative brands but alternative categories or subcategories, which is qualitatively different. The task is to build the category or subcategory even though a competitor could become relevant and benefit.

A category or subcategory is not a brand. A brand has a name reflecting an organization that stands behind the offering. Although a category or subcategory sometimes has a name, such as dry beer or happoshu, it often does not and has to rely on a description instead. More important, a brand has an organization behind it, whereas a category or subcategory in general does not. The exception is when the category or subcategory is represented by a single brand and its organization.

Nevertheless, a category or subcategory shares some similarities with a brand. It is defined by a set of rich associations that need to be prioritized and managed. It is the object of choice decisions. People can have varying degrees of loyalty to it.

It is defined by its associations. The management of a category or subcategory is also similar to managing any brand. In particular, the firm needs a plan to make the category or subcategory become visible, to identify its aspirational associations, and to design programs to realize them. These challenges will be discussed in detail in Chapter Eight.

A basic task is to identify the priority aspirational associations, usually one to five in number, which will define the new category or subcategory. These associations, which can be selected from a larger set of aspirational associations, can include features, benefits, personality traits, values, user imagery, applications, or any other descriptor that is capable of defining a category or subcategory and attracting people to it. The association set should differentiate the category or subcategory from alternatives, appeal to customers, deliver functional and, if possible, provide self-expressive and emotional benefits, and drive choice decisions. It should also be designed to include the brand as a relevant option and provide barriers to other brands to gain relevance. The definition should be clear as to what brands qualify as relevant to the category and subcategory and which do not because they are deficient on one of these associations.

The dry beer subcategory might be defined as crisp with less after taste, Western, and cool. After the reposition, it could add global presence and fresh product to the defining set. The lager category might be defined as the beer drinkers favorite, lager taste, and the beer my father drinks.

A second task is positioning. One or more of the defining associations should be identified to guide the short-term communication task. With a new category, the challenge is to identify one or two associations that will tell a compelling story and frame the category in such a way that the brand will have an ongoing relevance advantage. A brand such as TiVo, which had a host of advantages surrounding the complex DVR (digital video recorder) had trouble finding the right position and thus struggled at exploiting its first-mover advantage.

In the case of a subcategory, the positioning will usually be based on those associations that are driving the definition of the subcategory. For example, Bud Light Golden Wheat has all the associations of Bud Light including the fact that it is a light beer, but the driver of the subcategory is the fact that it is a wheat beer with a hint of a citric taste.

The positioning might differ by segment. One subset of the defining associations might be used for one segment and another for a second segment. Thus Asahi could have emphasized the young, Western, cool personality for those in their twenties and the crisp clean taste for older beer drinkers.

The third task, to build the "brand," is to communicate the category and subcategory and make it appealing. That means it needs to break through the clutter and perceptual barriers by leveraging the substantial or transformational innovation to create a buzz, a feeling that this new category or subcategory is interesting and worth talking about. It also means an understanding of perceptual cues that will stimulate people to think about and perhaps talk about the category or subcategory. If possible, metaphors, stories, and symbols should be employed.

How can a category or subcategory be built? In general, the best way is to use the brand and its brand-building programs to create the category and subcategory visibility, image, and loyalty. The ultimate is to have the brand represent the category or subcategory as its exemplar, a concept described in more detail in Chapter Two. In that case the category or subcategory will be referred to by the exemplar brand such as iPod, Jell-O, or A.1. steak sauce. A customer will describe the category or subcategory in terms of the exemplar: I want Jell-O, A.1., an iPod, or a comparable product.

The brand in assuming the exemplar role will need to focus on defining and building the category or subcategory. The brand attributes will tend to be implied rather than explicit taking on the characteristics of the category or subcategory. The idea is to sell the category or subcategory rather than the brand.

Such a tack, of course, runs the risk of being suboptimal when the brand encounters a brand preference context. There are advantages, however, in promoting the new category or subcategory rather than the offering brand.

First, a new category or subcategory is inherently more interesting and newsworthy than another offering, even a new one, and can be in a better position to deliver self-expressive benefits. A customer may have a relationship with a category or subcategory that is stronger than that with a brand. A person might believe that attending a high-end spa says a lot about him or her and that the spa brand is less important. A mountain climber will get respect from engaging in the activity, and the equipment brand will be of lesser importance.

Second, information about a category or subcategory can be more credible than a communications campaign promoting a brand, which can appear self-serving. The brand message is then implied rather than stated. Any brand that is so knowledgeable and excited about a new category or subcategory will likely be perceived as an innovative and capable exemplar, a brand that represents the category or subcategory. The exemplar role will be described in more detail in Chapter Two). If Fiber One cereal communicates that high fiber is a good characteristic of food rather than that Fiber One has more fiber than other cereal brands, the message will be more credible.

Third, using the brand as a vehicle to promote the category or subcategory will create a link between the two. For a brand to be relevant to the new category or subcategory, there needs to be a link established. For a firm to establish a new category or subcategory and fail to link its brand to it would be tragic; the brand would not then be relevant. The Asahi Super Dry brand by promoting the new subcategory became closely linked to it and reinforced its role as subcategory exemplar.

The exemplar role may not emerge because the brand is not successful at gaining an early market leadership or because the category or subcategory is fuzzy or ill-defined. In that case the brand role might be a bit less ambitious—to shape rather than define the definition of the category or subcategory emphasizing those elements to which the brand has an advantage and linking the brand to the category or subcategory. There still should be a clear concept of what the aspirational associations of the category or subcategory are and how they should be prioritized so that the brand can have an active if not dominant relevance leadership position.

Whether an exemplar role is assumed or not, it is helpful to attach a label to the category or subcategory such as dry beer, happoshu, or *cloud computing*, described in Chapter Nine. A label can be a powerful device if it is descriptive and gets traction. It can aid the challenge of creating visibility, the right image, and loyalty. However the ascendance of an accepted label is relatively rare. When it is missing, the defining associations need to be clear so that the brands or offerings that are excluded are clear.

The psychology concept of framing provides insights into both the sensitively of customers' response to apparently minor changes in the way the category or subcategory is presented and the importance of cuing the right associations. Framing is described in Chapter Two. In Chapters Three, Four, and Five several case studies describing the creation of new categories or subcategories will illustrate how they have been defined.

The First-Mover Advantage

Creating a new category or subcategory is strategically attractive in part because of the potential first-mover advantages that can result. One of the most appealing is the possibility of earning significant returns on investment because, with little or no competition, margins can be attractive. The tenure of this marketing position will depend on the barriers the firm creates, which are detailed in Chapter Nine. Many of these barriers are directly related to the first-mover advantage and include customer loyalty, an image of authenticity, scale economies, preemptive strategies, and competitor inhibitions.

The first mover has an opportunity to create customer loyalty to the new offering and brand. If the exposure to and experience with the new offering are appealing or even satisfactory, there may be no incentive for a customer to risk trying something that is different. Loyalty can also be based on real customer-switching costs, perhaps involving long-term commitments. Or there could be network externalities. If a large community begins to use a service, such as eBay, it may be difficult for another firm to create a competing community.

The innovator can also earn the valuable "authentic" label described more in Chapter Nine. This was a factor facing competitors such as Kirin when they tried to duplicate Asahi Super Dry's success in Japan. Being authentic is not only appealing, it provides credibility to the innovator and interjects uncertainty into the offering of any follower.

There are also scale economies available to the first mover. The early market leader potentially could have scale advantages with respect to logistics, warehousing, production, back office support, management, advertising, and brand recognition and perceptions. It is simple math. Spreading fixed costs like warehousing over a large sales base will result in a lower per-unit cost.

Early market leaders can also preempt the best strategies. For retailers that could mean securing the prime locations, for others it could mean attaining the prime brand position. For chocolate, for example, a prime position "a glass of milk in every bar" and could be unavailable to the second brand into a market. Preemption is particularly important if it results in a natural monopoly (an area might be able to support only one multiplex cinema, for example).

A competitor may be unable or unwilling to respond to a first mover's offering. Technology may be a barrier, as when competitors lacked the technology to respond to Kirin's Ichiban innovation. Or there could be organizational limitations. Many retailers attempted to duplicate Nordstrom's customer service but were unsuccessful because, although they could copy what Nordstrom did, they could not duplicate what Nordstrom was as an organization—its people, incentives, culture, and processes.

Competitors may also be unwilling to respond. They may believe that the new business is simply too small to be worthwhile, that it might cannibalize their existing business, or that it could tarnish their brands. All these concerns inhibited Xerox in the 1970s from entering the emerging low-end desktop copiers that were being offered by Canon, even though Xerox had access to one from its Japanese affiliate Fuji-Xerox. The result was an erosion in the Xerox business from the bottom up as Canon and others extended their product lines upward.

Perhaps the most important potential advantage of a first mover is to represent the category or subcategory and thus shape if not define it. The first mover will be able to highlight and frame the key associations. Others will then have to adapt to the first mover's conceptualization. Further, once the first mover has taken control of the category or subcategory, it has the ability to change its definition over time to reflect its innovation thereby creating a moving target.

The term *first mover* refers to an entry that is able to get traction for the new category or subcategory, an early market leader that is seldom the pioneer of that category. The pioneer, the very first entree, is usually an insignificant player because it lacks financial resources to make an impact, it has an offering flaw, enabling technology is not there yet, or the market is not ready for the new offering. Research on category after category demonstrates that the pioneer is rarely the early market leader but rather is swamped by a player that has resources and has created a superior offering. Such pioneers as Dreft in laundry detergent, Gablinger's in light beer, Royal Crown Cola in diet colas, Star in safety razors, Ampex in video recorders, Chux in disposable diapers, and Harvard Graphics in presentation software did not or could not capitalize on their pioneer status.[5] The list is virtually endless.

Trend Drivers

Trend drivers are those organizations that actually spearhead trends and participate in the creation of new category or subcategory definitions, thus gaining first-mover advantages. They anticipate and influence what people are buying instead of what brands they are choosing. Few firms have the opportunity or capacity to be trend drivers, and even those firms have only a few windows of opportunity.

The timing needs to be right. Bad timing is often the cause of an offering's failing to capture an opportunity. A premature effort to create a category or subcategory can fail—perhaps because the underlying technology is not ready, perhaps because the market size has not reached the tipping point. Recall the Apple Newton's premature effort to create the PDA (personal digital assistant) category. And being late can be equally fatal. It is important to have both the capability of being knowledgeable about markets and technology and the instinct to know when the time is ripe for a new offering.

There are two types of trend drivers. One will be willing to test the waters with new ideas but will maintain the flexibility to withdraw. The other will commit. Certainly Asahi was in the latter category, making enormous bets involving investments in plant, process, and brand building. As the brand got early acceptance, Asahi "doubled down," even in the face of a response from Kirin.

To be a trend driver, the firm needs to either be an extremely strong player or have the potential to become a strong player. In either case a firm must have real ammunition to work with, such as a breakthrough product like the dry beer innovation that allowed Asahi to define a new subcategory. Further, the firm needs to be capable of turning a first-mover advantage into a sustainable position by actively managing perceptions of the new product category or subcategory and asserting a dominant position of the brand in the new arena. That requires not only resources and recognition of the expanded brand-building task but also organizational will and competence in brand building.

Another option is to be a trend responder, a firm that is a fast follower rather than leader. Such firms track trends and events, evaluate their future impact, and create response strategies to deal with relevance challenges. In some cases they can enter and take over an emerging category or subcategory. However, trend responders are usually playing defense. They are keeping up so that they can take action to avoid irrelevance. Chapter Ten details trend responder strategies.

There is a third organization type that can be labeled as the "trend unaware." These firms are simply unaware of market trends and risk waking up surprised to find its brands are no longer relevant. The trend unaware often have inadequate external sensing systems, executives who are not market driven, organizational inflexibility, or an excessive focus on strategies that have worked well in the past. There are actually two types of trend-unaware firms. One is a "turn-the-crank" firm that simply does this year what was done last year. The other is the "committed" firm that has a single-minded focus on a business strategy and continually improves its competitive position by enhancing the value proposition, reducing costs, refusing to be diverted by market dynamics.

The Payoff

If you can create or own a new business arena in which your competitors are not relevant, as did iPod, Cirque du Soleil, Prius, Asahi Super Dry, and eBay, then you have the potential to make exceptional returns, sometimes for many years. Richard Rumelt, the UCLA strategy guru, talked about how the most feasible pathway to substantially higher performance for most firms is to "exploit some change in your environment—in technology, consumer tastes, laws, resource prices, or competitive behavior—and ride that change with quickness and skill. This path is how most successful companies make it."[6]

The financial success has some elements that are not often so obvious. First, a new category or subcategory can represent a growth platform of its own capable of spawning new businesses. Second, the new category or subcategory can create new customers who may have been sitting on the sidelines because of their perception that existing competitors lack offerings that fit them or their needs. Before the Luna energy bar for women came along, customers were uninterested in the products that were designed and positioned for men, for macho men in fact. Before ESPN sports fanatics were confined to newspapers and magazines.

In fact, there is empirical evidence supporting the proposition that, on average over many decades, an abnormal percentage of profits come to those firms that have dominated a new business area. This evidence comes from a variety of studies that involve different perspectives, databases, and time frames. We will review the evidence from financial performance research, new product research, and perceived innovativeness data.

Financial Performance Research

McKinsey has collected a database of over one-thousand firms (all with sales of over 50 percent in one industry) from fifteen industries over forty years. One finding was that new entrants into the database (84 percent of the firms were new entrants at one point) each achieved a higher shareholder return than their industry average for the first ten years after entry.[7] That return premium was 13 percent the first year, falling to 3 percent in the fifth and never rising above that level for the second five years. Further, there was an extremely high correlation between industry newness (defined as the number of new firms entering, less the number of firms leaving, during a seven-year period) and industry profitability. It is well documented that new categories and subcategories tend to be created by new entrants. A reasonable conclusion is therefore that those creating new categories or subcategories will earn superior profits.

Firms with established businesses struggle to grow and thrive no matter how excellent their management. An analysis of a database of some 1,850 companies in seven countries followed for ten years revealed that only 13 percent of companies were able to achieve modest growth (5.5 percent real growth) and profitability targets (exceeding the cost of capital) over a ten-year period.[8] If a firm has performed well for several years, the chances are high that it will falter soon. Studies of the dynamics of companies provide supporting evidence. Of the S&P 500 in 1957, only 74 firms remained in 1997, and these firms performed 20 percent under the S&P average during that period—meaning that the newer firms performed at a higher level.[9]

Another study of fifty venture capital firms found that six had abnormally high profitability. The common characteristic of these six was that they had identified prospective areas of promise, such as Internet supporting technologies and seeded companies around the area. They were thus investing ahead of others who waited for trends to become more visible and mature. Consequently, these six firms undoubtedly were more likely to be creating new categories or subcategories than the others and the resulting first-mover advantages probably accounted for their financial success.

More direct evidence comes from a study that considered strategic decisions within a firm. Kim and Mauborgne looked at strategic moves by 108 companies; the 14 percent that were categorized as creating new categories had 38 percent of the revenues and 61 percent of the profits of the group.[10]

A series of studies examining the effect of announcements of R&D activities on stock return has shown a significant relationship, announcements had a positive impact on stock return. One such study of over five-thousand announcements from sixty-nine firms in five high-tech industries, such as printers and desktop memory, found that when the announcements involving selecting a technology, developing it, and bringing it to market were combined, the response of the stock market was prompt and substantial.[11] Because many of these developments involved a new category or subcategory, this study provides evidence that the stock market believes such activities will pay off.

Most of the economic vitality in the United States comes from new businesses. In fact, from 1980 to 2008 the net new jobs were created by firms under five years old.[12] It is reasonable to assume that a large percentage of this set of successful new firms, in order to gain sales growth, had to generate new, differentiated offerings that created or nurtured new categories and subcategories.

Although these studies do not distinguish between new categories and new subcategories, it is certainly true that there are many times more subcategories created than new categories. However, because the same fundamental profit drivers—reduced or nonexistent competition and compelling value propositions—will be in place, abnormal profits should ensue for each.

New Product Research

New product research, whether it takes the form of test markets or product or service introductions, suggests that new offerings creating new subcategories receive abnormally high profits. Dozens of studies have shown that new product success is substantially driven by differentiation—it must be one of the most robust empirical relationships in business. Differentiation affects not only the value proposition but also visibility, the ability of the new product to gain attention in the marketplace. New products tend to fail if they are not sufficiently differentiated from the existing offerings.

A highly differentiated new product offering, which we know from research is, on average, highly profitable, is likely to create a new category or subcategory because differentiation is often a key definer of a new category or subcategory. A failed new product, in contrast, is very likely to be undifferentiated and be part of the brand preference battlefield. A product failure will not only have a direct, adverse effect on profitability because of the cost of developing and introducing the offering, but also it will represent significant opportunity cost. That investment in people and resources could have gone elsewhere.

Perceived Innovativeness Data

Being a first-mover and owning an emerging category or subcategory, a brand is perceived to be associated with innovativeness. Gaining perceptions of innovativeness is a priority for nearly all businesses because it provides brand energy and credibility for new products. But few brands break out and reach that goal. Examine the top fifteen brands on an innovativeness scale, according to the 2007 Brand Asset Valuator (BAV) from a Young & Rubicam (Y&R) database covering over three-thousand brands, which is shown in Figure 1.5.[13] Nearly all have created or owned a new submarket using transformational innovation.

Figure 1.5 Perceived Innovativeness–2007

1. Bluetooth	6. DreamWorks	11. Disney
2. Pixar	7. TiVo	12. Google
3. iPod	8. iMac	13. Swiffer
4. IMAX	9. Discovery Channel	14. Wikipedia
5. Microsoft	10. BlackBerry	15. Dyson

Creating New Categories or Subcategories—Four Challenges

Marketers are preoccupied, often obsessed, with brand preference competition and give it way too many resources and too much attention. Brand relevance, in contrast, gets way too small a role in strategy and way too little funding. Business, marketing, and brand strategies without a doubt would benefit from elevating brand relevance in their game plans. My objective is to make this happen by presenting evidence, methods, theories, frameworks, and role models that will point the way.

The centerpiece of a brand relevance strategy should be an attempt to create a new category or subcategory in which the competition is reduced, weakened, or even nonexistent. There is little question that success will result in a huge payoff if barriers to competition can be created or if the competition is diverted by other opportunities or threats.

The question is how to do so. How can a firm create and dominate a new category or subcategory? How can you assess the risks that the subcategory will be insufficiently appealing to customers or unable to withstand immediate competitor attacks? Can the firm actually produce and market the offering? How do you create an Asahi Super Dry beer, a Kirin happoshu beer, a Plymouth Caravan, a Toyota Prius, an Enterprise Rent-A-Car, an iPod, a Kindle, or any of the other examples of successful category or subcategory creation?

Creating a new category or subcategory is not at all easy. It involves the emergence of a new, different value proposition that is capable of generating visibility, energy, and a group of loyal customers. The resulting customer benefits need to be new, different, and meaningful, because the charge is to change perceptions and behavior with respect to what is being bought and used.

Benefits need to be relevant to customers, they should resonate. Benefits that seem significant to a firm, particularly to the champions of the new offering, may not be meaningful enough to customers to create a new category or subcategory. It is not just logic that is involved, because even with a compelling story around the new offering, customers must be motivated to pay attention and change behavior. What is the problem for which this is a solution? The "problem" may not be obvious.

Even if the benefits are worthwhile, the communication task might be too difficult to overcome. An indicator of success is often whether or not the new category or subcategory gets enough interest and energy that it self-propels, that there is a buzz that drives and supports the emerging loyal customer base and makes them part of the creation force. Without that energy it can be difficult. How, then, does a firm, aspiring to change what customers buy, proceed?

Most successful efforts at creating new categories or subcategories in one way or the other have addressed four interrelated tasks or steps. As summarized in Figure 1.6, they are:

1. *Concept generation.* Good options are needed and are more likely if they are generated from multiple perspectives. It is better to make inferior choices from great options than to make great choices from inferior options. Like a football

Figure 1.6 Creating Offerings That Will Drive New Categories or Subcategories

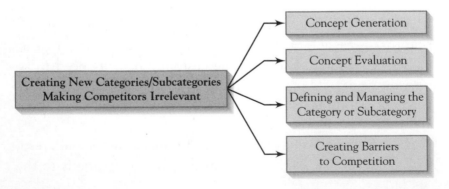

Creating New Categories/Subcategories Making Competitors Irrelevant

Concept Generation

Concept Evaluation

Defining and Managing the Category or Subcategory

Creating Barriers to Competition

coach who believes that competition at every position makes players better and provides backup if the first stringer falters, the strategist will do better when there are several good alternatives.

2. *Concept evaluation.* Evaluation provides tools to focus efforts on the best concept prospects. A fatal mistake is to get bogged down with too many options, which means that none may get the commitment of resources needed to win, or to cling to a concept whose prospects are fading.

3. *Defining and managing the category or subcategory.* In addition to managing the brand, managers now need to define and manage the category or subcategory The key is to identify priority aspirational associations, develop a positioning strategy based on those associations, create innovations to advance the category or subcategory, and use the brand and its brand-building programs to create visibility and image for the new category or subcategory.

4. *Creating barriers to entry.* Creating barriers is the ultimate task that will turn a new category or subcategory into a profit stream. If that stream can be extended, the results not only mean more resources recovered but also a better marketing position and momentum.

The Brand Relevance Model Versus Others

What is different about the brand relevance model of competition? After all, there are countless authors with theories that advocate transformational innovation or other strategic avenues to growth. *Blue Ocean Strategy* by Kim and Mauborgne, *The Growth Gamble* by Campbell and Park, Gary Hamel's *Leading the Revolution*, Chris Zook's *Beyond the Core*, *Creative Destruction* by Foster and Kaplan, *Winning Through Innovation* by Tushman and O'Reilly, and *The Innovator's Solution* by Christensen and Raynor make up a partial list.[14]

These works and a dozen others that are not mentioned are, in my view, excellent books that have on the whole made substantial contributions to the strategy literature. I have learned from all of them. They are all different, of course, and each has a point of view. However, it is possible to identify four interrelated aspects of this book and the brand relevance model that are not covered in these other books. This brand relevance book emphasizes the importance of defining and managing the new categories and subcategories. They should not be developed and then just sit there defined by the marketplace. Rather, they need to be actively managed just like any brand is managed. The new category or subcategory needs to be defined, to have its perception actively managed, and to be linked to the brand. In contrast, the other major strategy books either take this task for granted and fail to mention brand at all or fail to consider it as an aggressive part of strategy.

This book also emphasizes the need to create barriers to the category or subcategory formed. It is classic economics. Create a competitive arena and then build a fence around it so that others are kept out. There are a variety of barriers that can be created, but the brand, in addition to being a barrier itself, can serve to organize and leverage other barriers. For example, a distribution advantage can be a key barrier to competitors and also become part of the brand vision and serve to create and communicate a value proposition.

This book explicitly includes substantial innovation as routes to new categories or subcategories. The other books largely focus on transformational innovations like a Cirque du Soleil or incremental innovations as in "just execute better and better" and "leverage success by entering adjacent markets." There are many more substantial innovations than transformational, and incremental innovation is at the heart of the brand preference model.

This book also explicitly suggests that creating new subcategories in which competitors are less relevant should be a goal of the brand relevance strategy. It is not necessary to hold out for a home run in the form of new categories. The reality is that for every opportunity of creating new categories, such as a sports TV channels or cruise ships, there are dozens of opportunities for creating subcategories, such as a golf or tennis channel or cruise ship for kids or singles. The inclusion of subcategories gives the strategic thrust of the relevance model a wide scope. Nearly every business can continuously be looking for subcategory opportunities.

What is Coming

The next chapter will elaborate on the relevance concept. Drawing on theories and findings in social and consumer psychology, the discussion will help us understand and use this concept.

Chapters Three, Four, and Five consider the development of new categories and subcategories in three very different industries—retail, automobiles, and packaged goods. In describing twenty or so case studies I will attempt to show where ideas come from, how categories or subcategories are defined, why competitors respond or fail to do so, what barriers are erected, and the underlying causes of success or failure.

Chapters Six through Nine will examine how to create a new category or subcategory. Four mission-critical tasks—finding concepts, evaluating concepts, defining the category or subcategory, and creating barriers to competitors—are discussed. Readers for whom these chapters are of immediate practical interest are welcome to skip directly to them.

Chapter Ten examines the other side of the coin. What is the threat to firms facing emerging categories and subcategories that are making their existing business areas vulnerable? How do they best respond? Chapter Eleven details the characteristics of an organization that will support innovation. Without an organization that encourages and enables, creating substantial and transformational innovation is difficult indeed. The book concludes with an epilogue that puts all this into perspective by pointing out the risks and challenges that must be addressed to successfully win the brand relevance battle.

Key Takeaways

The brand preference model, in which brands compete in established categories, is a recipe for static markets and unsatisfactory profits. The brand relevance model, in which new categories and subcategories are formed, provides the opportunity for dramatic changes in market position, reduced or even no competition, and superior financial performance. A new category or subcategory will have no or weak competitors, a clear point of difference from other categories or subcategories, a new value proposition, a loyal customer base, and a set of barriers to competitors. It will usually be based on substantial or transformational innovation. The brand challenge is to manage not only the brand but also the category or subcategory and the link between the two.

There is considerable evidence that the successful creation of a new category or subcategory will result in superior financial performance. Studies show, for example, that new entrants to an industry, who usually will be forming new categories or subcategories, do markedly better than their peers. It is well known that new product success is directly proportional to the degree of differentiation from other products and thus to the probability that a new category or subcategory is formed. Much of this success is due to such first-mover advantages as scale effects, preemptive strategies, brand loyalty of early adopters, and brand equity.

For Discussion

1. Identify categories or subcategories for which the brand relevance model has prevailed. What are the characteristics of those markets?

2. Identify examples of substantial innovation that created new categories or subcategories. Was the TV channel ESPN a substantial of transformational innovation? Why? What was its first-mover advantage?

3. What firms have done well at creating and managing new categories or subcategories?

2

UNDERSTANDING BRAND RELEVANCE

Categorizing, Framing, Consideration, and Measurement

It is kind of fun to do the impossible.

—*Walt Disney*

I realized that my competition was paper, not computers.

—*Jeff Hawkins, inventor of the first personal digital assistant, the PalmPilot*

In this chapter we take a deeper look at relevance. Consumer psychologists and marketing theorists have done extensive work over the years using clever experimentation and insightful theory building that are germane to the relevance concept. Tapping their efforts will provide knowledge of the scientific underpinnings of relevance and add deeper and more textured insight into the concept and its applications.

The chapter starts with a discussion of categorization. At its essence relevance involves forming categories and subcategories and using them to organize brands. The categorization headline is that a brand should aspire to be an exemplar of the new category or subcategory. In the second section framing is explored. Framing research insights provides guidance to those defining, positioning, and communicating new categories or subcategories. Studied extensively by psychologists, framing suggests that small cues can have a big effect on perceptions, information processing, attitudes, and behavior, and how the choice of which associations to use to position a category or subcategory matters. The third section discusses research on consideration sets. What evidence is there about the inclusion of a screening step in brand choice in which a brand is deemed to be worth considering or not? The final section discusses the measurement of relevance, giving the concept the ultimate level of specificity.

Categorization

Categorization, how people form categories and subcategories, is at the heart of brand relevance. Consumer researchers and psychologists have studied categorization, which is defined as the process of grouping objects and events into categories on the basis of perceived similarities.[1] Some psychologists, in fact, make the argument that categorization is a fundamental human mental activity that is at the basis of all situations and activities. A person is always trying to make sense of people, contexts, and things by categorizing them with respect to some schema. People use categories to structure and simplify the myriad of stimuli with which they are continuously bombarded. Whatever the general importance of categorization, research in this area provides several insights and constructs helpful to understanding and managing brand relevance.

How People Categorize

People categorize in two ways. One approach, "attribute matching," uses a rule-defining process. A category or subcategory will have a set of ideal characteristics. Having or not having four-wheel drive may define a car subcategory. Another subcategory could be defined as being an SUV with a stylish exterior, good gas mileage, and a comfortable interior. A new offering would then be evaluated as to whether it had or did not have those characteristics. If any were missing, the new offering would not be perceived to be in the SUV subcategory.

Instead of being "in or out," alternately, the offering might be judged as to how close it is to the category (employing the concept of fuzzy sets). The result is a "goodness of fit" judgment. Distance from the category might be based on the number and identity of characteristics for which a match is missing. Or it might be based on how far the offering is from the ideal on dimensions for which the match is less than perfect. The gas mileage may be lower than would be desired, for example, but not so low as to exclude the offering from the category.

In contrast, the "exemplar" approach is based on the premise that the category or subcategory can be represented by one or more "good examples," or exemplars. So for compact hybrids, the Prius may be the exemplar in that it basically defines the category. Similarly, iPod and TiVo define their own categories, as do Jell-O, Gortex, Google, and others. New offerings are then evaluated as to how similar they are to the exemplar. Again, instead of being in or out of the category, a brand could be measured according to a "closeness" scale.

Which approach will be used when? One factor is whether an accepted and visible exemplar exists. If so, the exemplar approach is most likely to be used. However, if the identity of one or more exemplars is unclear or not well known, then the customer will be less likely to use the exemplar approach. If a category, such as low-fat food, evolves based on consumer trends, and no exemplar has played a defining role, then the customer is likely to employ the attribute-matching approach.

Research also suggests that the attribute-matching process is more likely to be used when the context is simple, whereas the exemplar approach will be more likely if the context is more complex in terms of the number of alternatives, the number of defining dimensions, and the difficulty of evaluating options with respect to the dimensions. So if a four-wheel-drive sedan defines a category, a car will be determined to be in or not in the category—a simple, unambiguous determination. However, if a category is described with multiple dimensions that are not based simply on "have" or "have not," then the customer is more likely to use an exemplar approach. Safety, for example, can be ambiguous. If a category is defined by car safety standards, Volvo might be an exemplar. The question then becomes whether a car brand is close enough to the Volvo exemplar to be considered a part of the category.

Gaining Exemplar Status

Clearly there is a big payoff for the firm that can establish a brand as an exemplar. First, the firm can help create the category by providing a defining anchor. Without an exemplar, the very existence of a category and its staying power can become problematic. Second, the brand that is an exemplar is by definition relevant, and any competitors are in the awkward position of defining their relevance in a way that only reaffirms the authenticity of the exemplar.

How can a brand become an exemplar? Some guidelines. First, advance the category or subcategory rather than the brand. Understand that the goal is to define the category or subcategory and make sure it wins. Be an advocate. Don't worry about the brand. If the category or subcategory wins, the brand will also win. Asahi Super Dry was an advocate of dry beer, and when the subcategory won, Asahi Super Dry won.

Second, be a thought leader. Think about the definition of the category and subcategory and its underlying motivation and logic. What is the why behind hybrid cars or organic food? Can the conceptualization of the category or subcategory be productively refined or enlarged?

Third, continue to innovate. Don't stand still. Innovation, improvement, and change will make the category or subcategory dynamic, the brand more interesting, and the role of the exemplar more valued. Disneyland is the exemplar of theme parks, and it is always innovating.

Finally, be the early market leader in terms of sales and market share. It is hard to be an exemplar and to leverage that role without market share leadership. Sometimes being first into the market gives an edge. However, there are other contexts in which the pioneer brands set the stage by introducing the area, and the timing is right for another firm with resources and an improved offering to become the exemplar and be the early market leaders.

How Categorization Affects Information Processing and Attitudes

Categorization has a substantial impact on information processing and attitudes. In some cases, individuals have been shown to categorize an object on the basis of a few key dimensions and then stop further information gathering and processing. Assigning an object to a category may simply be based on a cue. For example, a private-label grocery product with a package similar to that of the category's exemplar may be assumed to be in the category without the customer's analyzing more detailed information. People often lack the motivation and sometimes the ability to conduct a detailed analysis of an object's suitability to be classified as a member of a category or subcategory. The person makes the assumption that further research costs time and money and will be unlikely to change his or her initial judgments.

When an object is categorized, whatever the process, perceptions of the category will influence if not dominate perceptions of that object. It is the typical problem of stereotypes in all contexts, whether it be women, ethnic minorities, retirees, hunters, performance cars, department stores, or bakeries. In fact, consistency theory from psychology posits that there is a cognitive drive toward consistency that would explain why people deemphasize differences and assume similarities when considering members of categories. Thus, it may take extraordinary efforts to get a customer to recategorize a brand.

Categorization can also affect attitudes. If a brand is believed to be in a category or subcategory, even if objective analysis would show it is not, than attitudes toward that category or subcategory will dominate attitudes toward the object or brand. In a classic experiment, Mita Sujan showed people who were not camera experts two alternative cameras, one labeled a 35 mm and the other a disposable 110 model.[2] Even when the specifications were reversed, the subjects still preferred the one with the subcategory label they knew to be superior. Their analysis was subcategory based. This finding is similar to research in psychology that shows that initial attitudes toward people depend in part on the category into which those people are classified. A person will be perceived differently if assigned to a stuck-up, sophisticated category, for example, rather than an outdoorsy, energetic category.

Overlapping Sets of Categories

Eleanor Rosch, the pioneer of categorization, asserted that object categories are organized in a hierarchical fashion.[3] A basic categorization, such as fast-food hamburger places, could have a supercategory of fast-food restaurants and a subcategory of fast-food hamburger places with good salads available.

The schema could involve multiple supercategories and the category structure that prevails will affect the customer's perception. Febreze, the P&G fabric refresher that removes odors from fabrics, could be linked to laundry detergents because it works on fabric and to air fresheners because it eliminates odor. The relevance and credibility of the brand will depend on which supercategory a consumer comes to believe is applicable.

The first formulation of the supercategory in a customer's mind often prevails. One study compared linking a digital camera to film cameras as opposed to digital scanners.[4] They found that whichever association was first exposed would dominate perceptions, expectations, and preferences.

Categorization need not be restricted to nominal product categories or subcategories, such as compact cars or potato chips. If the consumer goals driving the decision are ambiguous (for example, avoid unhealthy food) or in conflict (for example, cars that are safe and fun to drive), then alternatives might well be drawn from more than one nominal product class. In one study using ice cream and granola bars, participants tended to select options from both categories when the goals of nutrition and "cooling off on a hot day" were salient or when there was no goal at all specified.[5] However, when a single goal (nutrition or cooling off) was emphasized, the participants tended to consider options from one nominal product class.

It's All About Framing

New categories or subcategories need to be defined and this definition needs to be communicated to customers. The concept of framing, studied extensively by psychologists and linguists, has implications for both tasks.

Framing is about influencing the perspective on an object, in this case a category or subcategory. What association should be front of mind? For a hybrid car, for example, should it be saving money, conserving energy, or saving the planet? How should the association be stimulated given that subtle differences can affect perceptions? Framing recognizes that associations do not exist independently but rather are in a network. Stimulating one association can indirectly stimulate others that may or may not be helpful for a firm attempting to manage a category or subcategory.

There are two frame metaphors that help illuminate the concept. The first is a picture frame that provides a border, showing what is in the frame and what is not. It delineates the scope of the category or subcategory—whether it is beer or light beer or wheat beer. The second metaphor is a frame of a building under construction, it is a structure that ties the components together and provides a foundation. So the framing of a product category or subcategory specifies a framework or structure that can involve a combination of attributes, benefits, applications, or users.

Framing, it turns out, can affect how a person perceives an offering; talks about an offering; develops attitudes toward an offering; and, ultimately, buys and uses an offering. The same information will be processed or not processed, be distorted or not distorted, affect attitudes and behavior or not affect attitudes and behavior, depending on the frame. The perception that the objective of washing clothes is to get colors more vivid will affect the way that a person processes ads for detergents and views a wash. The person will be sensitive to the vividness dimension, whereas with another frame that person might not notice such a dimension. A frame can affect purchase decisions, even when there is no information processing going on, because of the perceived credibility of a brand with respect to criteria made salient by the frame.

There is an illusion prevalent in organizations that customers are rational and seek out relevant information, establish clear objectives, weigh functional benefits heavily, and make logical decisions. Such a model of the world is appealing. It matches our instinct, especially if we reside in the high-tech or B2B sector, that the winning strategy is to develop and communicate logical, functional benefits. Further, customers, when asked why they buy this brand or avoid that one, give functional reasons because they can and because anything else would not reflect well on them and their decision making. But, unfortunately, this model is wrong.

Customers are far from rational. Even if they had the motivation and the time, which they usually don't, they often lack credible information, memory capacity, computational ability, and even sufficient knowledge about a product area to obtain relevant information and use it to optimize decision making. There is little doubt that even the executives at Singapore Airlines charged with buying planes, supplied with piles of proposal details on options, will in the end be influenced by their gut feel. Customers, instead of optimizing a purchase decision, rely on surrogates of perfect information and cues that signal outcomes. That is why framing is so important. A frame, by influencing the dialogue surrounding a product or service, can affect the whole decision process and user experience. It can trump logic, even for those who are informed.

George Lakoff, the Berkeley linguist, talks about framing in the political sphere and how influential it is in terms of managing the discussion.[6] Consider the difference in perspectives on taxation stimulated by a phrase that frames the debate. "Tax relief" engenders the metaphor of a hero who is relieving people of a burden and suggests that anyone who would obstruct that noble quest is at best naive. "Tax as investment in the future" produces the image of roads built, children educated, and a defense force enhanced. "Tax as dues like you pay at a club" is a metaphor associated with paying your fair share for services benefiting you and others close to you. Each frame influences the discourse very differently by implicitly altering the objectives.

It matters whether you are buying an energy bar for athletes, an energy bar for office workers, an energy bar for women, a nutrition bar, a breakfast bar, a protein bar, or a diet bar. It really matters. It affects the information you process, your evaluation of a brand, your purchase decision, and your user experience. If you are going to buy an energy bar for women, a product that has a man's look and feel may not be appropriate, even if it has the right ingredients. It just never has a chance, even though objectively it may have been a good choice. It ran into the wrong frame, which rendered it irrelevant.

Lakoff observes that frames are often cognitively unconscious in that people don't necessary even realize that there is a frame or that the frame influences.[7] That is in part why framing is so powerful. The frame does not achieve dominance because it is logically appropriate or fair; it just slips in there because one competitor exploited a first-mover role, created a vivid metaphor to represent a frame, or was simply louder and more persistent than the opponent.

A frame, once established, can linger. It is hard to change even when first introduced. Lakoff likes to start off his Berkeley classes with the admonition not to think of an elephant. Of course, students find it impossible to get the elephant out of their minds.

Empirical Evidence

A host of experiments have demonstrated that people process information and make choices that are affected by framing. A study showed that if meat is framed according to how lean it is rather than how fat, it will be preferred.[8] People consistently prefer 75 percent lean to 25 percent fat. The number 75 percent seems high, and so the judgment is made that the fat content is relatively low. When the label says 25 percent fat, the fat statistic is in your face. In general, attributes that are portrayed positively have a greater impact than the same attributes portrayed negatively. In general there is a preference for positive framing over negative framing.

Another study showed the difference in customer opinions that occurs when a firm is framed as a not-for-profit instead of a for-profit institution.[9] Researchers showed and described to one experimental group a women's bag by Mozilla.org. The use of the .org suggests a not-for-profit. Another group had an identical experience, except the bag was reported to be by Mozilla.com.

The ".org" firm was perceived to be warmer but less competent than the ".com" firm. Subjects were more willing to buy from the for-profit firm, unless both were endorsed by the *Wall Street Journal*. In that case, the perceived competence difference faded, as did the difference in willingness to buy.

Framing can dictate a person's perspective, a point of view about an evaluation or decision. Sometimes that perspective is in the form of an anchor in mind, whether it be a price or level of service. In a dramatic illustration of the power of an anchor, a group of graduate students were asked if they would pay for a nice bottle of wine an amount equal to the last two digits of their social security numbers, a completely arbitrary number.[10] Researchers then asked the students to bid on a bottle. The bid number was significantly affected by the social security number; it became an anchor even though it was obvious to all that these numbers were unrelated to the value of the wine. Another illustration—people tend to believe a glass described as half full started out empty, whereas those who had the same glass described as half empty believed that the glass started out as full.

If there is a key dimension that defines a category or sub-category, it is important to understand and manage the significant anchor. Is it premium delivering prestige? If so, a category or subcategory wannabe might be excluded if it had cues that signaled a bad fit. If the anchor was exceptional quality based on performance, however, it might not.

The product category membership can affect perceptions, attitudes, and behavior. Dan Ariely and his research colleagues did a series of experiments that illustrated this point rather graphically.[11] They told volunteers, who numbered in the hundreds, that they could each have a free glass of beer. They only needed to select from two pitchers based on a small taste sample. One of the pitchers had a premium beer, such as Samuel Adams, and the second had the same beer but with some balsamic vinegar added. When both pitchers were represented as beer, the great majority of respondents chose the beer with the vinegar. However, half the sample was told that the second choice consisted of a beer with vinegar added; the vast majority then chose the unadulterated beer and in fact were repulsed by the beer with vinegar. So when one option was clearly not within the scope of the product category it was rejected as unacceptable, even though objectively it was superior.

The beer experiment of Dan Ariely and his colleagues had a sequel. They sought to determine what would happen if they told respondents that one of the beers had vinegar added after they had tasted the beers and selected the vinegar-added beer as the better of the two.[12] It turned out that the attitude toward the vinegar-added beer did not change and, in fact, many volunteers, when given a vinegar dropper, added vinegar to their beers by choice.

One takeaway from the beer experiment is that the brand that is defining a product category or subcategory should make that definition clear so that a competitor's flaws are visible. The customer should be motivated to avoid a competitor brand because it is irrelevant. If the category or subcategory definition is ambiguous and a customer ends up trying a competitor's offering, the flaws may not be as pivotal. Another takeaway is that a brand trying to break into an emerging category or subcategory should hide any potential flaw until after there is a trial experience, at which time its emergence will be less damaging and could be an asset, just as vinegar in beer was considered positive by those that preferred its taste.

Frames can affect the emotional experience, as a study of Heineken and Coors showed.[13] The Heineken beer-drinking experience was associated with a warm, approachable, social group of upscale people. The experience of drinking a Heineken in that type of setting created a warmth emotion quite different from when Coors was placed in the same context because Coors was framed very differently. The Coors beer-drinking experience was associated with the outdoors and a campfire setting and thus did not create the same emotions in the social setting as Heineken.

Such associations as the area or country of origin also affect the frame of a set of options. In one study, one set of diners was given glasses of wine from a new North Dakota winery named Noah Winery.[14] Another set had the identical experience, but the same wine was purported to be from California rather than North Dakota. The former group not only enjoyed their wine more but believed their food tasted better, ate 11 percent more of it, and spent 15 percent more time at the table—perhaps because the enjoyment of the wine made them want to prolong the eating experience. None believe the wine label influenced them in any way.

The Scope of the Offering—Adding Options

One competitive strategy is to reduce the number of competitors by defining the category or subcategory to minimize the number of relevant options. However, there are contexts in which expanding the number of options can actually by helpful. That is the case with the inferior alternative effect and the compromise effect.

The appeal of a brand can be enhanced if an inferior alternative is included in the consideration set. Williams-Sonoma, the upscale kitchen appliance store for people into cooking, offered a home bread bakery priced at $275. When they added a larger unit priced at 50 percent higher, it did not sell significantly, but sales of the original item nearly doubled. The original bakery seemed more reasonably priced when there was a high-priced alternative that was inferior because of its size. This phenomenon has been replicated in many experimental contexts. For example, in a classic study, Simonson and Tversky gave one experimental group a choice between $6 and an elegant Cross pen and found that 36 percent chose the Cross pen.[15] In another experimental group, when a second, less-appealing pen with a lesser known brand name was included as an option, the percentage selecting the Cross pen went from 36 percent to 46 percent, and only 2 percent selected the inferior pen. When the inferior option was included, the Cross pen became more appealing.

Kraft's DiGiorno introduced in 1995 its "rising crust" pizza, the first pizza with a fresh-frozen, not precooked crust.[16] Rather than competing in the frozen pizza section, DiGiorno chose to reframe the category to included delivered pizza. With the tagline "It's not delivery, it's DiGiorno," the brand was a success for Kraft with $125 million the first year and a remarkable 50 percent repurchase rate, a record at Kraft. To make the new category more vivid, the DiGiorno delivery person was created who, of course, has nothing to do. One promotion involved a $100,000 salary to be a DiGiorno delivery person, the winner could collect a salary and had no job to do. By reframing the category to include delivered pizza, DiGiorno, instead of being a premium priced frozen pizza, now had a decided price advantage by being often half the price of delivered pizza. Further, its quality was now suggested to be comparable to delivered pizza and thus far above other frozen pizzas. The successful framing persisted as DiGiorno retained the leading brand status, enjoying a substantial price premium.

There is also a compromise effect. People generally like to compromise, choosing between the highest premium offer and the lowest value one. Taking the highest can seem indulgent or might risk not getting a good value. Taking the lowest offer, in contrast, risks getting an inferior option. Best Buy has two private-label offerings, Insignia and Denox. Insignia, which is priced below the national brands, looks like a more comfortable choice with Denox at an even lower price. There is a feeling that the final choice is not the cheapest alternative. In another study of Minolta cameras, the more expensive of two cameras saw preference for it increase when a higher-priced Minolta camera was added to the choice set.[17] The higher-priced camera was inferior in that its price was perceived to be excessive, but it allowed another camera option to become a compromise choice. More generally, people tend to avoid extreme choices, so if options can be added to the choice set such that a brand no longer represents the top or bottom option, its appeal will increase.

Which Frame Wins?

So which frame will be the dominant influence of the perspective of the category or subcategory? The most appropriate one should win and sometimes does. However, in many cases it is the last frame standing, and in more cases it is the one that is the most commonly used.

A student of mine once hypothesized that the last metaphor wins. If during a discussion someone puts forth a metaphor and there is no counter-metaphor on the table, the argument is often over with. In a discussion of brand pricing if someone says, "We are at war and our competition has attacked us with a price drop," the implication is that we need to be aggressive and angry. That framing will be influential. If, however, someone else at the same meeting characterizes the same event by suggesting the metaphor that the competitor was losing the battle and, desperate to survive, chose to reposition as a price brand, the discussion will take a very different course. Which frame or metaphor will survive, the attack or the survival? The last metaphor standing has a big advantage for sure.

In many cases, however, it is the frame that is used most often that wins. Returning to Lakoff's political landscape, phrases and associated frames, such as "tax and spend," "death taxes," "pro-abortion," and "tort reform" have been successfully used by Republicans to manage the discussion and frame the issues. They did this in part by being disciplined and repetitive. After these terms are out there so pervasively, their opponents, the Democrats, started using them as well. When the Democrats start using the Republican metaphors, the battle is nearly won.

Consideration Set as a Screening Step

The concept of relevance is based in part on the premise that the judgment as to what brands are in the consideration set is a screening step that brands need to pass before a person more extensively evaluates them. The selection of the preferred brand then follows. Only those brands that pass the screening test qualify to participate in this brand preference step. It turns out that this idea of a screening step has substantial support in the literature pertaining to consumer behavior, psychology, and economics.

There is empirical evidence in business-to-business (B2B) and consumer contexts that, indeed, customers often do engage in a screening step in which they select the brands to be considered. It is not just a theoretical hypothesis.[18] The screening step involves the elimination of those options that do not pass a minimum threshold on a certain number of attributes or dimensions. The screening step in buying cereal, for example, might involve eliminating all cereal products with more than 5 grams of sugar per serving. It is termed *noncompensatory decision making* because there is no possibility that being high on one dimension will compensate for being unsatisfactory on another. Having better taste and texture will not compensate for a deficiency in regard to sugar content if the latter is part of the definition of the subcategory to be purchased: high sugar content will exclude the brand no matter what other brand characteristics it might have.

The decision process then turns to the brand preference phase, an evaluation of those brands that pass the screening test and are thus relevant. This evaluation and decision to buy could be based on any number of decision strategies, including a compensatory process whereby a deficiency on one dimension can be overcome by a positive evaluation on other dimensions. So a cereal choice might be evaluated by taste, texture, fiber content, and nutritional value, and a deficiency on one dimension could be compensated for by high ratings on the others.

The concept of a noncompensatory screening step is based in part on the fact that customers are limited in their ability to receive, process, and recall information and to engage in computational efforts to support decision making. Even if customers were able to engage in the analysis needed to make the perfect decision, common sense as well as cost-benefit economics would suggest that it is simply not worthwhile to conduct an in-depth analysis of a decision that is trivial or repetitive. A chewing-gum decision just doesn't merit a lot of effort. As a result, customers accept less-than-perfect decisions and seek out ways to cope with an excess of information and complexity.

Herbert Simon, who was awarded the Nobel Prize in economics for work that repositioned conventional views of customer decision making, termed this set of customer limitations *bounded rationality* and the acceptance of imperfect decisions as *satisficing*.[19] His view was that people had bounds on their ability and motivation to be rational to make optimal decisions by processing all available information. They instead satisfice, or use decision heuristics such as the noncompensatory model that eliminated brands from consideration, even though that might result in nonoptimal, albeit satisfactory, decisions. Purchase decision makers recognize that optimality requires time and effort that are not worthwhile or even feasible. The use of a noncompensatory screening model is one mechanism that will reduce the number of options and therefore reduce the information involved and the decision's complexity.

Empirical research has showed that a noncompensatory screening step is more likely to occur as the number of alternatives gets larger, as the number of dimensions increases, and as the decision becomes complex. If there are few alternatives and few dimensions as well, then a screening step to simplify may not be needed.

The noncompensatory stage will be affected by the context. The more uncertainty that exists, the more brands likely to be included in the consideration set. If a dimension is binary, for example, a car is or is not a hybrid, then the screen is easily applied. However, if the criterion is low versus high gas mileage, and there is uncertainly about the gas mileage of alternatives, the screen may allow more brands to pass. The screen may also depend on the reliability of the data. A study of apartment choice revealed that more apartments tended to be screened out if the information as to size or location was reliable.[20] If the information was less reliable, then more alternatives were likely to be included. Respondents were reluctant to exclude options when the information was uncertain.

The challenge for the brand manager or marketing executive seeking to define a new category or subcategory is to position the category or subcategory around one or more clearly defined dimensions, with a bar set as unambiguously as possible. It is thus helpful to find a feature or use context that is connected with little ambiguity to the brand and not to other brands.

One option is to elevate a dimension and then suggest that only the best brand on that dimension should be considered. So Hyundai's "America's best warranty" and General Mills' claim that no brand will have more fiber than Fiber One both provide a criteria cutoff that is clear—accept only the best on key dimensions. By accepting this argument, the consumer may not feel that the brand is delivering what is literally the best but can be sure that the brand is at least very close to the best and that it is simply not worth the trouble to fine-tune the analysis.

Measuring Relevance

The measurement of relevance needs to start with a well-defined category or subcategory. If there is a label, such as energy bars or minicomputers, that is helpful. If no label is accepted by the marketplace, then a tight description is needed—"shaving products for women," for example. Then the first dimension of relevance would be measured by a series of questions reflecting the probability that the respondent will buy the category or subcategory. Have you bought? Will you buy? Are you interested? The second dimension of relevance will determine what brands are in the consideration set. If you are going to buy the category or subcategory, what brands would you consider?

The pages of the Techtel high-tech tracking database illustrate how relevance-based measurement can yield strategic insights. During the 1990s, Intel wanted to be associated with such attributes as fast, powerful, and having industry-standard processors. Tracking data showed in the late 1990s that the Intel Inside program had worked well for these criteria but was not working well for a new criterion, the search for powerful solutions related to the emerging Internet. Whereas over 55 percent of respondents found IBM strongly associated with such terms as *e-commerce* and *e-business*, both Intel at 12 percent and Dell were low by this measure. Thus Intel and Dell had a problem in that few thought them relevant to an emerging category, Internet-based applications. Over time Intel attempted to respond by expanding the Intel Inside brand to be relevant beyond microprocessors inside computers, and Dell sought to dial up its high-end server line.

An alternative to the consideration set question that is sometimes easy to fit into a survey instrument is to ask prospective customers unaided recall questions such as, What brands can you think of that are capable of providing the category or subcategory offering? This question demands that brands be salient enough to be recalled without any prompting. Although the unaided recall result can include brands not in the consideration set, there is often a close relationship between the two. And if a brand does not make the unaided recall test, it will probably not be in the consideration set.

Simple recognition (what brands from this list are associated with this category or subcategory?) is generally too weak a measure. In fact, brands with high recognition and low recall are termed *graveyard brands*. These are brands that people have heard of but are so low on the relevance scale that they do not come to mind when considering a product category or subcategory. Suppose an audience segment were asked to name compact cars, and later were shown a list of twenty compact brands and asked to check those that they recognized as makers of compact cars. If Dodge was recognized by most but few had named Dodge in the recall task, then Dodge would have high recognition but low recall.

Being in the graveyard is much worse that being completely unknown, because it is hard to create news around a graveyard brand. Because the brand is familiar, audience members assume that they know enough about the brand and fail to attend to "news" about it. A brand that is unfamiliar, however, has more potential to be newsworthy.

A common mistake is to use categories or subcategories associated with the brand as a measure of relevance. Such associations do provide clues as to the brand's current image and barriers to changing it. The image of Sony can be understood better by knowing that it is associated with television sets, consumer electronics, movies, music, and games. However, the more strategically important association—and the one that drives relevance—is what brands customers are associating with the category or subcategory. If a customer mentions Sony as an option when considering video cameras, then Sony is relevant to video cameras regardless of whatever other products the customer assumes that Sony makes. In fact, a brand that aspires to be relevant to multiple categories or subcategories may find that some people may not be able to recall all the categories to which the brand is relevant when the brand name is the stimulus. That doesn't really matter, because it is category- or subcategory-driven brand recall that determines market power.

With the concept of brand relevance now elaborated, we turn to two dozen or so case studies of brands that have attempted to fight and win the brand relevance battle. Most have attempted to create new categories or subcategories. The idea is to create a set of contexts that will illuminate the issues, the challenges, and the rewards of becoming the early market leaders and the exemplar of a new category or subcategory.

Key Takeaways

Categorization, how people form and define categories and subcategories, is at the heart of relevance. If a brand can become the exemplar brand that is used to define the category or subcategory, other brands will be at a disadvantage. Framing, which influences the way a category or subcategory is perceived, affects information processing, attitudes, and behavior. Subtle differences in presenting the category or subcategory can have differences in perceptions. People often use a screening step in brand choice to determine whether a brand should be considered. A brand will be screened out if it has a category or subcategory relevance issue or if it lacks visibility and energy. The measurement of relevance is based on whether the category or subcategory is selected and then given that choice will the brand be considered.

For Discussion

1. What are some exemplar brands? What impact has that status had on their marketing programs?

2. For the automobile or some other industry, describe how its subcategories are framed. Is there a brand that is driving that framing?

3. Identify a brand that often fails to be in the consideration set for a category or subcategory but that most know makes an offering that should qualify as being relevant.

4. Pick two brands and design a relevance measurement system for them.

3

CHANGING THE RETAIL LANDSCAPE

I don't know the key to success, but the key to
failure is trying to please everybody.
—*Bill Cosby*

If there is no differentiation, there is no innovation.
—*A. G. Lafley, former P&G CEO*

The next three chapters will describe a set of twenty case studies of brands that attempted to develop new categories or subcategories in three industries, some not so successfully. These cases provide a good perspective of the challenges and the complexities of the task plus the huge upside of a successful effort. Collectively, the goal is to gain insight into where ideas come from, the role of trend interpretation and projection, how categories or subcategories are defined, how firms achieved success or why an idea faltered or failed, why competitors fail to respond, and how barriers to competitors are built.

The three industries provide very different contexts and efforts. In particular, Chapter Four (the automobile industry) provides insights on competitor response and how it is intertwined with each competitor's own overall business strategy. Chapter Five (the food industry) provides a look at the complexities and dynamics of a megatrend, namely healthy eating, which should be instructive to any firm trying to interpret and maybe influence a trend in the marketplace. In this retailing chapter, we see up close the power of culture and values and how categories and subcategories are defined.

Retailers have several advantages in creating new categories or subcategories. They have a lot of variables to work with, including product selection and pricing, product presentation, store ambiance, and ways to involve and interest customers. Further, a retailer can refine the new concept while still under the radar. Pret A Manger, the enormously successful U.K. sandwich chain, refined the concept over five years when it was still a single storefront. Finally, a retailer can experiment, try out many concepts with modest investments, and wait until one hits. The Limited tried out many concepts within an existing store and created chains, such as Bath & Body Works and Structure, out of those that showed promise.

Of course, it takes insight to know what concepts should be tested and judgment to decide if a successful local test will travel over different geographies and through time. Further, scaling a good retail idea, expanding its footprint, can take a long time. During that time, competitors can observe the business model and operations that are driving the potential new category or subcategory. There is little to prevent them from being first movers in another city or country. To find a winning concept and scale it across markets while holding back competition is thus very difficult. Yet there are a host of retailers that have done just that. Their stories are instructive. How did they come up with the concepts? How were they scaled? How did they avoid having others copy the concepts?

Among the role-model retailers that have pulled it off are Victoria's Secret and Zara in women's wear; Eddie Bauer and L.L.Bean in outdoor clothing and accessories; The Body Shop and Bath & Body Works in toiletries; Amazon and Japan's Rakuten, an online mall, in e-commerce; IKEA and La-Z-Boy in furniture; Apple and Best Buy in computers; Walmart and Target in discounting; McDonald's and Subway in fast food; and more. Each has been able to scale, often based on a story and distinct offering and supporting culture. We will take a closer look at Muji (clothing and home furnishings), IKEA, Zara, H&M (women's clothing), Best Buy, Whole Foods Market, Subway, and Zappos (an online shoe site), each of which has established and dominated a new subcategory and has a set of characteristics that represent sustainable differentiation.

Muji

One of the strongest retail brands in Japan is Muji. BrandJapan has measured brand strength for 1,100 brands in Japan for nine years. Muji is always in the top 30 and usually in the top 20, a spot shared by only 3 other retail brands. It started as a sales corner of the Seiyu department store, with a lineup of nine household products and thirty-one food products. After opening its first stand-alone store in 1983 it became an independent company in 1990, and now have over 330 stores, nearly one-third of which are outside Japan. Few brands deliver more emotional and self-expressive benefits than does the Muji brand. Yet the Muji brand vision is to not be a brand!! It is the no-brand brand.

Muji, short for Mujirushi Ryohin, is represented by four characters that mean literally "no-brand quality goods." Their values are all about simplicity, nature, moderation, humility, and self-restraint. The Muji philosophy is to deliver functional products that strive to be not the best but "enough." "Enough" does not mean compromise and resignation but rather a feeling of satisfaction from knowing that the product will deliver what is needed but no more. Superfluous features and attributes that are unrelated to function are omitted. The aspiration at Muji is to achieve the extraordinary by modesty and plainness in the pursuit of the pure and ordinary. Not a contradiction at Muji.

A visit to a Muji store is an eye-opener. One of the first things you notice is that the clothes are all bland, mostly white or beige and never bright. Beige works. And there is no logo on the front of the shirts, in fact there is no label at all—not even on the inside of the garments. Why would you want a label? The furniture, cookware, and office equipment are plain but functional. The designs are simple, not for some minimalist statement but in order to provide just what is needed to deliver functionality. Periodically there is a Muji design competition that regularly gets two thousand entrants and results in products for the store that support the Muji beliefs and lifestyle. The prices are low, not by using cheap materials or inferior designs but by cutting out frills and using designs with the right objectives.

The store setting supports the products and the philosophy. The music in the background is soothing. The ambiance is relaxing and delivers emotional benefits that are very Japanese but also travel well. Actually, in Japan, unlike in the United States, a personality dimension that appears relatively frequently is calmness. Muji has it.

Not surprisingly, Muji is sensitive to the environment. They aspire to live in compatibility and sensitivity with the earth. Toward that end they developed a set of three large campgrounds that allow people to enjoy nature that is undisturbed. The campsites host Muji summer camp jamborees, which are events that bond Muji and the participants to undisturbed nature.

Muji can be described as a reaction to the glitz of the Ginza and other shopping centers that are filled with brands each trying to be more upscale than the next. Muji is anti-glitz. It explicitly desires to eliminate the self-expressive benefits to which people usually aspire. The badge of Louis Vuitton is the polar opposite of Muji's. Ironically, this desire to eliminate self-expressive benefits actually provides self-expressive benefits. Shopping at Muji and using Muji products make a forceful statement about who you are. You are above looking for badge brands. You are, rather, a rational person who is interested in the right values, connecting with a firm that is about function, antiprestige brands, calmness, moderation, and nature.

The fact that Muji has seen little real competition shows the strength of the barriers that Muji has created. These barriers are based not only on the products, but also on all that emanates from its core values and culture including its people, ambiance, programs, and philosophy. It would be impossible for Macy's to carve out a section with a subbrand and deliver the Muji spirit, lifestyle, and products. It just could not happen.

The brand Muji has a most unusual brand story—a nonbrand that delivers emotional and self-expressive benefits. Today's trends make the story even more interesting. Consumers have seen the downside of the excesses of debt-driven materialistic purchasing. There is almost a craving for simplicity, a move away from prideful and self-absorbed brand benefits toward more satisfying values. Desires for fewer additives in food, for entertainment systems that that are easy to operate, for less product confusion, for sustainable consumption, and on and on are becoming visible. It may be that the simple and unassuming may become more of a mainstream formula rather than a niche strategy. If so, the Muji brand may become a role model toward which others look.

IKEA

The founder of IKEA started selling pens, wallets, and other products at low prices as a seventeen-year-old boy in a village in Sweden in 1943. By 1953 he had added inexpensive, locally made furniture and opened a store to demonstrate the quality of his goods in the context of a price war. Three years later an employee removed the legs of a table in order to get it into a car. That event led to the concept of packing furniture in easy-to-transport containers and outsourcing assembly to customers.

Today IKEA, with over three hundred stores, is the largest furniture retailer in the world. Like Muji, IKEA features affordable products with materials selected with cost in mind and with designs that are simple but of high quality. There are also sharp differences between the two. IKEA delivers fewer emotional and self-expressive benefits than Muji, and buying at IKEA is not a statement against ego-enhancing brands. IKEA signature stores have efficient warehouses at which customers pick up unassembled items they selected from displays that mimic home settings. Each store has a huge footprint, oversized and visible signage, unique layout, and restaurants that provide instant energy, visibly, and often buzz for the IKEA brand. Further, the bulk of the marketing budget, some 70 percent, goes into a 350-page catalogue that provides in-home visibility plus a link between the customer and the store. The idea is to make good furniture available to the widest possible customer group.

IKEA leverages its Swedish background. The designs, many of which are branded, fit into a Swedish design tradition that makes simple and functional seem clever and more appealing. Swedish food, such as meatballs and loganberry jam, are served inside the store and provide both charm and a link to Sweden.

IKEA thus means affordable furniture because of scale, design, and being unassembled plus wide selection, easy shopping, informative displays, and a Swedish look and feel.

Zara

Zara, which opened its first store in Spain in 1973 and now has over 1,500 stores around the world, along with the Swedish firm H&M, pioneered and refined the concept of value-priced, fast fashion and are its exemplars. "Fast fashion" means that just after the fashion show is over or a trendy fashion emerges, a fast-fashion retailer offers the latest styles at an extremely low price. Customers, particularly young women who are fashion conscious, view this proposition as compelling.

Fast-fashion retailing requires an integrated design and supply chain. Clothing stores, even today, generally plan ahead six to nine months, in part to make the supply chain, usually based in China and other low-cost countries, work. Zara operates differently. They are vertically integrated, with design and manufacturing done in Spain or Northern Portugal (where wages are low) for the fashion-forward merchandise. Their knowledge of dyeing, cutting, and materials along with their design flare provide a significant edge. As a result they can create designs and supply stores with merchandise in two to five weeks, garnering process economies along the way because the communication and logistics challenges are reduced.

In addition to providing access to the latest fashions, the fast-fashion model has another important benefit to customers: there is always something new in the store. The merchandise profile at Zara changes continuously. Most designs last only a month, and those that don't perform are gone within a week. Shoppers are attracted to visiting Zara frequently in order to see what is new. One study found that the average Zara shopper in Spain visits Zara seventeen times a year versus three times for some competitors because of the continuous refreshing of the line.[1] The resulting buzz plus the sheer retail presence have driven the brand. As a result, Zara does not need an advertising budget.

One of the enablers of the Zara method, in addition to their integrated design-and-supply system, is their ability to detect fashion trends and respond rapidly. Competitor stores rely on the instincts of an insightful merchant to forecast six months in advance or more. However good he or she is, that task is nearly impossible. Zara has a much less demanding forecast horizon and several useful inputs. One is the experience of its stores, especially the fashion-forward ones at which customers tend to be fashion sensitive. When a design does well in those settings, it is a signal to be aggressive about extending the design placement to other stores. Another is the sales consultants in the stores, who are in daily contact with customers and can cumulatively provide ideas. A third is the Zara offices around the globe, which have fashion-sensitive people observing—particularly in countries and segments that typically lead fashions.

Success and scale, however, provide both advantages and challenges. It is helpful to have a sales level with enough size to be efficient and a barrier to competitors. However, when a business grows beyond that point and is no longer a regional operation, it becomes harder to maintain the integrity of the business model. Zara has indeed struggled to scale the model as the capacity of the Spanish core to serve the global reach has become stretched.

H&M

H&M, a Swedish retailer that has enjoyed 20 percent growth for decades and now has close to two thousand stores, also features trendy fast fashion, but generally operates at even lower price points than Zara. About 25 percent of the H&M stock is made up of fast-fashion items that turn over quickly. The aim is to have something new in the store every day. These items are designed in Sweden and sourced in lower-wage European countries by suppliers directly connected to and tightly integrated with H&M.

To create interest, H&M was a pioneer in the use of designer brands. The Italian designer Roberto Cavalli and the Parisian designer Sonia Rekeil both have clothing lines at H&M. Further, celebrities, such as Madonna and singer Kylie Minogue (H&M loves Kylie was an H&M brand), have endorsed limited, one-time collections that often sell out in days. The rest of the product selection—basic, everyday items that can have longer lead time—are sourced in Asia. H&M also put fashion magazine *Elle*-endorsed items at the front of its U.S. stores in order to provide interest and credibility.

Zara and H&M both have experienced a stunning growth rate in the last twenty-five years. Their value proposition surrounding fast fashion—namely the latest fashion at a low price and a continuously new product profile in stores—had traction among the clothes-buying segments. Their supply chain that delivers speed and low cost and their fashion sensitively represent formidable barriers to other clothing retailers.

Best Buy

Best Buy has a heritage as a small, regional retail chain called Sound of Music that begin in 1966 in Minnesota. However, it was in 1983 that Best Buy opened its first superstore and began its rise to becoming a national player. By 2010 the firm, still headquartered in Minnesota, had well over one thousand stores, was estimated to have around 20 percent of the U.S. market for consumer electronics retailing, and had a firm toehold in China and Europe. Along the way a major competitor, Circuit City, fell by the wayside.

Best Buy had always offered the value that comes from the scale of being a big-box retailer with warehouse distribution. However, it also always had a feel for customers as well and strove to reduce customers' stress and frustration in dealing with relatively complex decisions and products. A policy adopted in 1989 to eliminate sales commissions supported a very different customer relationship than was the norm in similar stores. The salesperson became an adviser, and the customer felt a reduced pressure to buy and to remain attached to someone who may not have been a good match—a gutsy move because suppliers could have rebelled. They were used to having the commission structure as a lever to target merchandise that they wanted to move, whether because of a high profit margin or obsolete design. The commission structure was an important part of their marketing. Best Buy did end up retaining suppliers and fundamentally changed the buying experience. Years later, in 2005, Best Buy eliminated mail-in rebates, another change that ultimately made the customer's life easier but again disrupted the promotions of suppliers.

After 2000 the aftermath of the high-tech-bubble meltdown, together with the 9/11 incident, made the market environment difficult. Further, Walmart and Amazon as well as Costco and Dell had emerged as huge threats because they all were entering the consumer electronics space with substantial advantages. So how was Best Buy going to compete with these firms that had virtually destroyed competitors in books, music, videos, and toys?

The answer that emerged after Best Buy had examined customers, trends, and competitors was to create a new subcategory, selling service instead of or in addition to products. Customers were extremely frustrated by products that were hard to evaluate and impossible to set up. There were too many extra features that contributed to hypercomplexity and total frustration when it came to installing and operating the products in the home or office, especially when they were expected to work with other products. Best Buy aimed to provide a service surrounding the buying and installation of the equipment that would reduce the time, bad decisions, and stress involved. The cornerstone of these strategies was the Geek Squad and such customer-centric programs as the Twelpforce.

The Geek Squad was an eight-year-old, fifty-person Minneapolis startup that installed and repaired computers when Best Buy bought it in 2002. It was founded by Robert Stephens, like Microsoft's Bill Gates a college dropout, with $200 and a bicycle.[2] The firm was tiny and local but had established some credibility with its fixed-price offering by serving some big customers, and Stephens was a talent. It was expected to provide the foundation for a service that would address the unmet need of painless selection, installation, and repair of computer products. The Geek Squad provided a start-up core of people but also a brand, personality, and logo (see Figure 3.1) that fit into the Best Buy effort to imbue its brand with fun and irreverence. Because much of the Best Buy product line was about entertainment,

Figure 3.1 The Geek Squad Logo

it seemed like a good idea to move the brand away from the serious preoccupation with functions and price that dominates stores in their genre.

The Geek Squad developed a whole family of tongue-in-cheek characters. There were the special agents who would go on home cases, counter agents who would help in stores, double agents who would go to both, and covert agents who would assist over the phone. They drove in Geekmobiles, VW bugs with colorful Geek Squad graphics. Stephens once described the Geek Squad as a "living comic book."[3] They dressed in uniforms that were impossibly geeky, with clip-on ties, black pants, and white socks included. Over time they expanded their portfolio to include home theaters; car installation services; iPod and MP3 services. There is now a Web site; a way to check the progress of your order on the Internet; a route to priority service (911 repair); a blog; and a partnership with the TV show, *HouseSmarts*.

The Geek Squad, an IT staff for the individual and a trusted advisor, became a determinant of store choice. Circuit City tried to copy with its Firedog in 2005, but it was too weak, too little, and too late in terms of both substance and brand. Walmart announced a plan to offer similar services via outsourcing, but that route has significant limitations. The Geek Squad in 2010 had over twenty thousand people, around 13 percent of all Best Buy employees, and drove a very profitable, fast-growing business.

Another element to support service orientation, called "customer centricity," was stimulated by the insight that the best customers should be identified and the buying experience should be tailored for them rather than for some average customer.[4] The archetypes of the primary customer sets might be the affluent tech enthusiast; the busy suburban mom; the young, gadget-oriented gamer; the price-conscious family man; and the small-business owner. A store would specialize in one or a small number of these segments depending on its clientele, and that would affect the layout, store features, and the type and training of people. In particular, stores that went after the busy suburban mom had personal shopping assistants who would guide, recommend, help with the transaction, and load equipment into vehicles. Stores after the young gamer have a good selection of games and an area where the games can be tried out.

Still another initiative that fits with the new thrust was the Twelpforce, whereby hundreds of employees interact with customers via Twitter. They can answer questions in real time about service or application issues. The tweets are aggregated and available for the customer interested in a particular issue on the Best Buy Web site. The Twelpforce reinforces the fact that Best Buy has knowledgeable employees who will help you have a better purchasing and user experience and provides a useful information platform that for some will be a go-to source.

In 2009 Best Buy embarked on a program that potentially could create a new subcategory: stores that have taken the leadership on recycling electronics and have a concern for the environment.[5] It's management recognized that sustainability is a rising social value and thus a business opportunity. Best Buy had experimented with small recycling efforts since 2001, but in March 2009 they launched a program, ultimately branded as Greener Together, to take almost anything electronic at no cost. TV sets, computers, and monitors required a $10 recycling fee that was balanced by a $10 discount coupon. Unlike the Geek Squad, this effort will not make money, but it provides a service to customers and validates a claim to having a cradle-to-grave relationship with customers. It also gets customers to make a store visit, which is an important part of store marketing. More important, it helps the brand. It makes Best Buy stand out as a green leader in environmental sensitivity and sustainability and thus for many provides another basis for a relationship. People like to do business with firms they respect and admire.

There is a possibility that the recycling effort may lead to eventually to such offerings as solar panels and windmills.

Credibility in the energy space could also lead to products by which energy use could be monitored and controlled by a home computer system. Best Buy is already selling electric motorcycles, perhaps the ultimate energy-conserving mode of transportation.

The Best Buy breakthrough move to a service offering involved several drivers. First, there was an obvious unmet need. It did not take a lot of insight to know that customers were incredibly frustrated installing and using consumer electronics and became even more so when the components had to work together. Customer research, while not providing the driving insight, did quantify the unmet need and make it more visible internally. Second, the recycling program was driven by a major trend toward being green and was influenced by the desire to deepen the brand-customer relationship by being a part of the process from selecting a product to disposing of it after its life was over. Third, there was the specter of large, formidable competitors moving into the Best Buy space with the ability to price aggressively. A new point of differentiation that would make competitors less relevant was needed. The consulting relationship with customers, the Geek Squad, and the recycling programs did just that. Finally, Best Buy was internally motivated to take its customer relationship to a new level, and they committed to invest in stores, people, and processes to make it happen.

Whole Foods Market

In 1978 John Mackey and a partner opened a natural food store in Austin, Texas, under the Saferway brand, which was a spin on the Safeway brand. Two years later a merger with another small, local brand prompted the first Whole Foods Market store. From this beginning, Whole Foods Market, under the leadership of Mackey, became a major grocer that is a source of natural food (food with no additives, preservatives, or sweeteners) and organic food (food that has not been exposed to chemicals and related contaminates during production). Its success has been in part based on an ability to acquire or merge with other like-minded regional supermarkets and imbue them with the Whole Foods Market culture, operations, and features. In 2009 Whole Foods Market had around two hundred seventy-five stores, some in Europe, and was approaching $10 billion in sales. In the process, it became very different from other grocery chains in at least three ways.

First, it is a visibly socially responsible firm with a stated purpose to care about communities, people, and the environment. The tagline is "Whole Foods, whole people, whole planet." Although all firms aspire to be socially responsible, few deliver, and even fewer get market credit for what they do. Whole Foods Market has tangible programs that make a difference. Further, these programs are cumulatively visible and reinforce its reputation as not only going further than others but really caring. The result is a connection with the prime target segments that is based on shared values and respect for effective programs.

The Whole Foods Market social programs and related customer information and protection initiatives are impressive. It has enforced farmed seafood standards and was the first U.S. retailer to offer seafood certified by the Marine Stewardship Council, an independent organization that fosters sustainable fishing practices and has created and enforced extensive aquaculture environmental standards for farmed seafood. It changed its buying to reflect more humane treatment of animals. In 2006, Whole Foods Market became the only Fortune 500 company to offset 100 percent of its energy with wind power credits. In 2007, it created the Whole Trade Guarantee programs, which affirms that the identified products involve good worker wages and working conditions and sound environmental practices plus 1 percent of the retail price goes to the Whole Planet Foundation for poverty relief. More visibly, the firm eliminated the use of disposable plastic grocery bags, in part by selling large, colorful bags made out of recycled bottles, a designer version by Sheryl Crow is shown in Figure 3.2. These programs and others were so on-brand and cumulatively visible that Whole Foods Market garnered a host of associated awards.

Second, Whole Foods Market has and conveys a passion for food and health. They aspire to satisfy and delight, to make the shopping process fun and interesting. The product assortment contains items like fresh soup, bakery goods, and food to

**Figure 3.2 Sheryl Crow Signature
Reusable Shopping Bag**

go that involve the customer with aromas, tasting opportunities, and a wide selection. Shopping becomes a stimulating adventure. A host of items that are first seen at Whole Foods Market and others are unique to its store. The availability of healthy items makes it clear where its interests and priorities lie. The "team members" reinforce the core values around natural, organic, and healthy eating because they are informed, involved and clearly care.

Third, Whole Foods Market has developed the capability of providing organic and natural food with consistent quality and extensive selection. It has a program to actively manage the handling and labeling of organic and natural products. Its experience with sourcing and presenting such food products is not easy to duplicate. For the growing segment that looks for organic and natural products, Whole Foods Market becomes the go-to place.

Other stores are trying to respond by increasing their organic and natural selections, but it is a struggle because Whole Foods Market not only has the competence to deliver but also has an authenticity that comes from its legacy and values. Others can copy what they do but not who they are. The reality is that many of Whole Foods Market's competitors are more interested in logistics, warehousing, checkout efficiency, and making money than in food, and it shows.

Whole Foods Market represents a commitment strategy. It has a passion about its business that shows up in its culture and operations and is hard to duplicate. The horizontal merger and acquisition strategy has enabled the firm over the years to build what was a local business into a national and potentially global business, thereby creating scale advantages. Whole Foods Market kept its eye on the ball and did not get diverted by other business ventures not related directly to its business and its passion.

Whole Foods Market had the timing right and developed advantages hard for competitors to overcome. The demand for natural and organic food enjoyed years of 20 percent growth, spawned in part by a revolution in sensitivity and attitudes toward eating, and became hard to ignore. Healthy eating and environmental issues were in the news and in the bookstores and affected attitudes toward brands. Despite these increasingly visible trends, the natural and organic movement was below the radar screens of most major food retailers for many years. It was considered in large part a quasi-hippy niche that was happily delegated to small fringe retailers. The niche grew, however, and some of those fringe retailers ended up joining Whole Foods Market.

It was not until around 2005, when the sales of natural and organic products reached about $14 billion, that the major supermarket chains took notice and began to ramp up their offerings. The established chains recognized that a looming relevance problem faced them. There was a growing segment that wanted credible natural and organic food. In addition, the presence or absence of such food was a signal that the store was or was not interested in healthy food. Because the trends had reached a tipping point, the food chains had to act by adding natural and organic food to their selections. The problem then was branding, because they did not have adequate brand platforms to support credible organic and natural offerings.

One supermarket branding route was to use subbrands. In 2006 Safeway launched the O Organic brand, which was so successful that it was sold outside the Safeway chain. That same year Kellogg's developed an organic version of its major cereal products, such as Organic Raisin Bran. The chains, however, had several problems. Their brands, even with a strong subbrand like O Organic or a supplier brand like Kellogg's, were at a disadvantage compared with Whole Foods Market, who not only had credibility of delivering but also of believing. The food chains were at best going to deliver functional benefits. And delivering was not that easy, because the supply was limited and the operations involved in maintaining organic purity were daunting.

The Subway Story

Subway has now over thirty-two thousand restaurants in over ninety countries, doing over $90 billion in sales. It is consistently ranked number one in *Entrepreneur* magazine's list of top franchises.[6] Started in 1965, it grew to sixteen outlets in 1974 when it decided to convert to a franchise model. During the 1980s and 1990s Subway was a submarine sandwich shop offering good value with fresh ingredients, baked bread, an ability to have the sandwich made "your" way, and an obvious emphasis on cleanliness and food safety. As the leader in the subcategory, Subway had a value proposition that was all about the heartiness and freshness of sub sandwiches. The signature sandwich was the BMT, which meant "biggest, meatiest, tastiest," and included salami, pepperoni, and ham.

In 1999 everything changed. First, there was the trend during the 1990s toward healthy eating, and the role of fat, particularly saturated fat and trans fat, had become visible. Second, a 1999 article appeared in *Men's Health* about a college student, named Jared Fogle, who lost 245 pounds by walking and by eating a Subway diet consisting of two Subway sandwiches each day, a 6-inch turkey at lunch and a foot-long veggie at dinner.[7] Third, Subway had a latent ability to deliver healthy meals as compared to the pizza, hamburger, fried chicken, and taco alternatives. Something clicked at Subway—these three facts came together. The result was the creation of a new subcategory, healthy fast-food meals. The new subcategory was a portion of the submarine sandwich market and a small part of all fast-food offerings, but it had substance and momentum.

The relatively easy first step was to exploit the existing Subway menu. In 1997 Subway developed a logo around its "7 under 6" menu—7 of its sandwiches had fewer than 6 grams of fat. This became the centerpiece of its healthier fast-food brand. Of course, most of its customers order more indulgent sandwiches, but the healthier choices were very visible.

Subway surrounded the "healthier" claim with nutritional information that is on signage out front as opposed to hidden behind the counter.

Over time Subway buttressed the substance and appearance of its healthier menus. In 2003 they added a Kids Pak with a juice box, a fruit roll-up, and an active toy. The next year Subway introduced a line of carb-controlled wraps with under 5 grams of net carbs and created a school curriculum with the tagline, "One Body? One Life? Eat Fresh! Get Fit!" aimed at elementary students supported by a subwaykids.com Web site. In 2007 Subway launched its FreshFit and FreshFit for Kids meals, which feature healthier-for-you side options, such as apple slices, plump raisins, low-fat milk, bottled water, and Dannon yogurt. Subway developed the meals to fit into the American Heart Association's approach to a healthy lifestyle. To support FreshFit, 150 Subway brand ambassadors awarded bicycles and thousands of Subway Cash Cards to consumers and spectators for their "random acts of fitness"—such as climbing stairs or power walking. That same year Subway removed all trans fat and added higher-fiber wheat and honey oat breads.

The key to the creation of the healthy fast-food subcategory was Jared Fogle, his Subway story, and the symbol of his huge pants. He became a centerpiece of the advertising and a spokesman, spending two hundred days a year representing Subway. He has done a lot more than tell the story. He has gotten involved with programs to turn his story into progress on helping kids turn to healthier choices that provide nutrition and energy. Among the kids' programs were Jared's Steps to Healthier Kids information cards and a Jared and Friends School Tour, which stressed the importance of healthy eating and exercise. In addition, the FreshFit launch teamed Jared Fogle and musician LL Cool J on a double-decker bus for a TV and print media event in Times Square in New York City.

The totality of the program worked. Subway became the healthy fast-food alternative. In 2009 Zagat Fast-Food Survey rated the Subway brand as the number-one provider of "healthy options."[8] The three drivers were the substance behind the menu; the brand behind the "7 under 6"; the symbol of Jared's story backed up by a real person; and the vision that generated an ongoing stream of programs that supported the healthy eating position. The menu plus advertising would not have led to success.

A side story about how Subway needed to be concerned with staying relevant in the face of an emerging subcategory. Subway became conscious of the appeal of the fast-growing rival Quiznos, who had created its own subcategory—toasted submarine sandwiches—and had become the number-two brand. Started in 1981, by 2000 they had one thousand stores, and by 2003 that number had doubled. In response, Subway installed ovens in all its units in 2005 and offered its customers the choice of toasted versions of its sandwiches. Subway did not promote this additional feature; the intent was not to join the toasted subcategory but to remove a reason not to choose Subway, to maintain its relevance to those attracted to toasted sandwiches.

Zappos

A brand about happiness? Disney? Actually, it is Zappos.

In 1999 Nick Swinmurn spent a frustrating day trying to find shoes. Stores were out of his size or color or model. Reasoning that an online e-commerce retailer could stock a wide range of shoes and remove this source of frustration, he started a firm called Shoesite.com. In part because 1999 was at the height of the Internet boom, Swinmurn sold the idea to the venture firm Venture Frogs, who funded it with a $500,000 investment under the proviso that he hire someone who knew shoes.

Venture Frogs was cofounded by Tony Hsieh (pronounced Shay), who was also the cofounder of LinkExchange, which was sold to Microsoft for $275 million even though the firm only had $10 million in sales and Hsieh was only twenty-four years old. Hsieh, a computer science major at Harvard, was at the right place at the right time. Those were the days. With his share of the money, Hsieh decided to start Venture Frogs as a fund that would incubate Internet startups.

Swinmurn found that, even with a shoe person from Nordstrom on board, the operational task was too much. Shoe firms were reluctant to participate, associating the Internet with low prices and wanting to protect their existing retail relationships. Also, the use of local retailers to fill orders via dropshipping, the only feasible operating model, was expensive and did not provide good service because too often the ordered models were out of stock. After six months and with only three manufacturers on board, the company was failing. It was the story of most start-ups with great ideas capable of creating new categories or subcategories: underfunding, real barriers to execution, and inadequate staffing and leadership. In this case, however, Hsieh, tired of financing troubled firms and desiring to create a place where work would be fun, gave the concept a chance by stepping in to underwrite the firm, and, as important, becoming the co-CEO.

The name was changed to Zappos, stimulated by the Italian word for "shoes," *zapatos*, and by the realization that in the long run the firm should not be locked into shoes. In fact they eventually went into eyewear, handbags, apparel, watches, and electronics and even had backburner ideas to go into service-intensive industries like banking, hotels, or airlines. The name was not the only change. Because of the difficulty of obtaining a broad array of shoe manufacturers, a decision was made to change the firm's brand essence to over-the-top service rather than broad selection. A tagline of "Powered by service" was ultimately created. The manufacturer scope did, however, grow.

There were fifty manufacturers on board after a year and a half, and one hundred a year later. However, it would take seven years before Nike became a participant.

The mission was to have the best service in the industry. The signature policies were free shipping (customers expecting five or six days were surprised to get shoes by air); a 365-day return policy with free shipping; and a call center that was open 24/7 and staffed in the United States with involved, informed, customer-oriented representatives. Zappos, unlike other e-commerce firms, actually encourages customers to call in, with a visible 800 number believing that the resulting personal contact with its sales reps will foster the relationship with the brand. Zappos also departed from most e-commerce firms by not competing on price. It was about service and selection. In order to deliver the service expected, in 2003 Zappos opened a warehouse in Kentucky and basically stopped all drop-shipping, allowing them to control the logistics and reduce the out-of-stock incidences.

This level of service was expensive. It was financed in part by foregoing profits and having a reduced marketing budget. The firm did not turn profitable until 2006 when sales reached $600 million. Hsieh reasoned that the marketing budget was better spent on free shipping and a 24/7 call center, which would generate word-of-mouth advertising. Further, search-engine marketing was extremely effective and inexpensive—Zappos simply bought the brand names of shoe manufacturers so that when a customer searched for a shoe brand on Google, a Zappos ad would appear.

The real secret to the service level is not so much the policies and the programs as the culture and values of the company. The first value is to deliver WOW customer service. The up-front goal is to exceed expectations and to generate customer loyalty. One story, among many, is that when Zappos was informed that shoes were ordered for a husband who died in a car accident, the call center rep not only refunded the purchase price but sent flowers to the funeral. On her own.

Other values encourage employees to drive change, be creative and open minded, pursue growth, build open and honest relationships, build a family spirit, be passionate, and be humble. But the value that defines the atmosphere more than the others is to create fun and a little weirdness. The ability to be offbeat and quirky, thereby making life in the office fun and unpredictable and encouraging innovation, is not only tolerated but communicated externally as well as internally and rewarded.

The hiring and training process and the reward system help make it possible to maintain a strong culture even though wages and perks (except for generous health care) were below average. The hiring process includes a culture-matching section. For example, applicants are asked to describe how weird they are on a 1-to-10 scale—the number is not as important as the reaction to the question. A humbleness test involves asking whether the last title the applicant had was appropriate. Applicants, particularly senior ones, are evaluated in informal social settings. There is a two-week culture-training session, followed by two weeks in the call center and one week in the warehouse. After that time, employees are given $2,000, no questions asked, to leave the firm if they do not feel comfortable with the culture. Unlike at most call centers, the representatives are not measured by the length of call or by sales. Rather, there are spot checks of their conversations, and representatives are measured to the extent to which they make the customer feel happy and connected. The goal is personal emotional connection (PEC). A failure to fit the culture is grounds for dismissal.

The culture is supported as well with a host of activities that reinforce the values. Hsieh, whose modest desk is tucked into a row of cubicles, twitters regularly to the employees and some 1.6 million followers with thoughtful notes that are designed to inspire, inform, connect, or entertain. Employees contribute each year to a culture book with a one-hundred- to five-hundred-word comment on what the Zappos culture means to them. The book is sent to anyone interested. The office has jungle creepers that hang from the ceiling, and some have bells or pompoms used to greet visitors. Visitors coming to see great service in action are common. Managers are expected to spend 10 to 20 percent of their time socializing with those working for them.

Zappos, like Disney, is selling its culture programs and tricks to others. They have a two-day, $4,000 seminar on how to create a strong culture. A Web site, Zappos Insights, offers management videos and tips from staffers at a cost of $39.95 a month. This effort reinforces the culture internally and provides credibility and buzz around the service mission of Zappos externally.

Back to happiness. Hsieh has taken a professional interest in happiness and concluded that the Zappos vision should be to deliver happiness to customers and employees. He noted that the many happiness studies and theories from psychology and elsewhere suggest that happiness is influenced by four basic needs: perceived control, perceived progress, connectedness, and being part of a larger vision. He has attempted to make sure that Zappos has responsive programs and policies.

Perceived control is achieved in part by allowing Zappos employees to have control over the customer relationships. The call center representatives, for example, are not tied to scripts but are encouraged to be themselves and let their personalities show through. Further, they have as much authority to handle customer problems as Hsieh has. Employees also have some control over their compensation, in that they can earn raises by completing courses in some twenty skill sets.

Professional progress is ongoing at Zappos both in terms of training and advancement. Those with two years of experience or more can choose among a host of professional development programs, from specialized training to personal development, for example in public speaking. Promotions happen more quickly because they are broken down into six-month increments that make progress more continuous, and there are a variety of recognition opportunities.

The last two dimensions of happiness are driven by the culture. Connectiveness is encouraged with a familial social atmosphere, events, and the culture hiring screening. It is measured by how many best friends are within the firm. The values, in particular delivering WOW service, provide the larger vision. Zappos was never about sales goals but, rather, about delivering the best service possible.

Happiness applies to customers as well. In particular, the customer has a great deal of control, is part of an interactive family of customers and employees, and is often aware that the Zappos relationship is about more than transactions. The customer-driven architecture of the Web site allows customers to control the shopping experience. They are encouraged to call if they need advice or assistance. The passionate customers that resonate with the Zappos values and experience can create or view videos with commentaries on Zappos and can put an "I love Zappos" button on their Facebook pages. The act of spreading the word about Zappos broadens and deepens the brand relationship. The culture, values, and happiness concepts enabled Zappos to create a new subcategory of retailing based on employee energy and empowerment to deliver WOW customer relationships. Interestingly, the strategy was pushed without the support of the venture capital investors, who felt it held back short-term profitability. In the long run, it has clearly paid off.

Zappos exceeded $1 billion in sales in 2008 and was sold to Amazon in 2009 for an estimated $1.2 billion. Amazon asked Heish to run Zappos independently with a mandate to maintain and enhance the culture and the delivery of high-touch, WOW customer service in the face of Amazon's focus on low prices. The substantial barriers that Zappos has created in the form of customer relationships are expected to be enhanced as Zappos accesses Amazon's technology and infrastructure to become more efficient and to deliver even better customer performance in terms of in-stock, fast, efficient order fulfillment. Sounds like a combination that might indeed create the elusive synergy that is so often assumed in major acquisitions. The fans and members of the Zappos team are looking forward to seeing this vision emerge.

Key Takeaways

- A strong vision and culture that connects to a core customer group, as we saw in Muji, IKEA, Whole Foods Market, Zara, H&M, and Zappos, provides energy during the early years and direction and commitment as the firm experiences growth and scope expansion.

- A vision-driven organizational culture that involves values, programs, and leadership, it is hard to copy.

- Brand equity, a significant barrier to competitors, can be based on brand visibility and on customer relationships involving emotional and self-expressive benefits that can run deep and are not easily disturbed.

- Timing is critical, because the task is hard enough without wind at your back. Whole Foods Market and Muji benefited from growing interests in their visions. Zappos would not have worked in another time when the Internet was at a different stage of maturity.

- Concepts evolve over time, especially during the early days of a firm's growth. Muji, IKEA, Best Buy, and Whole Foods Market all started small in scope and ambition and expanded the vision as they got traction and found things that worked. Zappos changed from assortment to service as the key value proposition.

- An unmet need that is not served well or is hidden from view will often drive the concept. Zappos, for example, was stimulated by a frustrating shopping experience that existing shoe retailers did not think to question.

- Operations, critical to success, are difficult, requiring financing, innovation, people with specialized skills who believe, and an inspiring vision and champion.

- Brands can carry the innovation message. The Geek Squad, for example, told the service story vividly with humor and personality. The "7 under 6" helped Subway communicate.

- Green values and social programs are popular with a growing portion of most markets, and few organizations have credibility in the space. Whole Foods Market and Muji have broken through with visible substance and are seen as sharing the values, interests, and even lifestyles of an important customer segment.

For Discussion

1. Identify some highly differentiated retailers. What makes them different? How do they achieve and maintain that difference?

2. Evaluate Best Buy's decision to buy the Geek Squad instead of building a capability from within. What are the pros and cons of the decision? What was the key issue that drove the decision?

3. Why didn't other shoe stores create the Zappos model when Zappos started? Compare Zappos to Nordstrom.com as a shoe site.

4

MARKET DYNAMICS IN THE AUTOMOBILE INDUSTRY

I'm going to democratize the automobile. When I'm through, everybody will be able to afford one, and about everyone will have one.

—*Henry Ford*

Daring ideas are like chessman moved forward; they may be beaten, but they start a winning game.

—*Goethe*

Consider the history of the automobile market during the last century. There were a dozen or so innovations that have created new business arenas, such as the enclosed car; the assembly line; the GM spectrum of cars from the Chevrolet to the Cadillac; installment selling; the automatic transmission; rental cars; the Japanese cars of the 1970s that came in standard and deluxe versions, eliminating a host of choices; station wagons; convertibles; minivans; SUVs; crossovers; luxury trucks; hybrids; and mini-cars. In addition, path-breaking cars that have changed the face of the industry include the Model T, Jeep, Ford Thunderbird, Ford Mustang, Fiat 500 minicar, VW bug, Pontiac Firebird, Dodge Caravan and Plymouth Voyager, Lexus LS 400, Mazda Miata, Saturn, Prius, Minicooper, Hyundai, and Nano to name a few. And in the auto rental market there have been Enterprise Rent-A-Car and Zipcar. In each case the innovators achieved above-average profits that sometimes extended for years.

We want to take a look at a few of these subcategories and the brands that created them—Toyota's Prius hybrid, the Chrysler minivan, GM's Saturn, Tata's Nano, Yugo, Enterprise Rent-A-Car, and Zipcar. The goal is to learn how firms were able to create and dominate new subcategories and why competitors stood by and watched. The automobile industry is a particularly good context from which to gain insights into competitors' reactions to clearly market-changing innovations. Winning the relevance battle depends a lot on what competitors do or fail to do. These stories illustrate that reality rather vividly.

Toyota's Prius Hybrid

The Prius was introduced into the United States in 2000 and became not only the dominant hybrid car in a growth submarket but the symbol of Toyota's technological leadership and ecological commitment. A decade after its introduction it had been improved in its appearance and performance and retained its dominance. The story is instructive.

The hybrid, it turns out, is not new. Ferdinand Porsche, then a twenty-three-year-old engineer, developed a hybrid car termed the Mixte, which was introduced in 1901 and had high marks for gas mileage and performance. It was developed at the behest of a coach builder in Vienna who wanted a silent, battery-operated car. Porsche concluded that a battery-only car was not feasible and that a hybrid was the only solution. Electric and hybrid cars had a niche during the first years of car production. In fact, in 1900, 38 percent of the cars were electric. However, the gas-powered car became dominant because of a demand for faster cars; the availability of cheap gasoline; the construction of highways; Ford's inexpensive Model T, introduced in 1908; and the invention of the self-starter, first offered by Cadillac in 1912, which eliminated a very annoying and dangerous design limitation of gasoline cars, the hand crank. For over half a century, battery-powered cars operated under the radar as cheap gasoline and improvements in gas-powered engines emerged.

The gas embargo of 1973 stimulated a government initiative to create more efficient cars. It led to the corporate average fuel economy (CAFE) regulation of 1975, which specified that the average mpg of each automobile firm must improve over time (although, somewhat strangely, heavy SUVs and trucks were excluded, in part because of the political influence of farmers and small businesspeople who used trucks). Complying with the CAFE regulations was a challenge for sure. Although the hybrid was a potential solution, there was little progress in Detroit.

A curious exception was the work of an engineer and inventor: Victor Wouk had been working on a hybrid under the auspices of the founder of Motorola, who was worried about air pollution as early as the 1960s. Wouk was drawn to a hybrid design because of the limitations of the battery-powered option. The Environmental Protection Agency, the driver of the initiative, tested a Wouk vehicle and found that it met the strict guidelines for emissions and was fuel efficient. Nevertheless, in a puzzling decision, the EPA rejected it outright despite the fact that the world price for oil had not declined substantially. There were undoubtedly political and interpersonal reasons based in part on the fact that Wouk was a Detroit outsider. It is not enough to have the best car if there are barriers to bringing the car to market that are not overcome.

Even more puzzling was why one of the U.S. manufacturers did not pick up on the innovation and create a subcategory and brand. There are a host of potential economic, political, technical, and market-based explanations. In particular, automobile manufacturers (who of course influence legislators in different ways) may have been concerned that success would create costly and inconvenient mandates. In addition, there were perceived corporate limitations, the risk-adverse culture of the U.S. firms, and strategic momentum toward existing technology. There might also have been a not-invented-here syndrome. In retrospect, it may have been an opportunity lost. Even if early models had not been profitable, improvements over time could have resulted in a dominant position in an attractive market, especially six years later when the price of oil nearly doubled again. But Detroit auto manufacturers, their customers, and legislators have again and again been unwilling to face such contingencies.

In 1978 an auspicious technological development occurred that was important to the hybrid's future. When a car brakes, power is dissipated into the air through heat and is thus lost. An engineer, David Arthurs, developed a way to collect this power and use it to recharge the batteries. Termed a regenerative braking system, it did much (along with a host of other innovations) to make the hybrids of today feasible.

A note about battery-powered cars needs to be inserted here, because their development is linked to the hybrid in regard to technology and politics. In 1990, influenced by a battery-powered GM prototype car sponsored by GM's then-CEO Roger Smith, the California Air Resource Board (CARB), searching for way to meet the state's Clean Air Act, declared that automobile companies doing business in the state would have to produce zero-emission vehicles that made up 2 percent of California auto sales by 1998, 5 percent by 2001, and 10 percent by 2003. That regulation stimulated activity in battery-powered cars.

The most notable battery-powered car was the GM EV1 subcompact. Just over one thousand cars were produced and leased from 1996 to 1999 at a substantial price premium. However, given the EV1 experience, particularly its high manufacturing cost, GM did not have confidence that a battery-powered car was viable. GM cars and those of competitors were ultimately used as evidence in court and in CARB hearings to successfully argue that the CARB standards were unrealistic and needed to be relaxed. When CARB relaxed the 1998 standards in a step toward getting rid of them on the basis that the technology, particularly in batteries, would not be ready, GM, Ford, and others gratefully killed the products. GM, in fact, tried to destroy all such cars on the road. Rick Wagoner, GM's CEO from 2000 to 2009, opined late in 2006 that GM's biggest blunder was to walk away from the electric car.[1] The year 2006 was a time when GM was making a big bet on another electric car, the Chevrolet Volt, introduced in 2010.

Back to the hybrid story. In 1993 the Partnership of a New Generation of Vehicles (PNGV) was formed, stimulated in part by the work of Vice President Al Gore and by the CARB regulations. A research program designed to develop 80 mpg cars that run clean brought together the three U.S. auto manufacturers (therefore excluding Toyota and the other foreign makers) plus some eight federal agencies and several universities. The intent was to jumpstart the technology development so that internal combustion engines would have a viable, clean-air competitor. Nearly $2 billion were invested, nearly half of which was paid by the government.

Diesel hybrids emerged as the best option after a variety of other paths were pursued to achieve the goal. All three manufacturers met or came close to the mileage claims with diesel-battery hybrid cars that were estimated to cost from $3,500 to $7,500 extra to make in production quantities. Despite that success, the program was terminated by the government in 2002 and replaced by one termed Freedom car, which focused on cars powered by hydrogen, a technology favored by GM, and which all agreed was the ultimate solution but was at least a decade away and probably much more.

Why didn't one of the three U.S. manufacturers use the diesel hybrid technology as a springboard to create and dominate the diesel hybrid area? The explanations are illuminating. First, the technology may not have been fully in place. In particular, the battery, a key component, was a barrier to mileage range and cost. A new battery technology that reduced the problem, the NiMH, only emerged in 2000 after the decision by the auto companies had been made to give up the chase. Second, the prototype cars, perhaps due to a spec mix-up, did not meet the current target level of emissions. So more work was needed. Third, in the small-car market, in which these cars would likely play, it was hard for U.S. manufacturers to make profits because of their cost structure, union wages, staff overhead, and expensive processes. And the cost premiums for hybrids were considered significant in a price-sensitive portion of the market.

The biggest barrier to U.S. participation in the hybrid market, however, was a mind-set against hybrids in favor of conventional gas-driven cars and trucks. The CARB regulations, the motivator for conducting research on hybrids, over time became diluted and less of a stimulus. It turned out that it was easier to get the politicians to change the regulations than to meet them. Further, there was the specter of hydrogen cars, so tempting even if they were off in the future. Among the problems were on-vehicle hydrogen storage issues and the formidable task of generating a system of stations to supply a driving public. As late as 2004 Bob Lutz, the influential vice-chairman of product development at GM, was quoted as saying that hybrids were an interesting curiosity.[2] But the hydrogen programs provided GM and the others with a story to tell to those who asked for a strategy. The reality is that the U.S. manufacturers did not believe in or want the hybrid. The commitment was not there. They just wanted to pacify the government.

In late 1995 Toyota's CEO Hiroshi Okuda, shut out of the PNGV research consortium, challenged his engineering team to develop a car that would double the mileage rating and to introduce that car in 1997. There is a colorful story about this decision that sheds light on Toyota. Okuda visited Daimler Benz in fall 1995 and was showed the A-Class car, which was intended to be the best small car on the road. Okuda was disturbed by the possibility that another manufacturer, particularly one from Europe, would take a leadership position in small cars. He was not going to have that happen! Hence the challenge. It was reminiscent of an initiative of another Toyota executive, Eiji Toyoda, who in August 1983 observed that car owners were growing more mature and affluent and challenged his organization to "create a luxury car to challenge the very best"—a challenge that resulted in the Lexus.[3]

Reacting to Okuda's goal, the chief engineer assigned to the job said it was impossible. However, given the choice of quitting or doing the job he decided to try. Getting inspiration from stories of others who did the impossible, he led the team to a successful introduction of the Prius in Japan in December 1997. To create that Prius, several technological advances and breakthroughs were required. Off-the-shelf technology was far from adequate. An improved version, with a much smaller and more reliable battery pack, was introduced as a compact car in the United States in 2000.

Toyota made the Prius a moving target with innovative features and improvements. The second U.S. generation, introduced in 2004, was now between the Corolla and Camry in size, with driving performance comparable to the 2004 Camry's. It featured a branded transmission, the Hybrid Synergy Drive, which optimizes the use of the battery, the gas engine, and the electric motor to recharge the battery. This branded component became a further point of differentiation and a statement of authenticity. The third U.S. generation came in 2009 with several models and options and was rated as the cleanest vehicle with the highest gas mileage sold in the United States. It is shown in Figure 4.1.

The Prius was an incredible success. By mid-2009 Toyota had sold over 1.2 million Prius automobiles. The Prius was by far the leader in the hybrid market with a share that was at 50 percent in 2008. And customers were loyal. Some 94 percent of Prius customers said they would rebuy the brand.[4] Although the early Prius cars lost money, by 2002 Toyota was reportedly making money on each Prius sold.

The Prius provided not only functional benefits but also the self-expressive benefit of doing something about the energy and global warming crises. In 2007 over half of the Prius buyers in one survey said the main reason they purchased the car

Figure 4.1 The Third-Generation U.S. Prius

was that "it makes a statement about me," a percentage that had grown over the years.[5] The Prius is only available as a hybrid. If a Prius is seen on the road or in a parking lot, there is no doubt that the owner has bought a hybrid. In contrast, buyers of a Honda Civic or Ford Escape SUV may or may not be driving a hybrid. You do not make a statement by buying a Civic or an Escape.

Further, the technology was expanded to other models, such as the Camry, the Highlander, and the Lexus. As a result, Toyota had sold over 1.7 million hybrids worldwide by 2009 and had close to a 79 percent share of the hybrid market. Also, the Prius enhanced Toyota's position as the most innovative brand in Japan and the most environmentally sensitive. Toyota has done many things in its factories and social programs to merit both claims. But it is the Prius that became a highly visible statement of Toyota's culture and values.

Where were Honda and the others? Honda actually introduced a hybrid into the U.S. market before the Prius. It was the Insight, a two seater that was in production from 1999 to 2006. During that time it sold only eighteen thousand units, so it was more of an extended test than a serious entry. In 2002 Honda introduced the Civic Hybrid, a more serious entry, but one that was tied to the Civic brand, which had a lot less energy than the Prius brand and struggled with 10 to 15 percent of the hybrid market. In 2009 Honda introduced another hybrid, under the brand Insight, meant to compete with the Prius in the U.S. market. However, the Insight, which challenged largely on the basis of price, had a disappointing start, perhaps because Prius buyers were not allowing price to dominate their decision making.[6] At least for the first decade, Toyota won both the technology and marketing battles.

Ford was the first U.S. manufacturer to release a hybrid, the Ford Escape hybrid SUV, which appeared in 2005 and was also the first SUV hybrid. Ford trailed Honda in the marketplace, however, and the other U.S. manufacturers were nonfactors. GM, after disparaging hybrids for years, in 2004 created a partnership with DaimlerChrysler to produce hybrid vehicles in 2006 that, at least initially, made little impact on the market.

Toyota dominated the compact hybrid subcategory for over a decade because of its ongoing innovations, both incremental and substantial, its strong brand, its marketing programs, its distribution strengths, and its commitment to the Prius. The commitment provided the resources for not only the initial success of the Prius but also the ongoing ability to create a moving target for competitors. The Toyota effort was aided by the mind-set of the U.S. manufacturers and the uncharacteristic inability of Honda to keep up technologically.

With Prius as the exemplar of the compact hybrid subcategory for the first decade of the century, another subcategory was emerging, all electric vehicles. Stimulated in part by the adaptation of lithium-ion batteries used in consumer electronics, a host of established and start-up firms, some in China, with dozens of brands are creating a market during the first part of decade following 2010. The challenge facing all electric car brands is to make consumers see that the fuel cost savings and contribution to the environment are worth the range limitations and the high cost of the vehicles. In part the range problem is perceptual in that most trips are short. Nevertheless, the image of running out of power with no convenient way to repower is a problem. A system of recharging or replacing batteries is emerging in some smaller countries, but for most, it will remain an issue. It is likely that electric cars will emerge as an option, but the nature and extent of their acceptance will depend on further battery development, recharging infrastructures, and the price of gasoline.

The Saturn Story

With the Prius initiative, Toyota showed what ongoing commitment to a new brand and subcategory means. GM showed a different kind of commitment in its Saturn venture to create a new subcategory of cars—U.S. compact cars with high quality and a different dealer experience. GM had a commitment to achieve success but a lack of commitment to perpetuate and leverage that success because of leadership changes, a focus on short-term profits, and the inability to fund so many businesses and brands.

On January 7, 1983, the GM chairman Roger Smith, the same Roger Smith who championed the GM electric car, announced the creation of the Saturn Corporation, calling it "the key to GM's long-term competitiveness, survival and success as a domestic producer." Their mission, in part, was to market compact vehicles developed and manufactured in the United States that "would be world leaders in quality, cost, and customer satisfaction."[7]

GM pulled it off by creating an independent, team-oriented organization with its own design team, a dedicated manufacturing plant in Spring Hill, Tennessee, with an informal partner relationship with the union very different from elsewhere at GM, and a completely new and innovative dealer network. It introduced a car in 1990 that for years was one of the quality leaders along with the higher-priced brands Lexus, Infinity, and Cadillac. The dealer experience, unprecedented in car retailing, with salaried, no-pressure salespeople, backyard BBQs, and the elimination of dreaded price negotiations. No-haggle pricing was made possible because adjacent dealers had common ownership, which meant that competitive dealers were not close by. Saturn sold the company—and its philosophy of treating customers with respect, like a friend—rather than the car. Saturn customers and employees truly believed the tagline—"a different kind of company, a different kind of car." It was done under the leadership of a charismatic though soft spoken CEO, Skip LeFauve, who broke a host of GM norms and procedures in the process. Saturn was an enormous success in terms of sales and resale value, and achieved remarkable customer loyalty. A few customers even got married in their Saturns. Saturn owners not only acted as advocates but as sales consultants to prospective buyers. And over forty thousand of them came to Spring Hill for a party in 1994. Shades of Harley-Davidson loyalty. Saturn owners were proud of the fact that an American company had made a quality car and created a customer relationship based on friendship and respect.

Competitors were stymied. The distribution model could not be duplicated by the others who were locked into their systems because of the dealer ownership history, which were protected by onerous state laws. Saturn had no legacy dealers, they started with a blank sheet of paper. Further, the Saturn group had cracked the quality code, virtually the only Detroit organization to do so except the Toyota-GM joint manufacturing effort (NUMMI), which was never successfully transferred to other GM plants. Saturn employees, including the union members, were all on the same team and made sure the quality never faltered. Finally, the intense, Harley-level loyalty of customers was not something another brand could capture, especially at the value end of the market. Saturn was not an expensive, prestige brand.

So what did GM do with this gem? Did it invest in a new model in the mid-1990s that would compete with the Camry, Accord, and Altima and therefore provide a platform to win against Toyota, Honda, and Nissan? No. For ten years, except for rather meaningless cosmetics, GM made no product investment in Saturn. Where did GM invest instead? In Oldsmobile!! GM created from scratch the Aurora, introduced in 1995, which lasted around four years except for a failed attempt to revive it in 2001. The Aurora was intended to save Oldsmobile, although, ironically, GM tried to eliminate any connection with Oldsmobile in marketing the Aurora because of Oldsmobile's image of being an old people's car lacking quality or design excellence. The Aurora failed in part because of its inability to create a new brand and because it simply was not a very good car with respect to quality. If the Aurora investment had been channeled to Saturn, the car would have been of superior quality—the Saturn family, the engineers, the manufacturing team, and the dealers would have made sure of that.

How could this have happened? What can be learned and applied today? First, GM had too many mouths to feed. Each brand would line up and say, "My turn." It was Oldsmobile's turn for a new model, and even though the Oldsmobile brand was in trouble, GM could not then bite the bullet and do away with the brand (although finally in 2004 it did die). Second, there was a preoccupation with short-term profits and a lack of strategic vision and scenario planning, a problem that is not at all unique to GM. For GM the Saturn line did not provide a healthy ROI, in part because it struggled to make money on lower-priced cars due to labor costs and because of the huge investment that was required to get Saturn off the ground (one estimate had it at $5 billion). Third, the Saturn champion Roger Smith was long gone and, worse, discredited because his policies (outlined in the next case study) of the 1980s turned out to be disastrous for GM. Fourth, GM's management at the top did not foster the kind of innovation and culture represented by Saturn, and the union at the corporate level was not a fan of the Saturn employee partnership with its flexible contract. GM failed to learn from Saturn, just as it failed to learn from its partnership with Toyota at the NUMMI plant in Fremont, California. Both were treated as entities removed from GM and the learnings from each could not penetrate the rigidities of the GM organization and culture.

GM executives in the 1990s did not share the dream of those who conceived the Saturn concept in 1985, that Saturn provided a platform to fight the Japanese brands, a platform that could be a key to the survival of GM, especially in the event of waning customer support for the big gas guzzlers. It was someone else's dream. The ongoing commitment shown by Toyota was missing. If Saturn had been given a set of larger cars to compete with Toyota, GM might have had a chance to win the war. Strategic vision was either absent or trumped by short-term ROI prospects.

In 2009 GM made the decision to close Saturn and walked away from a dealership asset that had created a completely different dealer experience.

The Chrysler Minivan

In 1974 a gifted Ford engineer, Hal Sperlich, with the support of marketing-oriented President Lee Iacocca, proposed that Ford build a minivan. Their research indicated that the market would be large if the step-up height were low enough to appeal to women, if the car could fit into a garage, and if there were a nose with an engine in front in order to provide protection for the driver in case of an accident. However, it would require a significant investment in tooling, and despite very promising research data such a new concept was not a sure thing. Further, the existing Ford platforms were all rear-wheel drive, and to get the roominess that would make the product most desirable required a front-wheel-drive system, which would be costly to develop. Henry Ford II, the CEO and part-owner of Ford, did not want to invest in the idea, especially at a time when Ford was somewhat financially stressed, and turned it down. He was influenced in part by his experience with the 1950s Edsel, which was one of the most disastrous car introductions ever; was reliant on the opinion of a risk-averse finance team; was irritated with the visibility of Iacocca and did not want another reason for him to gain the spotlight; and had a commitment to large cars, observing, "Small cars, small profits."

About five years later, Sperlich and Iacocca, having each been fired by Henry Ford, in some part because of their championing of the minivan, were at Chrysler. Both still had confidence in the minivan project and Iacocca as CEO now had the authority to go ahead with it. They were in the right place at the right time. Chrysler had just finished developing a front-wheel-drive platform, which was the basis for the successful K-car series. Further, Chrysler dominated the market for the full-size van, a truck-like vehicle too large for a garage with a share of some 45 percent, which gave them market experience and credibility. Their van product successes were based on car-like conveniences, such as power windows, good stereos, and rear-window defrosters, all features that would be helpful in the minivan arena. Perhaps most important, Chrysler was weak in the station-wagon market, in which both Ford and GM were making significant profits. The prospect of seeing a new minivan category take business away from station wagons was for Chrysler a good thing.

There was a problem. When Iacocca arrived in 1979, Chrysler was in bankruptcy and required a government bailout of some $1.7 billion (a lot of money in those days) in loan guarantees in order to finance the minivan and, in fact, in order to survive. Given the desperate need for new vehicles, Iacocca decided to spend $6.5 billion over five years on vehicle development, the first of which was the minivan. This rather gutsy decision might not have been made had Iacocca been a finance type who would look to restructuring and closing plants first, or if the situation had not been so dire that clearly some changes in the product profile were needed. So the crises may have helped.

On November 2, 1983, Chrysler introduced the minivan in the form of the Plymouth Voyager and Dodge Caravan, seven-passenger, front-wheel-drive, "garageable" minivans with roomy interiors, low step-in height, and removable seats. Termed the "Magic Wagon" by admirers, the new vehicle felt and drove like a car rather than a truck. It sold over 200,000 in the first year and over 12.5 million by 2009, by which time the Chrysler Town and Country had been added to the stable of brands.[8] With its early success, Chrysler made the tough decision to build a second plant, gambling that the initial sales results were not a short-term flash in the pan. It was exactly the kind of bet-the-firm decision Asahi made went they built additional capacity upon the initial success of Asahi Super Dry beer that was recounted in Chapter One. For at least sixteen years, Chrysler did not have a serious competitor, and over two decades later they were still the market leader. Everyone else was playing catch-up. In 2009, over twenty-five years after the minivan's introduction, Chrysler still had 44 percent of the market, more than Toyota and Honda combined.[9]

Competitors came up with inferior options to attempt to participate in the new category that Chrysler had created. It was not until Honda spent six months having its people study the experiences of U.S. drivers and came out with the second-generation Odyssey in 1998 that Chrysler had a real challenger. The first-generation Odyssey, which was not well received, was narrow, had four conventional doors, and had an underpowered four-cycle engine. Toyota introduced the Sienna in 1998, but it took a few years more until the car was improved to be a real alternative to the Chrysler products. Before that the Toyota offer was an odd-shaped, rear-wheel-drive, underpowered vehicle called the Previa.

The fact that Chrysler was the only viable option for the new category for some sixteen years and the leader after that time is remarkable. Its continuous improvement over time helped. Chrysler had many firsts in the minivan category. By 1990 the first all-wheel drive on a front-wheel platform and child-safety locks on sliding doors were added. A driver-side sliding door and Easy-Out Roller Seats were in place by 1995. During the next five years, wireless headphones and an LCD screen for in-vehicle entertainment systems plus three-zone temperature control became available. By 2009; the vehicles included a third-row easy-entry system, the Swivel 'n Go seat system, in which the second-row seats swivel, and an integrated child booster seat.

GM and Ford came out in 1985 with rear-wheel-drive, truck-like vans, the Chevrolet Lumina and the Ford Aerostar, which were perceived as lumbering and inefficient. Even in the mid-2000s, GM and Ford were not factors in the midsize minivan market, although they did have presence in the large-van market.

Why? Why did the major competitors allow Chrysler to own such an important segment for so long? The reasons differ a bit from player to player, but it boils down to investment priorities and strategic vision for their firms.

During the 1980s, under the finance-oriented CEO Roger Smith and his predecessors, GM was focused on cost reduction and high technology.[10] The bulk of the some $80 billion invested during the 1980s went to robots, most of which did not work or were actually destructive (one robot reportedly destroyed windshields while installing them), as a route to lower costs and smaller union payrolls. Another investment direction was into ill-advised technology firms, including $6.5 billion for Electronic Data Systems (EDS), Ross Perot's computer systems company, and some $5 billion for Hughes Aircraft. GM did invest in vehicles. There was a $7.5 billion effort to create a new midsize car that was needed but ultimately unsuccessful, the $5 billion invested in Saturn, investments in the truck and SUV markets, and efforts to increase the commonality across models to decrease costs. In addition, station wagons, competitors to minivans, were profitable—its business was a cash cow for GM.

Because of the GM strategy in the 1980s, there was no energy or vision directed at the minivan market created by Chrysler and no way to provide a vehicle that would be a competitor. The 1990s were a catch-up period for all GM models and processes given the mistakes of the 1980s that left no resources available to attack the minivan market, especially during the recession that began the decade.

In the 1980s and 1990s Ford prioritized three areas. First was the design project that resulted in the wildly successful Taurus (and Sable) car that was introduced in 1985 and became the largest-selling car until well into the 1990s. Second was the F-series truck, the largest-selling vehicle from 1978 into the 1990s. Third was the SUV-class vehicles built on the truck foundation. The Ford Explorer, introduced in 1990 as an SUV that provided extra comfort and amenities, led the category for many years. It was followed by a larger Ford Expedition in

1997 that was very profitable. The success of trucks and large SUVs was helped by the fact that the CAFE standards did not apply to them, an incredible loophole.

Ford's investment decisions were influenced by the biases of Henry Ford mentioned above and by two other factors. First, the Ford station-wagon business had been extremely profitable since the 1950s, generally selling over 200,000 cars a year and occasionally many more.[11] Throughout the 1980s Ford averaged 160,000 station wagons per year in sales. There was no incentive to help the minivans kill off the golden goose; rather, the more sensible strategy was to improve the station wagons and stave off the minivans. Second, Ford caught the diversification bug from GM and invested in financial services and high technology in addition to aggressively pursuing stock buybacks. There was little money left for a minivan, and they regarded the flawed Ford Aerostar as an adequate stop-gap product.

The reasons that the Japanese firms failed to offer minivans competitive to Chrysler for so long are very different. The Japanese manufacturers were hampered from 1981 to 1984 by voluntary quotas brought on by the fear that the U.S. government would do something extreme to reduce the threat of offshore products to the domestic industry. As a result, the efforts of the Japanese during the 1980s and 1990s were primarily aimed at creating entries into the high-priced car market so that each car shipped under the quota would provide more profit. As a result, the Acura, the Lexus, and the Infinity were introduced at the end of the 1980s. Another priority was improving the existing line of cars, because continuous improvement was a part of their DNA. Still another priority was to build a manufacturing capability in the United States in order to reduce the import stigma.

Chrysler had a sound, market-based vision and executed it flawlessly. They could not have done so unless a host of factors came together, financial and product crises, a gifted CEO and engineering executive, the existence of a front-wheel design at exactly the right time, and a very weak position in station wagons. They were also blessed with the fact that all five major competitors had different investment priorities and did not have the luxury to join the minivan surge.

Tata's Nano

The concept of a "people's car," one that has such a low price that it can open up the car market to the masses, has dramatically affected the industry at several points in time. In 1908 Henry Ford, inspired to create a car for the "great multitude," introduced the Model T, a car offered only in basic black that was based on a cost-sensitive, static design and the assembly-line technique. It sold over fifteen million cars over sixteen years, mostly to those who otherwise would not have been able to afford a car.

In 1932 Ferdinand Porsche had a vision of a *Volkswagen* (translated as "people's car") and designed what is now recognized as the famous Beetle. The Beetle sold over twenty-one million cars from 1946 to 2003, reaching its peak in the United States in 1968 when it sold 423,000 units, still a record. Remarkably, in a classic strategic blunder, Ford turned down the chance to take over the Beetle and its factories for nothing in 1946. Ford's right-hand man Ernest Breech reportedly concluded that the design would never sell in the United States and was not worth a damn. Like all such blunders, and there have been many over the years, the failure to project product evolutions and consider untapped markets was at the core of the tragic miscalculation.

In March 2009 history repeated as the new "people's car," the Tata Nano, aimed primarily at the Indian market, was commercially launched, having been announced just over a year earlier. It was a rear-engine, two-cylinder, four-passenger car designed for urban and rural use with a 52 mpg rating in city traffic. Scheduled to sell for $2,000 to $2,500, depending on the model, it was the least-expensive car made. This new "people's car" had the potential to disrupt automobile markets not only in India but also around the world.

The Nano concept was born when Ratan Tata, the chairman of the Tata Group, observed that two wheelers, with the father driving, a wife behind, and a child in front, was a common if not dominant transportation mode. He thought there had to be a four-wheel improvement that would be safer and more comfortable. Finding no interest in a cooperative development effort from partners throughout Asia, he decided that Tata should develop the car on its own (see Figure 4.2).

The initial idea, to base a vehicle on the two wheelers, was discarded as the existing parts were deficient and functional criteria steered the project toward a new, freshly designed car. As the process evolved, Tata upgraded the concept from a rickshaw-like vehicle without doors or windows to more of a modern enclosed car. The target price of $2,000 came from

Figure 4.2 The Nano

a casual estimate to the press of what it might be possible. This rather arbitrary estimate became the target for the design team. In addition, the team was charged with generating a design that would satisfy pollution and safety standards and achieve performance targets with respect to fuel efficiency and acceleration.

An intense focus on costs, based in part on restricting features to "essential" as opposed to "nice" and in part on sheer creative innovation, dominated the effort. Among the saving ideas were having only one windshield wiper, putting the instrument cluster in the middle of the dash so it would work for a both left and right-side drive, having common handle designs on each side, and designing a simplified engine-control computer with reduced sensors and functions. A mock-up of the car with its innards exposed was a centerpiece of an engineering team who were daily looking for ways to simplify and reduce costs. Tata did not do it alone. The suppliers were an integral part of the team and were the source of key cost-reduction approaches—over forty suppliers set up plants adjacent to the Nano plant to reduce logistics and inventory costs. The effort was global. The in-house design team was supplemented by an Italian-based design firm and the engine management systems was created by a supplier headquartered in Germany. In addition, government subsidies were obtained for building factories.

The Nano was able to leapfrog the Muruti 800, which was a popular four-passenger car in India. The Nano was much less expensive, however, and even had 21 percent more interior space because of its headroom, despite an 8 percent smaller exterior. It also scored high on fit and finish, and the deluxe version had many amenities, including air conditioning.

The Nano promised to greatly expand the market by bring automobile ownership to people who otherwise could not afford it—65 percent by one estimate. As a result it would obtain sales from new segments besides having an impact on sales of existing models. It was reminiscent of the inexpensive Swatch watch, which expanded the watch market without affecting the sales of the established Swiss watch manufacturers.

Demand was so strong that 206,000 people applied for a lottery to see who would get the first 100,000 cars during a three-week window in April 2009. A year later 45,000 cars had been delivered.

Yugo

Before the Nano was the Yugo, from Yugoslavia, which sold some 150,000 cars between 1985 and 1992.[12] A loser of historic proportions, it was poorly built, unsafe, broke down frequently, got poor gas mileage, and was dirty with respect to emissions. Over the years it has been repeatedly recognized with titles like "the worst car ever sold in America." There was no end to Yugo jokes.

- What is included in every Yugo manual? Ans: A bus schedule.
- What do a Yugo and a ceiling fan have in common? Ans: They both have the same motor.
- How do you make a Yugo go from 0 to 60 in under fifteen seconds? Ans: Push it off a cliff.
- How do you make a Yugo go fast? Ans: Use a tow truck.
- What do you call a Yugo with brakes? Ans: Customized.

The Yugo started off with excitement and sales. It had an auspicious introduction, with coverage in the media, lines at dealerships, favorable reviews from people who had not had a chance to drive the car, and a remarkable promoter. It was the fastest-selling first-year European import in U.S. history. But most of this excitement was in place before the car arrived. In fact, the scarcity helped the hype.

How could so many be so wrong? First, the Yugo was breath-takingly cheap, over 20 percent less than the least-expensive alternative, making a new car or second car much more afford-able. Second, it had the credibility of being based on a Fiat design and thus had an indirect endorsement from a major manufacturer. Third, it was made in the country that showcased a successful Olympics and that had a reputation, perhaps unde-served, of being able to make the buses run on time. Fourth, virtually no one questioned it. There was too much PR momen-tum. Everyone, even the experts, relied on the word on the street rather than actually testing the car.

The Yugo is a sobering lesson in how hype can take over. What you hear three times must be true. It is also a lesson in the importance of implementing the concept and delivering on the promise. The best idea poorly executed will fail.

Enterprise Rent-A-Car

Jack Taylor, the founder of Enterprise, started the business in 1962 with seventeen vehicles in St. Louis and the cus-tomer insight that people needed cars when theirs were being repaired. The business grew to nearly a million cars; a staff of 65,000; and a very different car-rental business model and strategy. Hertz, Avis, and the other rental car companies made the logical decision to focus on the heavy user, the business traveler, who would pay a premium for the conve-nience of airport rental facilities. They thus made a commit-ment to airport service and supporting facilities. Enterprise, in contrast, served those who needed cars in their home cities as replacement vehicles while their own were being repaired or for special occasions, such as weekend getaways. To serve its customer base, they developed retail sites all over each city and were able to claim that over 90 percent of U.S. citizens live within fifteen miles of an Enterprise loca-tion. Avoiding airport facilities gave them a significant cost advantage. Even when they started to serve airports in 1995, they used less-expensive, off-site locations.

Enterprise Rent-A-Car created a new subcategory of car rentals. With a series of innovations and programs that came to represent significant barriers to competition, Enterprise had its subcategory virtually to themselves for at least three decades, a recipe for profitability. The firm actually passed Hertz in sales during the mid-1990s, and in 2008 they had sales of $10.1 billion as compared to Hertz's $6.7 billion. Further, they were less susceptible to the ups and downs of the airline industry. The privately owned company was estimated to value at $17 billion in the last part of the first decade of the 2000s.[13]

Enterprise from the beginning has been highly entrepreneurial, with each of its offices representing a profit center. Because the customer base is local, the office manager and staff have room to build relationships and affect the business, much more so than a manager of an airport branch that serves out-of-town customers. There is an aggressive incentive program based on branch profitability, and employees are empowered to innovate. In fact, it was an Orlando office manger who in 1974 created the "We'll pick you up" program that has become an Enterprise signature promise.

At the same time, the Enterprise culture values customer service, emphasizing a distinctive professional dress, courteous demeanor, and personalized assistance. Jack Taylor started it all with this philosophy: "Take care of your customer and employees first, . . . and profits will follow." The incentive structure previously mentioned applies to customer service as well as profits. One of every fifteen customers is interviewed to determine if he or she is completely satisfied. The percent that check the "completely satisfied" box becomes a key performance measure for each branch, affecting promotions and compensation. This number approaches 80 percent across the company.

Recognizing that insurance companies, which generate one-third of their sales, and repair shops are important customers, Enterprise developed the Automated Rental Management System (ARMS) to provide an electronic interface for handling bookings, billings, payments, and more, making dealing with them painless and efficient. Its patents on the process provide potential difficulty for others encroaching on its turf. There is also a friendly Web site that puts the products and services at the fingertips of the insurance company as well as the end-user. Finally, Enterprise offers fleet management to larger companies, whereby they will manage the vehicle fleet, including deciding on the fleet profile, buying the vehicles, and managing the servicing that may be needed. The resulting infrastructure that Enterprise has developed generates a stickiness among the customer base that is difficult to overcome.

Enterprise has also created two additional barriers. First, its pervasive presence creates a significant value proposition around convenience, for customers and also for insurance companies who can deal with one firm for their rental car programs. It would be expensive for others to duplicate this level of coverage. Second, it has a cost advantage over its main competitors. Its profitability and balance sheet generate a credit rating of A, versus the B rating of Hertz, which means that the extensive financing of the car inventory can be done at a lower interest rate. Further, without the concession fees and staff expense of airport facilities, Enterprise has historically been at a cost advantage, although that advantage will be reduced as its program to enter airports grows.

Why did Hertz, Avis, and the rest allow Enterprise to become such a large, successful competitor? Could they not see the same opportunity? In part, the answer is no. The opportunity was for many years small relative to the total rental market, which was centered on airports, and Enterprise was thus just a minor curiosity. Hertz was virtually unaware of Enterprise as late as 1989, when Enterprise started advertising and was already a major force with some $600 million in sales.[14] More important, its eyes were elsewhere. Hertz was focused on and aggressively competing with the other airport brands, playing the brand preference game.

As Enterprise grew the market, its competitive advantages became significant such as its customer relationships, its insurance company service portfolio, its reputation among repair shops, its office coverage, and its cost advantages all provided barriers to competitors. When Hertz and the rest woke up, Enterprise was dominant in the major cities.

Zipcar

The major rental car companies were again blindsided by car sharing. Zipcar was started in 2000 in Boston on the basis of the completely new concept that people could share cars instead of owning them. Most cars in urban settings are used for only a few hours per week. Why should people pay for owning and maintaining cars when they are not being used? They could instead join a club and become Zipsters, allowing them access to cars located at sites around the city. Members can simply reserve cars online or by phone, any time of day or night, minutes or days or months before they need them. When they arrive at the cars, the microchips in their Zipcard membership cards will signal the cars to unlock. They then drive the cars for hours or days. All this can be aided by a Zipcar iPhone application. Parking, fuel, and comprehensive insurance are part of the deal. They pay for the use of the cars by the hour or day.

Zipcar members can eliminate the need for owning and maintaining a car, or at least a second car, thereby saving a significant amount of money. For each Zipcar, it is estimated that fifteen to twenty personally-owned vehicles are eliminated.[15] Plus, customers can drive a variety of cars depending on their moods and tasks. But there is more. Members can have a positive impact on the urban lifestyle and environment in several ways. For one thing, they tend to drive less. After joining Zipcar, 90 percent of members reduced their driving by over five thousand miles on average. Perhaps as important, older vehicles on the road are replaced with new cars that are less polluting, and people tend to drive smaller cars. The result is a visible way to express a personal concern for the environment.

The Zipcar vision, articulated by Scott Griffith who became CEO shortly after the firm started and required financing, is to be a global lifestyle brand.[16] Rather than being about renting cars, they're about urban life and the freedom of not owning and maintaining a car but still having access to one. In that spirit it provides a way to cope with urban living in a fun, upbeat, and environmentally sensitive way. Zipcar aspired to be a lifestyle brand. The Zipcar Low-Car Diet, a very on-brand promotion that gets people to blog about giving up their cars, fits the lifestyle. For the promotion, one bike brand partner gives away a bike in each city.

Zipcar was the world's leading car-sharing service in 2010, with over 350,000 members and 6,500 vehicles in urban areas and on college campuses throughout twenty-eight North American states and provinces as well as in London. Offering more that thirty makes and models, including electric vehicles, it is in the process of changing the automobile industry. Its ability to become the market leader is in part due to a strategy of buying smaller operations to establish its local or regional presence. One estimate placed the 2009 market at $150 to 250 million with a potential of growing to $3.3 billion in 2016.[17]

The rental car companies' response is to provide more flexible rental arrangements, including renting by the hour instead of by the day, and to enter as direct competitors in niche markets such as college and company campuses. But Zipcar has created a process technology, an infrastructure, and a lifestyle personality that represent significant barriers to others. They are the authentic car-sharing brand.

Key Takeaways

- An unmet need is sometimes hidden and sometimes very visible. An insight about unmet needs stimulated the concept ideas at Zipcar, Enterprise, and Chrysler. For the other firms, such as Prius and Nano, however, the need addressed was visible to all; the problem was creating and delivering an offering that is responsive.

- Timing with respect to the market, a firm, and a technology can play a key role. Chrysler had the front-wheel-drive K-car platform needed for the minivans already developed. The battery technology and regenerative braking system were in place for Toyota's Prius and not for forerunners. The Internet and card technology were available for Zipcar.

- It is possible to have a dream of a concept that seems infeasible and see it happen. Tata's Nano, Zipcar, and Toyota's Prius all experienced innovation that made the impossible possible.

- Government regulations played a central role in the hybrid story and an indirect role in the Saturn and minivan stories in that all were motivated by the need to provide better gas mileage that was encouraged by government regulations. Subsidies, such as those offered by local governments to influence factory location decisions, helped enable the Saturn and Nano.

- Decisive and forceful leadership by a CEO was the driver in each of these cases. Some had a forceful product champion for sure, but the CEO's support was still essential.

- All the winners except Saturn were committed to their insights and strategies. The Toyota CEOs created organizational challenges that resulted in the Lexus and then the Prius. Enterprise began and continues with some unshakeable tenets around service. The Saturn case shows that the commitment needs to be enduring.

- Each of the winners was highly differentiated. There was a substantial space between the existing products and each new subcategory on a host of dimensions.

- Each of the winners created meaningful barriers to entry. The Prius technology, the Saturn dealer network and culture, the Chrysler design, and the Enterprise and Zipcar operations and storefront presence all made it hard for competitors to respond. The Nano's cost difference, based on many innovations plus sourcing and manufacturing efficiencies, made it difficult to match.

- Competitor priorities rather than barriers were seen as the primary reason why competitors failed to respond in several cases. Competitors that focused on automation, on diversification, on such other product lines as trucks and SUVs, and on dealing with issues like voluntary quotas were not in a position to join a new subcategory. A strategic evaluation of a new concept should know that competitors will decide whether to participate in part by considering competing problems and opportunities.

- In each case to develop of a strong brand was crucial in creating a barrier to competitors and in defining the category or subcategory. In the case of the Prius, Toyota's decision to restrict the brand to hybrids enabled self-expressive benefits that never would have been possible had the new car been branded as a Corolla Hybrid, the route that Honda took.

For Discussion

1. What are other examples of cars that created a new category or subcategory? Were they able to avoid competition? How? What barriers did they create?

2. Consider the process of concept generation. How did each of the concepts emerge? To what extent was the stimulus an

"aha!" experience, an evolution, a technology, or a market insight?

3. Two firms, WhipCar in London and Relay Rides in Boston, have launched firms that allow people to rent cars from private car owners. These firms will check driver's licenses and the cars' registrations, and in the case of Relay Rides all participating car owners will have cars that are accessed using a card. How would you evaluate the potential for such a concept?

5

THE FOOD INDUSTRY ADAPTS

It is useless to tell a river to stop running; the best thing is to learn how to swim in the direction it is flowing.

—*Anonymous*

Oversimplification has been the characteristic weakness of scientists of every generation.

—*Elmer McCollum*, author of
A History of Nutrition, *1957*

People have always been interested in getting and staying healthy. Health gurus throughout history have been responsive to this interest and have employed, interpreted, and promoted science to uncover products and practices that will advance healthy living. Giacomo Castelyetro in 1614 unsuccessfully tried to get the English to eat more fruits and vegetables. In the late nineteenth century John Harvey Kellogg, a vegetarian, a surgeon, and the father of the modern breakfast cereal, advocated a diet high in vegetables, grains, fruits, nuts, and legumes, plus plenty of water and thorough chewing of food. There have been many more before and after these early nutritionists.

Scientists from a variety of disciplines have developed theories, and conducted experiments on those theories. Some consensus findings have emerged, but the overwhelming conclusion is that the body, the food that goes into it, and the lifestyle that surrounds it represent a highly complex system. As a result the science is often ambiguous or embryonic, and judgments are made that assume that findings are more definitive than they are.

In addition to health gurus and scientists, the government plays a role in the discourse by validating or countering positions, communicating ideas, and regulating products. A study of the roles of gurus, scientists, and the government not only helps put into context the strategies of firms in the food industry but also demonstrates why predicting and interpreting trends is not easy. Trends are powerful, ambiguous, and complex, and they ebb and flow.

Lessons about dealing with trends learned in the food industry can be applied elsewhere. Every industry faces the challenge of identifying, understanding, predicting, and sometimes influencing trends that affect markets. Retailers cope with fashion trends, material developments in clothing, consumer tastes, and so on. The automobile industry grapples with technology, government regulations, style trends, consumer preferences, demographics, and more.

The ultimate translators of these trends and the theories on which they rest are firms in the food industry who are sensitive to health issues. These firms have two challenges. One is to seize opportunities to own new subcategories as they emerge. Another is to avoid becoming irrelevant, to avoid standing on the platform as the train leaves the station, by adapting offerings to the new theories of the day.

This chapter has several objectives. One is to provide a close-up look at a megatrend, healthy eating, to appreciate its complexity and the political, cultural, technological, and marketing forces that influence it. Most firms will need to interpret and respond to trends and can learn from this case study. Another objective is to present a series of case studies of strategic responses to the growing but changing face of healthy eating to gain insights into what stimulates ideas; the risks involved; the brand strategy options; the competitor response factors; and the role of uncontrollables, especially the capricious trends, in the decisions and their aftermath.

We start with the fat battle. Many consider fat in food to be unhealthy. But which types of fat? In turns out the answer to that question is not simple and has changed over time. Examining the drivers of change and a few of the responses from brands such as Nabisco, Dreyer's, and Oestra provides insight into the difficulty of harnessing market trends and forces. We will then move on to look beyond fat to healthy eating more generally and will explore what two firms, General Mills and ConAgra with its Healthy Choice brand, have done to attempt to lead or respond to this force.

Fighting the Fat Battle

The fat battle has been at the core of healthy eating for a long time. Gurus have opined about it and created their own theories and diets to deal with fat in food. Scientists have studied fat and developed theories, which more often than not have been superseded by revised or completely different theories. The government has been an arbiter over time.

It will be helpful first to examine the roles and impact of gurus and scientists. Three fat-related theories will help explain the scope of and differences among ideas. The role of the government in regulating fat will then be examined. Finally, with the context in place, this section will detail efforts by three firms, Nabisco, Dreyer's, and P&G, to respond to theories and consumer trends relevant to fat.

Roles of Scientists and Gurus

Firms in the food industry need to follow the theories of the day that are getting traction and be prepared to offer responsive products when the timing is right. One source of such theories is influential scientists and gurus, who over the decades probably number in the thousands. To provide a flavor of their efforts and the resulting thought dynamics, we visit briefly three scientists who generated influential theories and diets centered around fat. Two of these, Nathan Pritikin and Dean Ornish, have diets that carry their name. The third, Ancel Keys, was the founder of the Mediterranean Diet.

Inventor Nathan Pritikin was diagnosed with heart disease in 1958 at forty-one years old. The medical advice of the day was to stop exercising and not worry about eating a pint of ice cream after lunch. Pritikin, however, gravitated toward a vegetarian diet that was low in fats and high in unrefined carbohydrates and began an impressive series of experiments to show that such a diet, when combined with moderate exercise, could reverse heart disease. He was influenced by knowing that heart disease and diabetes fell sharply during World War II, when high-fat food products were unavailable, and by other research showing that a low-fat diet could dramatically lower cholesterol and the probability of death. In 1975 he opened a longevity center and spa, and in 1979 he published a book based on his diet, *The Pritikin Program of Diet and Exercise* (coauthored by Patrick M. McGrady), which was a best seller.[1] Well over a dozen supporting books by Pritikin and others followed.

Dean Ornish got interested in preventing heart disease as a medical student in the mid-1970s. He subsequently conducted research exploring how a low-fat diet coupled with moderate exercise and such stress-reducing activities as yoga can reverse heart and other diseases. In 1990 he published a best-selling book, *Dr. Dean Ornish's Program for Reversing Heart Disease*, and followed that up with eight additional books on eating and his program.[2] The Ornish Diet is considered extreme by some, advocating that less than 10 percent of the diet should come from fat and that the dieter should avoid nuts and fish, which contain types of fat that many feel are beneficial.

In 1970 Ancel Keys published the results of a seven-country study involving twelve thousand men that focused on the impact of diet on cardiovascular diseases.[3] The inhabitants of

Crete had much better health outcomes, in part, it was hypothesized, because of their diet, which was high in olive oil and therefore fat. This study was followed by others concluding that a Mediterranean diet high in olive oil, vegetables, fruits, breads, nuts, and whole grains; moderate in dairy products, fish, poultry, and wine; and low in meat would result in a host of medical benefits. The headline was that fat from olive oil was not only OK but actually helpful. In the 1990s the Mediterranean Diet got traction and became a major player in the healthy-eating debate.

The Government's Role

One role of the U.S. government is to approve products for sale and to dictate how they are presented and labeled. Another is to legitimize the theories and scientific findings of the day—a tough job because the issues are complex and the science incomplete and uncertain. Nevertheless, the government is expected to be an objective and credible arbiter and thus has a big role in creating and influencing trends. Firms in nearly all industries, therefore, need to anticipate and influence not only consumer attitudes but also the actions of government.

The 1938 Food, Drug, and Cosmetic Act included an "imitation rule" that said that consumers needed to be informed if such food items as cheese and bread included cheap substitutes in place of "real" ingredients. Sounds like a reasonable effort to prevent adulteration of food, except that the rule inhibited the ability of the industry to reformulate the American food supply to get rid of the dietary evil of the time, fat. No firm could make something like nonfat sour cream without cream unless it was called "imitation" sour cream, which would be a fatal taint to the product. The food industry, with the support of the American Heart Association and other medical groups, worked successfully for the act's repeal, which occurred in 1973, and the floodgates of nonfat innovation began.

In 1977 another notable event occurred. Senator George McGovern, as chair of the Senate Select Committee on Nutrition and Human Needs, held hearings on heart disease, which was labeled by some as an epidemic. Although the presenters to the committee noted some complexities, the final report defined some dietary goals for the United States, one of which was "Eat less red meat."[4] However, after the meat industry had their say, the rule morphed into something like, "Choose meat that will reduce your saturated-fat intake." Although the prescription was no longer to eat less meat, there was now an official governmental spotlight on saturated fat.

Despite the definitive statement by the government about saturated fat, the evidence was not as clear-cut as implied. As late as 2001 an influential article in *Science* cited the ambiguities of the evidence and noted that although fat consumption had declined the incidence of obesity and diabetes had increased. The article also noted that although studies had linked saturated fat to higher cholesterol—and higher cholesterol to heart attacks and deaths—establishing the causal link between saturated fat and deaths has been more elusive. The relationship, it turns out, is complex. For example, an increase in heart disease could be caused not by the U.S. population's eating saturated fats but by the companion reality that Americans are consuming fewer fruits and vegetables. Nevertheless, the acceptance that fat and saturated fat in particular are bad for you spawned a host of nonfat and low-fat products. One estimate made in 2000 was that some fifteen thousand such products had been introduced over the years.[5]

The government played a key role in one solution to the saturated fat problem, namely by turning trans fat, or hydrogenated fat, into a villain. About one hundred years ago the discovery was made that hydrogen could be added to liquid oils, converting them to solid fats for use in food manufacturing. The first such product was P&G's Crisco, which was introduced in 1911 supported by free cookbooks showing how to use Crisco. The hydrogenation technology led to the development of margarine products, which were marketed as alternatives to butter and vegetable shortenings and which increasingly replaced animal fat in cooking. Because trans fat was an effective preservative and enhanced taste and texture, it was a welcome alternative for both processed-food and fast-food firms, who in the 1980s needed to deal with the purported harmful effects of saturated fat.

Trans fat was considered safe until 1990, even though evidence to the contrary was starting to emerge before then. By the mid-1990s, scientific evidence showed that trans fat had a deleterious effect on both good and bad cholesterol levels. The government passed a law in 2002 requiring companies to label the trans fat in food by 2005. Denmark in 2002 effectively banned the use of trans fat in food, and in 2006, after an unsuccessful public campaign to reduce consumption of trans fat, the New York City Board of Health voted to ban trans fat in restaurant food. Companies scrambled to remove trans fat from their products. It proved difficult but not impossible. Even Crisco, now owned by the J. M. Smucker company, got rid of trans fat in 2002. In 2009 an Interagency Working Group on Food Marketed to Children, representing the FDA and three other agencies, specified a standard for children of less than 1 gram of saturated fat and 0 grams of trans fat per serving.

Clearly the government has been highly influential in, if not a determinant of, the role of fat in a megatrend in food, namely healthy eating. If a firm is to be a trend driver in this context, it is necessary to anticipate government legislative and regulatory responses to issues and to influence them whenever possible by contributing scientific studies. Couple the ambiguity and complexity of the science of health with the political winds, and it is difficult and sometimes risky to become a trend driver. However, the first-mover advantages, especially with respect to brand equity, can be significant.

Nabisco Cookies

The cookie industry in the United States generates around $6 billion per year in sales but has been declining at a modest rate for the last decade. The decline has been driven by rising costs, the appearance of alternative snack options, and a concern for health. In fact, the percentage of kids eating cookies has declined from a historic 97 percent level to a current level of 90 percent. To examine the several health issues that have buffeted the industry, we now take a close look at two leading Nabisco brands, SnackWell's and Oreo.[6]

In the early 1990s low-fat diets, led by gurus like Pritikin, Ornish, and others, gained visibility, primarily because of their effectiveness at weight reduction. In response, in 1993 Nabisco introduced SnackWell's, a line of cookies and crackers that were largely fat free—"Live well. Snack well." Perhaps the most successful introduction of a packaged good in history, sales were so phenomenal that the product had to be rationed at times. In 1993 sales exceeded $200 million, and in 1995 they exceeded $430 million. In addition, the licensing of the SnackWell's brand brought in well over another $150 million in 1995. SnackWell's was at the right place at the right time.

However, the subsequent sales collapse was nearly as dramatic. One problem was taste, which after the excitement and novelty wore off became more visible. It turns out that fat enhances taste. By 1998, when sales had declined to $222 million, SnackWell's decided to reformulate the line by adding fat and becoming a low-fat instead of a nonfat option. In general, the new products had half the fat of its competitors although sometimes more sugar. An introduction with a large supporting budget reduced the rate of decline, but in 2000 sales were down to $160 million. A low-fat product is a compromise, and the key target market was not impressed with low-fat products. There are a litany of low-fat offerings that did not make it. The McLean Deluxe, a reduced-fat hamburger introduced by

McDonald's in 1991; the KFC skinless chicken option; and low-fat frozen deserts by Sara Lee all failed in the marketplace.

A second problem was that people who ate low-fat or low-calorie food items tended to eat more. Some would feel empowered to eat a whole box of SnackWell's. Tragically for Nabisco, this phenomenon was labeled the "SnackWell's syndrome," even though it applies to any product with a label that has a low-calorie connotation. Another curse of success. When people learned from firsthand experience or from reading about scientific studies that SnackWell's was not a route to losing weight, the energy was sucked out of the brand. SnackWell's is still a viable brand with a worthwhile business, but it is no longer a star. The SnackWell's brand, however, remains poised to capitalize on low-fat surges in the future and thus may be a significant asset beyond its current business.

A similar story played out over Nabisco's much larger brand Oreo. Oreo is the leading cookie sold in the United States—sales are not regularly publicized, but in 2002 Oreo sales were reported to be over $900 million. The current form of the Oreo cookie, introduced in 1952, was actually developed by Sunbeam in their Hydrox cookie, which lost market share to Nabisco and was ultimately withdrawn in 1999. The original Oreo was made with lard and thus had excessive saturated fat. When saturated fat became a visible health issue, Oreo switched to trans fat in 1992 without affecting the taste and texture of the original. However, when trans fat became a problem the remedy was not so easy. There followed an enormous R&D initiative over many years to find a replacement for trans fat. Finally, in 2006 a revised Oreo with acceptable taste and texture was introduced without trans fat, but by that time Oreo had lived under a cloud for several years.

Nabisco took another tack by seeking relevance to an audience used to indulgent eating but preoccupied by weight control. In 2007, Nabisco pioneered 100-calorie packs of snacks. In doing so it leveraged the equities of its brand portfolio.

Oreo Thin Crisps, for example, a cracker-like product with the taste of Oreo cookies, was one of the first. There was significant initial success, and the innovation created a position in a new subcategory. However, with few entry barriers other competitors were able to leverage their own brands into the 100-calorie-serving concept, and people even learned to prepare their own packs.

Dreyer's Slow Churned Ice Cream

William Dreyer, an ice cream maker, and Joseph Edy, a confectioner, opened the Grand ice cream shop on Grand Avenue in Oakland in 1928. That was the beginning of Dreyer's Grand Ice Cream. The legacy of its innovation in flavors began the next year when they invented Rocky Road. Dreyer's expanded to the East Coast in the early 1980s and took on the name Edy's for that market to avoid confusion with Breyer's, a major Unilever ice cream brand that was established on the East Coast. In 2002 Nestlé invested in Dreyer's, and four years later became the full owner of the business.

In 1987 Dreyer's, responding to the concern about fat, pioneered the light ice cream subcategory by introducing a low-fat ice cream. Although light ice cream gained a substantial part of the market, its taste and texture was decidedly inferior to full-flavor ice cream and it, like SnackWell's, hit a wall and fell back. The unmet need was clearly for a product that would deliver a low-fat benefit without sacrificing taste.

After five years of research, Dreyer's discovered the answer in the form of a new technology, low-temperature extrusion. In traditional ice cream production, the product needs to be frozen after it is done churning, a process that results in large ice crystals unless milk fat is added. With this new process, the freezing isn't necessary so neither is the added milk fat. The result is a product that has half the fat of regular ice cream and two-thirds of the calories. And in blind taste tests, eight of ten respondents found it indistinguishable from regular ice cream. The process supported by the brand name helped communicate the new technology while also making more difficult for competitors to introduce credible alternatives.

Dreyer's introduced Dreyer's Slow Churned ice cream in June 2004, and it promised to radically change the marketplace. Gary Rodgers, CEO of Dreyer's, called it the first major technological innovation in ice cream since hand-cranked churning and milk pasteurization.[7] It was introduced with over sixteen flavors at the outset plus some of Dreyer's trademark seasonal limited-edition flavors, such as Pumpkin and Eggnog. The new brand had an aggressive introduction, including a promotion that allowed people to write a proposal for an ice cream party in their home or neighborhood hosted by Dreyer's. Sales of the light category, which had been stagnating, increased by 75 percent. Six years later, the new product was increasing to the point where its potential to exceed the sales of regular ice cream seemed in sight.

Figure 5.1 Dreyer's Slow-Churned Ice Cream

The decision to use the Dreyer's (and Edy's) brand to represent the new product meant that another brand did not have to be introduced into the frozen food case, but it also meant that a strong subbrand was needed to represent the transformational innovation. The Slow Churned brand describes the process, which is important to the credibility of the product, in a way that is easy to understand. It also evokes an image of a simpler time when homemade ice cream was churned slowly by hand. It thus has associations of natural, unprocessed ingredients and family events.

Breyer's had a problem. They needed a response. Their solution was a product, introduced a year after Dreyer's Slow Churned, that was initially termed Double Churned, a brand that served to provide legitimacy in the new subcategory and diffuse the first-mover advantage of Dreyer's. The product performed well in taste tests but was a year late and lacked the flavor breadth of Dreyer's. A more serious problem was its use of a genetically altered additive.

Breyer's, with roots going back to 1866, had a legacy of being all natural. In fact, the product was called Breyer's All Natural. A classic ad showed someone trying to read the ingredients of a competitor's ice cream but then reading milk, cream, sugar, and vanilla on the Breyer's product. After being acquired by Unilever in 1993, it did add tara gum to its ice cream, which was arguably still a natural additive although the concept of a pure and simple formula was somewhat compromised.

Breyer's Double Churned had a more tricky issue to deal with. It used a patented additive that Unilever researchers, termed antifreeze proteins (AFPs). Made with genetically modified yeast in large batches, the additive mimics a substance that keeps some species of fish from freezing even in very cold waters and prevents the ice crystals from forming, negating the need for milk fat to be added. Articles from groups concerned with genetic modification opposed to such additives in food questioned the long-term safety of the product and, in particular, the possibility that the additive would cause inflammation.[8] Nevertheless, it was approved by the FDA and any risk seemed remote. The negative publicity was limited and may not have caused a major problem for Breyer's Double Churned, but it was at least awkward given the firm's heritage.

Breyer's Double Churned never could stop the Dreyer's momentum. In 2009 Breyer's reformulated the product and changed the name to Smooth and Dreamy All Natural. So it found a way to get rid of the AFPs and return to its natural roots, but in the meantime Dreyer's had gained five years' advantage, and the new Breyer's product had some uncertainties in regard to its taste dimension.

P&G's Olestra

The story of P&G's Olestra illustrates the risk of not only tracking trends but also predicting the acceptance of products that are responsive to trends. All products have pluses and minuses— and the associated risk that an innovation will stumble in the marketplace because the flaws end up swamping the positive attributes. The story also indicates how a third party, in this case the nonprofit Center for Science in the Public Interest (CSPI), can influence the positioning of a new product category.

In 1968 two P&G researchers, when researching fats that could be more easily digested by premature infants, discovered Olestra. This remarkable product was a fat substitute that, unlike others, had zero calories and delivered the same taste as any of the fats it replaced. Plus, it could be fried or baked, an extremely important attribute. The potential food applications were extensive. There was speculation that this was a $1.5 billion business and the ultimate solution to the saturated fat and trans fat problems.

After an abortive effort to get the product approved as a drug to reduce cholesterol, P&G sought FDA approval for Olestra's use as a food additive. Toward that end P&G did some

150 studies to prove its safety. In 1996, the FDA, under some public pressure to make their approval process more expeditious, finally approved Olestra for use in snack products only with the following warning to be placed on the label—"Olestra may cause abdominal cramping and loose stools. Olestra inhibits the absorption of some vitamins and other nutrients. Vitamins A, D, E, and K have been added." The warning reflected the fact that there were side effects. For some, these side effects, though not life threatening, were extremely uncomfortable and inconvenient.

Two years later Frito-Lay introduced its line of snacks under the WOW! subbrand made with Olestra branded as Olean. There were Lay's WOW!, Ruffles WOW!, and so on. One of the hit brands of the 1990s, the WOW! group sold some $350 million worth of product in the first year. However, complaints about the side effects affected the demand, and sales in 2000 fell to $200 million. In 2003, after some additional P&G studies convinced the FDA that the side effects were "mild and rare," comparable to food with high fiber, the labeling requirement was removed. The next year Frito-Lay rebranded WOW! chips as Light, and their sales again took off.

Throughout the process CSPI waged a relentless war against P&G and Frito-Lay. In 1996 they argued that the side effects were so bad that the product should be banned and pursued this point continuously and visibly. They claimed studies showed that the use of Olestra not only inhibited the absorption of key vitamins but also reduced markedly the incidence of carotenoids in the body. Researchers have hypothesized, on the basis of many studies, that carotenoids are linked to a variety of long-term health benefits. Some even theorized that, over time, users of Olestra would be more susceptible to developing cancer. They also pointed out that anal leakage, another possible side effect, was not mentioned on the warning label. CSPI, without question, succeeded in putting Olestra and WOW! on the defensive. When Frito-Lay changed the name from WOW! to Light, CSPI vigorously argued that Frito-Lay was deliberately deceiving consumers into believing that the snacks no longer contained Olean (Olestra).

P&G essentially gave up in 2002, selling the factory to a supplier firm and writing off a substantial plant investment, although they did retain the brand and technology rights. Further, Frito-Lay and P&G's Pringles continued to use Olean (Olestra) under the Light subbrand. Presumably those customers who experience side effects have learned not to use Olean, and the remainder can enjoy its benefits. In addition, there was a technological spin-off application that resulted in P&G's 2009 introduction of a paint additive using an Olestra-like substance with several good qualities, including the absence of toxic fumes.

In retrospect, the Olestra adventure cost P&G hundreds of millions of dollars and diverted resources from more productive options. P&G may have overestimated the appeal of the product and did not accept or take seriously enough the negatives or the influence of CSPI. However, given the unquestioned size and urgency of the problem to find a low-calorie, functional fat substitute and the competitive advantages for P&G had Olestra worked, there was an enormous upside, and the gamble must have been temping. There needs to be a distinction between good decisions and good outcomes. This is a case in which there might have been a good decision but a bad outcome.

From Fat to Health

Fats are not the only story in healthy eating. There have been a lot more chapters and characters. Among the most prominent healthy eating suggestions have been to reduce the intake of carbs, sodium, sugar, and, for some, glutens while increasing incidence in the diet of whole grains, fiber, soy, protein, probiotic cultures, vitamins, and fish oil, and to use food products that are natural and organic. These thirteen dimensions of food, only a partial listing, all have their adherents. The low-carb theories have received particular notice and have helped draw attention to weight control and healthy eating in general.

There were countless low-carb diet plans, including the Atkins Diet, the Scarsdale Diet, the Zone, Sugar Busters, and the South Beach Diet. The Atkins Diet, formalized in a 1972 book by Robert Atkins, featured severe reductions of refined carbohydrates with little fat restriction. The popularity of the Atkins diet has ebbed and flowed, but in 2003 something like one of eleven people in the United States were on some version of the program.[9] The South Beach Diet, described in a 2003 book by cardiologist Arthur Agatston and dietician Marie Almon, in part advised people to avoid food items like potatoes or alcohol, which have a high glycemic index, a measure of how fast a food turns to sugar in the bloodstream.[10] *The South Beach Diet* and its supporting books were said to have sold over twenty million copies.

Scientific studies have explored and tested directly or indirectly these diet plans, all on an ongoing basis. Although there are some generalized findings, there is a great deal of ambiguity about some of the specifics of the various diet plans and their efficacy. Further, these ambiguities fuel public perceptions and attitudes and create huge swings in behavior, making it hard for firms to predict and respond, to say nothing of leading the parade. One trend seems to lurch to another without much warning, a shift perhaps driven by a particularly well-written book or a specific government action. In this context, we look at the response to the increased interest in healthy eating of General Mills and ConAgra's Healthy Choice.

General Mills and the Health Trends

The General Mills story illustrates a variety of ways a firm can interpret and respond to a trend to win the relevance battle by staying relevant and creating contexts in which competitors are less relevant. A key to its strategy was the flexibility provided by having multiple brands and products and the capability represented by a creative kitchen.

General Mills has a heritage and culture that are oriented toward healthier products and health appeals. The Cheerios brand, first introduced in 1941 as Cheeri Oats, was the first oat-based, ready-to-eat cold cereal and has a history of health claims. In the early days General Mills stressed the whole oats ingredient in Cheerios. More recently, it promoted its studies that show that eating Cheerios regularly will reduce cholesterol. And multigrain Cheerios, introduced in 1992, is vitamin fortified and contains fiber. The Cheerios franchise is, with four entries, by far the leading cereal brand, with some 12 percent market share. It's perceived healthy benefits undoubtedly have made it relevant to at least some who are sensitive to healthy foods. However, some have observed that the sodium content of Cheerios is high (as is the case in other cereal products), and some challenge the cholesterol claims. Nothing is simple.

There were a series of brands introduced by General Mills that had healthy eating as their basis and provided platforms for health-oriented offerings. Their stories all have a learning message for firms responding to market trends.

In 1975 General Mills introduced Nature Valley Natural Crunch Oats and Honey Granola Bar, a product with real honey and brown sugar combined with rolled oats for a natural nutritious snack that is high in fiber and protein and low in saturated fat. Since then Nature Valley has expanded the line to include Trail Mix, Yogurt, Sweet & Salty Nut, and Roasted Nut Crunch Granola Bars plus Granola Nut Clusters, and has solidified the brand's natural associations with a thirty-year link to the American Hiking Society. For some people, its level of differentiation may be such that Nature Valley products represent a subcategory.

In 1985 General Mills introduced Fiber One cereal into the high-fiber arena. Its name reflected the fact that Fiber One dominated in terms of fiber content among cold cereals, with some 57 percent of daily requirements of fiber and 14 grams of fiber per serving. The brand was profitable in part because it had an intensely loyal following (the highest loyalty of any cereal brand) and required no marketing. However, sales were low and dormant.

In 2007, when the need for fiber got additional traction in part because of its role in balancing carbohydrate consumption in low-carb diets, Fiber One was aggressively extended. The Nature Valley team, realizing that the Fiber One brand could play in its arena, worked to develop a line of bars using the Fiber One brand and promise. In the first year the product line exceeded the coveted $100 million year-one sales mark. Building on that success, General Mills used the Fiber One brand to introduce high-fiber entries in other food categories including yogurt, bread, muffin mixes, toaster pastries, and cottage cheese. All these had sufficient fiber levels to make them the leaders of their categories on the fiber dimension. It was a good example of spanning business silos by combining and leveraging assets, in this case a brand, recipes, marketing, and production capabilities.

In 2000 General Mills introduced a soy-milk product branded 8th Continent in a joint venture with DuPont. DuPont had developed a sweeter soybean product and lacked access to the distribution channel, so the joint venture made good sense. The soy market was in total over $2 billion and growing rapidly; the soy-milk market was around $200 million, with the Silk brand having over 50 percent of that, and was projected to grow to $1 billion in just a few years. The opportunity was there. In 2004 General Mills introduced a light version of the product. However, it turned out that the soy-milk demand was not the growth area it had appeared, in part because of some uncertainty about its health claims and because the business required a substantial investment making the return marginal. Deciding that the investment dollars could best be used elsewhere, General

Mills sold the business in 2008. There was thus a twin lesson: optimistic projections can change and business considerations matter. A market supported by a real trend is not enough, a profitable business model must also exist.

In 2001 General Mills entered the organic food business by acquiring Small Planet Foods, a leading producer of organic food products based in Sedro-Woolley, Washington. Two brands arrived. The Cascadian Farm brand held the number-one or number-two share positions in the markets for organic frozen fruits, vegetables, juices, and entrées, and the company's Muir Glen line was the leading brand of organic canned tomatoes, pasta sauces, salsas, and condiments. General Mills introduced the brands, well known in organic and natural food channels, into traditional grocery outlets and extended the Cascadian Farm brand into cereals and the Muir Glen brand into organic soups. Although both brands were relatively small, they held the potential to ride a surge of interest in organics.

Wheaties was created in 1922, as a result of an accidental spill of a wheat bran mixture onto a hot stove by a Minnesota clinician working for the Washburn Crosby Company (later General Mills). Another initiative was the revitalization of the Wheaties brand, long the "Breakfast of Champions"—a brand that enjoyed extremely high awareness and even emotional benefits, a brand that everyone knows and respects but few eat. With such high awareness and great image, the brand had a lot of latent potential. Five top athletes, including football's Payton Manning and basketball's Kevin Garnett, formed a panel to help. As a result of their first task, to specify what they wanted in a cereal that would enhance their performance, a set of ingredient parameters were created. The athletes also helped create three candidate formulas to deliver these ingredients. Readers of *Men's Health* helped select the final choice. The result was Wheaties Fuel, delivered in a black package with Manning on the front cover and the panel pictured on the back that was on the shelves in January 2010. It was a rare cereal, one designed for and directed toward men. Virtually all other cereals had women as the main target. Its healthy message was geared toward athletes, an association that resonates with a lot of men, especially those in their thirties and forties.

In addition to the new master brands General Mills had created, the firm also made an effort to upgrade the healthiness of all their products.[11] Some of these changes were in response to competitor actions. For example, Green Giant Valley Fresh Steamers, a product making it easier to prepare frozen vegetables with natural sauces, was one of the top five new products of 2009 and served to energize and enhance the General Mills Green Giant brand.[12] It was stimulated by Birds Eye Steamfresh introduced in 2006. The General Mills Yoplait line added a Yo-Plus product in 2007, which included probiotic cultures, fiber, and vitamins to help the digestive process. This was in response to Dannon's Activia, introduced in 2006, which enjoyed considerable first-mover advantages.

Other General Mills initiatives to make their products healthier were not stimulated by competitor's products but by its belief that health, along with taste and convenience, was a prime motivator for customers. Among the notable incremental innovations were the following:

- By 2005 all General Mills cereals used whole grains, and a consumer (who typically cycles between a half dozen brands) could rely on any cereal under a "Big G" (logo for cereals from General Mills) brand to contain whole grains.
- Progresso Soups in 2006 added a light version and received an endorsement from Weight Watchers, affirming the claim that Progresso's soups should be assigned zero points in the diet system. Shortly after, Progresso created a low-sodium version of several of the light soups.
- Yogurt Kids had 25 percent less sugar as well as added cultures that made it easier to digest, even for those who are lactose intolerant.

- In 2009 Yoplait stopped sourcing dairy products from cows exposed to a controversial hormone.
- Bisquick Heart Smart reduced sharply the amount of saturated fat and trans fat in Bisquick.
- In 2007, General Mills introduced 100-calorie portion sizes for products including Chex snacks.

One initiative that created a subcategory was the introduction of Betty Crocker Gluten Free desert mixes in 2009, made possible by the arrival of newly developed gluten-free ingredients. The effort was so promising that General Mills either changed, recognized, or promoted other products as gluten free. Some, such as the Chex cereal family, got a subsequent sharp boost in sales. It turns out that the incidence of concern for gluten is much larger than originally assumed, and it is very hard for those with a gluten-sensitive condition to determine whether a product is gluten-free not. Launched in 2010, the General Mills gluten-free informational Web site, which lists some 250 General Mills gluten-free products along with recipes from the Betty Crocker kitchen, thus had the potential to become a go-to source for information. Further, this success shows that niche health markets, previously considered too small, have now become accessible because of the power of digital media.

The General Mills strategy involved developing a series of brand platforms with the power and flexibility to adapt to health trends. The major brands with such subbrands as Cheerios Multigrain, Wheaties Fuel, and General Mills Gluten-Free provided platforms to support product refinements that created or participated in new subcategories. The Betty Crocker brand platform had permission to be a partner in healthy cooking. Further, General Mills invested in products and brands such as Fiber One, Muir Glen, Cascadian Farm, and Nature Valley not central to its business but relevant to niche markets. They stuck with those niche products and in the process built strong brand platforms. As the general category of healthy eating in its various forms emerged, General Mills had the brands, the expertise, and the market knowledge to move forward. There is little question that it is easier to make a new offering fly with an established brand that has credibility in niche areas.

Healthy Choice

Healthy Choice represents a rare case in which the origins of a brand and its value proposition are clear. The story involves three phases: pioneering, maturity, and revitalization.

In 1985 Mike Harper, the president of ConAgra, a diversified firm that markets a host of food brands including Hunt's and Orville Redenbacher's, had a heart attack and became motivated to change his diet. He was stunned to learn that many processed food products, including those made by ConAgra, were high in fat and sodium and thus were unwise food selections for anyone concerned about heart disease. The options in the supermarket for those looking for heart-healthy food were limited. The specialty products that did apply had the justifiable reputation for tasting bad.

Consumers by and large were unconcerned, in part because they were not sensitive to heart risk factors and because the fat and sodium content of brands was communicated only in fine print on packages. But the situation was changing: heart risk factors were becoming more widely known, and the concerned segment was growing. The processed food industry, however, had yet to get the message.

As a result of Mike Harper's wake-up call, ConAgra changed its mission from "We build on basics" to "Feeding people better." The commitment was made to market even more nutritious and healthy consumer products. ConAgra Frozen Foods first laid the cornerstone of the strategy with its 1987 introduction of Healthy Choice frozen dinners. The brand's objective was to minimize fat and control the level of such other components as cholesterol and sodium. However, the products also had to have a taste that was competitive with other national brands. Thus Healthy Choice's core identity was great taste and good nutrition.

Purchasers of competing brands such as Stouffer's Lean Cuisine and Weight Watchers, which were positioned as provided weight-control benefits, represented the target consumers because many interested in weight control were also attracted to overall health. Healthy Choice appealed to this large and growing subsegment.

The Healthy Choice frozen food line was successful for several reasons. First, its products were not perceived to have a taste liability, they were at least comparable to competing products on that key dimension. Second, because of its established lines, ConAgra Frozen Foods had access to distribution channels, thus ensuring that major supermarket chains would try the new products. Third, the timing was right. Healthy Choice appeared just when those interested in health and heart risk factors were growing from a small segment into a large, mainstream market. Fourth, their competitors were committed to a different, more narrow position (weight control), in part because of their prior success, and were slow to respond. Weight Watchers, in particular, was not motivated to undercut its franchise by leading the market in another direction.

Soon after Healthy Choice appeared, competitors did retaliate with such subbrands as Stouffer's Right Course and LeMenu Light Style. However, each had positioning problems. The Right Course subbrand was tied to Stouffer and appealed mainly to Stouffer users. LeMenu Light Style targeted Weight Watchers and was not well positioned to compete with Healthy Choice. In fact, recognizing the weight control connotations of the "Light Style" brand, it later was reintroduced as LeMenu Healthy. In contrast, Healthy Choice was a new brand that could develop a strong position with appeal for a broad market.

Other subbrands were later introduced, such as Budget Gourmet Hearty and Healthy; Tyson Healthy Portion; and finally, in mid-1992, Weight Watchers Smart Ones. These late-comers had the difficult job of enticing away members of the Healthy Choice segment. Meanwhile, the Healthy Choice team continued to expand and improve its dinner and entrée lines with such offerings as Fiesta Chicken Fajitas, Country Glazed Chicken, and Cheese French Bread Pizza.

The power of a brand to extend depends on the core brand associations, and basis of a relationship with customers. The Healthy Choice core associations of taste and nutrition was not tied to the frozen food area but rather traveled well throughout the store. In this case, the core associations was broad indeed, providing the foundation for a powerful range brand, a brand that ranges over products.

Various ConAgra operating units started to look to other product areas on which to apply the Healthy Choice brand and associations. Product classes in which there was an absence of a brand with a strong heart-healthy dimension were prime candidates. Frightened competing firms nervously reexamined their brand offerings and product class profiles to see if they were vulnerable. The answer was usually yes. In order to preempt Healthy Choice and respond to the growing consumer concern with more nutritious food, there was a flurry of new products, often using subbrands like Lite, Fresh, Healthy, Right Choice, or Fat Free, designed to preempt or respond to Healthy Choice. However, Healthy Choice, because of its strong associations and presence in other food categories, was formidable even when others had developed "healthy" subbrands.

In 1995 Healthy Choice had estimated retail sales of $1,275 million, up from $858 million in 1993, $471 million in 1991, and $30 million in 1989. In 1993 Healthy Choice was called "the most successful new food brand introduction in two decades" by *Advertising Age*. The brand appeared on over three hundred products, including soups (the Healthy Choice soup line was named as product of the year in 1992 by *Progressive Grocer* magazine), ice cream (the number one national brand of light ice cream), and cold cuts. Whereas Weight Watchers was one of the most successful new range brands in the 1980s, Healthy Choice earned that claim in the 1990s.

During the ensuing decade, Healthy Choice lost momentum, in part because ConAgra was looking at efficiencies and cost control instead of the menu and product appeal. As a result, the offerings began to be tired. As the Healthy Choice team's focus was on limiting undesirable characteristics such as fat and salt, its offerings began to develop a significant taste disadvantage in relation to competing products that did not have that goal. As a result, the Healthy Choice frozen dinners, in particular, were considered irrelevant by many. Further, there was little innovation or news.

In 2004 and 2005 the Healthy Choice team undertook a major study of customers to explore what consumers were looking for in frozen food. A takeaway was that a major unmet need was to obtain the same food freshness that is available from prepared meals. Freshness was associated with a good eating experience in regard to taste, texture, and health benefits. Another insight was that steaming was a strong freshness cue. Steamed frozen vegetables, for example, were perceived to result in freshness characteristics. Bird's Eye Steamfresh, a line of vegetables, came out in May 2006, and customer acceptance of that product reinforced the study's insight.

One challenge for Healthy Choice was to create a steaming technique for frozen dinners, in which the sauce is typically frozen with the other ingredients. The R&D solution was a two-tiered set of trays, by which the sauce on the bottom tray would both steam and add aroma to the food on the top tray. The result was a steam-cooked experience that retained the color, texture, and flavor of the food, resulting in crisp vegetables, juicier meats, and al dente pasta. The other challenge was to create more appealing recipes. Toward that end the concept of removing things like fat and salt from food was replaced with a focus of putting in healthy ingredients, such as whole grains,

Figure 5.2 Healthy Choice Café Steamers

extra virgin olive oil, and large vegetable bits. The result was Café Steamers, which were introduced in 2007 and became not only a sales success, named the number-one food launch in 2008 by the research firm Information Resources Inc (IRI), but also an important part of turning around the Healthy Choice brand. Café Steamers was followed by Asian Inspired Cafe Steamers in 2009 and by Mediterranean Inspired Café Steamers in 2010, reflecting the fact that "Asian" and "Mediterranean" both have healthy connotations.

Change and innovation appeared in other Healthy Choice products as well, including a new line of all-natural entrées with varieties like Portabella Spinach Parmesan and Pumpkin Squash Ravioli that were high in fiber, were low in saturated fat, and contained antioxidants. Healthy Choice also introduced another line of self-staple fresh mixers (with a significant shelf life in the store and at home), in which a compact container contains sauce, pasta, and a strainer so you can make it at your desk with no refrigeration or freezing. Healthy Choice Hearty 7 Grain bread was another healthy option.

The revitalized brand was signaled with new packaging, which included an exclamation point. There was also a humorous advertising campaign with a story line involving the comedian Julia Louis-Dreyfus, who in deciding whether to be a spokesperson was gathering information about the new Healthy Choice. The invigorated Healthy Choice brand had regained its mojo and was gaining market share. Going forward, Healthy Choice aspires to be known for healthy food that tastes good but, more generally, to be a brand that supports healthy living. To live in such a way as to get as much out of life as possible. To do things. To revitalize.

With the perspective provided by these case stories from three industries—retailing, automobile, and food—we now turn to the four tasks associated with creating new categories and subcategories. The first, finding the concept, is discussed in the next chapter.

Key Takeaways

- Trends can be complex and ambiguous, and, worse, their directions and intensity can change quickly, driven by forces outside the control of a brand. Detecting, monitoring, and understanding such trends is challenging, as is any effort to drive them.

- Such influencers as gurus and such objective arbiters as the government matter. However, gurus can be trumped by other gurus and by other credible sources of information. Further, the government can lack certainty and timeliness and is subject to political pressures unrelated to the issues at hand.

- A strong brand or subbrand that can represent an innovation is necessary for success. An established master brand such as Healthy Choice, Cheerios, or Dreyers or strong endorser brand such as Betty Crocker will provide credibility, familiarity, and useful associations. Creating a new brand from zero such as Fiber One and Nature Valley did can be expensive, time consuming, and difficult but may be necessary and, if successful, can itself be a platform for future extensions.

- Having a portfolio of brands, as do General Mills, ConAgra, and Nabisco, may provide flexibility because their portfolio brands can become candidates for powering new offerings. It is hard to know for sure where the market is going. Having brand options is one route to winning in dynamic markets.

- A variety of offerings, as we saw in the case of Dreyer's flavor selection and the Healthy Choice line, can provide important barriers to entry because more offerings provide more links to customers, more innovation and energy, and more brand exposure and enhancement.

- An offering with big potential can be accompanied by high risk, some of which is hard to quantify and can be out of the control of the firm. In the case of Olestra and Breyer's Double Churn, a third party affected perceptions.

- Creating an offering can entail anticipated and unanticipated difficulties in design, delivery, and competitor response. Any uncertainties should be recognized, accounted for, and managed.

- Unmet needs are central to new offerings. In some cases determining unmet needs will be a key success factor but in most of the cases described in this chapter, the unmet need was clear—the problem was delivering an offering that addressed the unmet need.

- Ideas for new products can come from other silos within the firm. Such a source is not available to competitors. The idea for Fiber One snack bars, for example, came from the Fiber One cereal group.

For Discussion

1. How does a theory or idea about eating get traction? To what extent does it depend on objective facts? There is a school of thought that people do not process or respond to facts. Comment.

2. What are some firms in the packaged-food sector that have created new subcategories? How did they do it? What barriers were involved?

3. What firms attempted new subcategories but failed? To what extent was the failure due to poor timing, bad execution, inadequate demand, or competitive response?

6

FINDING NEW CONCEPTS

The best way to a good idea is to have lots to
choose from.

—*Linus Pauling*

The question is not what you look at, but what
you see.

—*Henry David Thoreau*

The strategic goal should always be to develop a new category
or subcategory so that the difficult and destructive brand preference competition is no longer the norm. That involves several
tasks that Apple does very well: find and evaluate new concepts,
define them, and create barriers to competitors.

Apple

In October 2001 Apple launched the iPod, which combined
Apple's technological flare, its easy-to-use vision, and its eye for
design.[1] It was an instant success. Over the years Apple added
such variations as the iPod shuffle, nano, and touch. Eight years
later, having sold over 220 million units, the iPod led to the
creation of four additional new subcategories in the form of
the iTunes store, iPhone, Apple Store, and iPad.

The iPod had a design that was breathtaking in its aesthetics
and functionality. The clean lines; the color; the feel; and the
wheel all made it stand out in the world of consumer electronics. Its functionality, from the interface to the speed of downloading music, was far beyond that of the existing MP3 players.

It was a product that you only had to see once to appreciate—it was simply cool and was clearly viewed as being used by cool people.

The timing was right. Steve Jobs recognized that there was a window of opportunity for the iPod. There was a need, the competitive entries were seriously flawed, and the combination of Apple technology and new hardware options created an opening. In particular, an inexpensive, 1.8-inch hard drive from Toshiba became available that could hold over one thousand songs, a key enabling advance. In order to react fast to the market and to access competencies in key areas, Apple employed partners in the development process.[2] The team was under the leadership of PortalPlayer, which provided the base platform, and generated a product that included a stereo digital-to-analog converter from Wolfson Microelectronics, a flash memory chip from Sharp Electronics, a Texas Instruments interface controller, and a power management integrated circuit from Linear Technologies. Apple was not alone.

The introduction was embedded in a crazy amount of buzz. The product was introduced into TV shows and movies without any placement pay simply because it was cool. The power of the Apple brand, having been revitalized by the distinctive iMac design that appeared in 1998, only one year after Jobs returned to Apple from his forced exile, was a crucial ingredient. The buzz and brand were complemented by an effective marketing program.

Another critical component of success was the easy-to-use iTunes application for organizing and listening to music on computers. In April 2003 Apple introduced the iTunes store, which allowed a user to buy (as oppose to steal) recorded songs and later books, podcasts, and TV shows, and which itself was a new category. Steve Jobs and his team accomplished what seemed impossible. In addition to creating enabling software, they pulled off the delicate task of getting the five major music companies to agree to sell single songs for 99 cents over the Internet. In addition, the whole iTunes store operation was not only linked to the iPod, it was part of iPod. You simply selected the iTunes store from the iPod menu on your computer. Jobs's ability to get music companies and musicians on board with the idea of selling songs was due in part to his credibility and salesmanship but also in part to the fact that their inability to control Internet piracy had made them desperate. Even Sony Music fell into line. Less than three years after the start, the iTunes store sold its billionth song.

The role that Steve Jobs played in the iPod's success was pivotal, as it was in the other Apple successes. He enabled the project to begin when he realized that the existing MP3 software was slow and deficient in its interface. During the development process his style was to push his team toward greatness, exhibiting a stubborn unwillingness to compromise. His management style is reminiscent of that of the Toyota CEO who charged his team with a seemingly impossible task that led to the Prius.

A side story. At the huge Las Vegas Comdex trade show in fall 1999, Sony, the long-term leader in portable music dating from the Walkman's emergence in 1979, introduced two digital music players two years before Apple brought the iPod to the market. One, developed by the Sony Personal Audio Company, was the Memory Stick Walkman, which enabled users to store music files in Sony's memory stick, a device that resembled a large pack of gum. The other, developed by the VAIO Company, was the VAIO Music Clip, which also stored music in memory and resembled a stubby fountain pen.[3]

Both failed for several reasons. First, the technology was just a few years too early. Each had 64 megabytes of memory that stored only twenty or so songs, and each was priced too high for the general market. Second, because of Sony's long-term tendency to avoid industry standards, both products featured a Sony proprietary compression scheme called ATRAC3. Software to convert MP3 files to the Sony standard was not convenient and, worse, resulted in slow transfers. Third, the fact that Sony promoted two different devices created by two fiercely independent silos confused the market as well as the Sony organization. Worse, another silo, Sony Music, was more concerned with avoiding piracy than with the success of the new digital product and inhibited access to a broad array of music, leading to the use of the cumbersome uploading process.

Apple too was not without premature products. One of the most visible was Apple's Newton, a personal digital assistant introduced in 1993 when John Scully was CEO. It was designed to manage schedules and a name list, support note taking using a human writing recognition system, and a variety of other tasks. Despite terrific introductory marketing, the product failed and was killed when Steve Jobs returned to Apple in 1997. The Newton was priced high, was both unreliable and sluggish, and had a hard-to-read screen. If the product had waited for only two years for the technology to improve and the design to be made more reliable, it would probably have been a success. In 1996 Palm, with more advanced technology and a less ambitious product vision, came out with the PalmPilot, a simpler PDA that was a resounding success.

In one of the most remarkable strategic decisions, Jobs decided to have Apple become a retailer, not just a seller of product but a chain of stores that would represent the Apple brand, present and communicate the products, and create a more intimate relationship with its customers. The decision, which was widely criticized, was based in part on an observation that existing retailers would not or could not represent the Apple products and brand in an authentic manner. The Apple Store, opened in May 2001, confounded skeptics by surpassing GAP as achieving the fastest growth of any retailer—in three years it was doing $1 billion and in five it was exceeding $4 billion. By 2010 there were over three hundred stores in ten countries.

The stores are clean, elegant, and spacious and located in prime, high-traffic areas. They include "genius bars" at which technical help hangs out, theaters for presentations, studios for product training, and solution zones for such elements as digital photography and video editing. The stores go beyond the shopping experience to the ownership experience and lifestyle of the customers. The idea that Apple's going retail would fail because retailing requires different skill sets or because its entry would antagonize its existing distribution channel was proven wrong. The remarkable success of the Apple stores was in part due to the design and layout, the energy of the Apple brand and products, the power and penetration of the iPod, and the crazy loyalty of the users. In sharp contrast, Gateway Computers closed its chain of 250 stores because its undifferentiated products, unappealing locations, and the lack of inventory—customers could only order computers.

Two other major new subcategories that emerged were related to the iPod phenomenon: the iPhone introduced in January 2007 and the iPad in March 2010.

The iPhone is an iPod with internet connectivity and a phone. It is very Apple, providing a simple, elegant product that is easy to use and contains features that combine to create a very different user experience. Although not the first, it quickly became an exemplar for smart phones. Interestingly, the iPhone's development started with an objective to build a tablet computer with touch technology, in part because the mobile phone business was messy. However, the product evolved to include a phone and a connection with AT&T, and was a runaway winner. The hype around the product's introduction by one estimate was worth $400 million of advertising. And after two years something like 150,000 applications had been written for it all readily available from the Apple "App Store." Because it is linked to the iTunes store and Apple software, the iPhone is not easily matched.

The iPad is a new type of tablet computer, which Jobs called a "truly magical and revolutionary product."[4] The iPad connects to a Web store and thus allows access to a host of books, magazines, newspapers, movies, and video games. It is positioned to challenge the Kindle for e-book supremacy. Except for a camera it is similar to a giant iPhone, with much of the touch-screen controls familiar to iPhone users and access to all the iPhone applications. There is speculation that the iPad will replace not only notebooks but also some portable computers not used for extensive word processing or data handling.

Another side note. A host of touch-screen tablet computers preceded the iPad. In the 2000 Comdex event, the leading electronics trade show, Microsoft's Bill Gates unveiled a Tablet PC, a computer without a keyboard. It never caught on, in part because the technology was not ready and in part because it lacked any hint of coolness. Panasonic and Toshiba have been making such tablet computers in relative anonymity for years for primarily business users. In spite of the early market presence of competitors, Apple again took over an exemplar role, this time for tablet computers.

A remarkable story—arguably five new subcategories within ten years by the same firm and same CEO—the iMac, the iPod, iTunes, the iPhone, and the iPad. And that doesn't count Jobs's Pixar, the remarkably successful animated film studio that was sold to Disney in 2006. Several takeaways. First, in each case the final product evolved over time, the final vision was not in place at the outset. Each involved building on innovations that existed in prior products. No product started from scratch, and none stood still. Second, the customer's unmet need was rather obvious; the challenge was largely technology, which was resolved by exploiting a combination of outside and inside products and talent. Third, strong barriers succeeded at keeping competitors at bay for an extended time period. One barrier was the creation of an ecosystem including an Apple operating system, iTunes, and the App Store where applications can be obtained. Others, including the Apple brand, a committed customer base, and ongoing product energy and news, added up over time to make Apple a moving target.

Where did the ideas for the iPod, iTunes, the iPhone, and the iPad originate? Not from customers. They came rather from market insights on the part of Jobs and colleagues, who famously believe that customers cannot help with concepts that are not already on the market. These market insights were based on a confluence of factors: a belief that customers would respond to a suite of applications, a knowledge of evolving relevant technology, the fact that current products on the market were hopelessly deficient, and confidence in their ability to improve and add features. Timing was critical. The technology and market needed to be in place, which meant that close tracking of both was needed.

The role of Apple's CEO, both as a visionary and as a force reaching for greatness, was pivotal. However, another lesson is that no firm, even one with Steve Jobs, will bat a thousand over time and across products. Jobs, extraordinary at creating uniquely designed, easy-to-use products for individuals, had less success selling to companies that were not creative service companies. Apple has long been on the outside looking in with respect to the business market for computers. Jobs's effort to create a computer for companies during his Apple exile, NEXT, never did make it, although NEXT's software became a ticket back to Apple. So even Jobs had a mix of disappointments sprinkled in with his stream of successes.

■ ■ ■

The preceding five chapters have presented over twenty cases in which brands have developed offerings with the potential to create new categories or subcategories. Each case provides a different perspective on both how it was done and why it was successful or unsuccessful. One overall theme is that there are complex market dynamics, formidable creation and implementation challenges, and considerable uncertainty surrounding efforts to transform markets.

With that background, what guidance is there for those who would like to move from the brand preference competition to create market arenas in which the relevance of competitors is reduced or eliminated entirely? How can a firm create and dominate a new category or subcategory with a different value proposition and group of loyal customers?

The answers to these questions can be structured into the four interrelated tasks or challenges that all organizations, from start-ups to mature firms, need to address. As summarized in Figure 6.1, they are concept generation, concept evaluation, defining and managing the new categories or subcategories, and creating barriers to competitors. This chapter will cover concept generation. The following three chapters will discuss and elaborate each of other three tasks.

Chapter Ten will discuss the challenge of gaining and maintaining relevance. In Chapter Eleven the characteristics of a supporting, innovative organization are detailed. In an epilogue, the whole process will be put into perspective. The reality is that although the payoff is high, the process is both difficult and risky with an uncertain outcome.

Figure 6.1 Creating Offerings That Will Drive New Categories or Subcategories

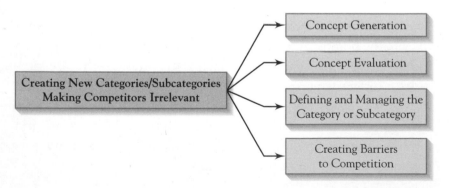

Concept Generation

We start with concept creation. Where do those ideas come from? How can a flow of new concepts be generated? Although we will detail several specific approaches that can be used, it is first helpful to understand two key constructs that drive the process: unmet needs and organizational creativity.

Unmet Needs

A driving concept that can result in a substantial or transformational innovation usually centers on an unmet need. A focus on customers' unmet needs as opposed to, for example, their motivations is useful because responsive products or services are highly likely to be relevant to customers and can lead to new categories or subcategories because they represent unserved or underserved markets. When Best Buy, for example, changed the customer relationship to one of helping in the store and later, with the Geek Squad, one of helping at home, they were addressing a significant unmet need. Betty Crocker's Gluten Free cake mixes addressed a real unmet need as well. In each case the firm created a new, well-defined subcategory, and competitor brands were rendered less relevant.

OfficeMax found that people, especially women professionals, each wanted a workplace, often a cubical, with color, patterns, and textures. The result was four product lines that promised to enliven and personalize cubicle environments, delivered under the tagline, "Life is beautiful, work can be too." An unmet need provided not only a route to a successful offering but also lead to the creation of a new subcategory. Ariat broke into the market for equestrian footwear by providing high-performance athletic footwear for riders who were not well served by traditional riding boots. Driven by the belief that riders are athletes, Ariat developed a brand and product line that was responsive to an unmet need.

Sometimes there is an obvious unmet need that provides the basis for a driving concept. The problem is to overcome the technical problems in order to deliver on that concept. The desire for low-fat foods is there, for example, but delivering low fat without sacrificing taste is difficult, as SnackWell's found out. Further, the need for better gas economy has been well known, but the Prius team, with some help from others preceding its work, had to overcome several technological hurdles. Everyone knew that the car dealer experience was painful, but the assumption was that people needed to live with it because there was no practical solution. Then Saturn came up with the regional dealer concept, which made no-haggle pricing with consultant as opposed to pressure selling possible.

Other times the unmet need is known but is dormant because investment is incorrectly assumed to be too great or the demand wrongly thought to be too small to take the risk. That may have been the case for the Chrysler minivan or Best Buy's Geek Squad before these concepts were proved in the marketplace.

However, in many cases some insight is required to identify an unmet need that is not obvious. That may have been the case for Enterprise, Muji, and Zara, whose founders recognized unmet needs that were not visible to the larger market. Market insight then results in the potential for a pioneering advantage because others may not recognize the same need.

A good exercise is to create a list of the top five to ten unmet needs in the marketplace. Categorize each as to whether it is obvious but lacking a solution, whether it is dormant, or whether it is below the radar screen. Keep monitoring each to determine when the time might be right to actively explore a responsive offering.

Even when an unmet need is targeted, it is still a challenge to understand its impact and trajectory. Will it support a business if solutions can be found? How substantial an innovation will be required? Is the problem so meaningful that any progress will be helpful and result in a successful new entry? To answer these questions, it is helpful to put the unmet need into a larger context and to determine what the offering would look like and what its value proposition would be.

Organizational Creativity

How does an organization or a person generate concepts with the potential to create new categories or subcategories? How can an organization foster conceptual creativity that will result in an offering that will drive a new business? It turns out that creativity has been studied extensively. Drawing on this research there are certain observations and guidelines that apply to the search for market changing new offerings.

Be Curious. Curiosity is the mother of invention. It is important to be curious about why a weird, unexpected event happens, why an unexplained observation appears, or why a certain constraint exists. Toyota famously has the five-why approach—a problem is addressed by successfully posing the question Why? until the most basic issue is uncovered (I know a two-year-old who would be a terrific innovator by this logic).

Soak in Information. Information is the lifeblood of invention. Those people and organizations that have wide knowledge bases will be able do the mixing and matching that is often the basis of innovation. An organization needs to be a bit like an ant colony with tentacles continuously determining what is changing in the environment and what could be changed. As in an ant colony there should be a relentless pursuit of useful information and an ability to act on that information in a timely fashion.

The story is told of Charles Draper, who spent twenty years going to school, mostly at MIT, gaining knowledge in fields like psychology, electrochemical engineering, and physics. One of the most inventive scientists of his day, he has been called the "father of inertial guidance," and the scope of his knowledge base was undoubtedly one reason for his success. Overburdened managers often feel like it is wasteful to absorb information not immediately applicable. However, information outside a firm's boundaries can play a key role when it comes to that firm's creative thinking.

Access Diverse People. Different people and organizations bring different knowledge bases, experiences, and perspectives to the table. Having people from different backgrounds or being able to access them means that different ideas and perspectives will enrich and deepen the process. The challenge is then to get them into the same actual or virtual room to focus on an issue. Multiple parties not only can contribute ideas but, perhaps more important, can refine ideas. Most new offerings start in forms that are unfeasible or easily rejected. Refinement by various partners makes offerings viable.

Know and Use Brainstorming. Many people and organizations feel that they know how to brainstorm but few make it a part of their management rhythms or do it well. The innovation firm IDEO provides some guidelines to effective brainstorming beyond simply doing it regularly. First, have a good, motivating problem statement. The best usually center on a customer need. In addition to getting early ideas out, brainstorming can be used to address sticky issues or barriers that arise as offering ideas emerge. Second, make sure that there is a suspension-of-evaluation period during which the goal is to generate a high volume of ideas and allow weird ideas to build toward better ones. It helps to count ideas. Aim for 100 to 150 in a one-hour session. Third, when flow of energy and ideas slows down, find another starting place even if it is fanciful. Fourth, unless the group is experienced, have a warm-up period.[5]

Force New Perspectives. Each different perspective provides a source of ideas. The idea is to challenge ideas and stretch thinking. What can the manager of a five-star hotel learn from a zoo?

What can an emergency-room doctor learn from working in a fast-food restaurant? At Prophet, a brand and marketing consultancy, the innovation practice teams sometimes encourage clients to start by describing the worst idea possible. The worst concept extension for a popular doll, a prostitute, led to a brand-appropriate line of nighttime apparel. It can even help to start over at the same point. In one study a group that worked on a puzzle uninterrupted was outperformed by another that was asked in the middle to do a brainteaser.

Don't Look Only for Breakthrough Ideas. Innovation can be a simple idea. It doesn't need to involve transformational technology. There is a misconception that innovation needs to be dramatically new and different. That is not the case. Most innovators just combine what is available in a new form or apply an existing technology or component in a different way or for a different application. The container that revolutionized shipping was just a modification of the familiar truck trailer. The iPod was really a collection of developed components and technology. So the trick is to know what is available and have the insight to put different elements together in a new way.

Sourcing Concepts

There are several approaches or methods proven useful in generating new offering concepts, as summarized in Figure 6.2. Each represents very different perspectives on the marketplace and its dynamics and thus provides an impetus and enabler for creativity. Most innovative organizations are very skilled at many of these approaches. There is a learning curve, however, and building competence in a few can be productive. However, they are complementary, so the challenge is not to pick one but to work with a set.

The first portion of this group of approaches looks to customers or potential customers for insights. The other approaches

Figure 6.2 Finding New Concepts

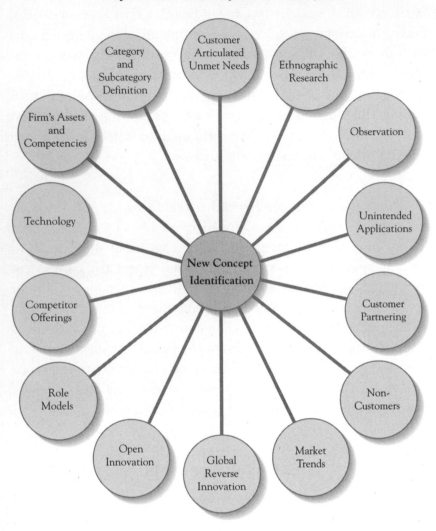

look to market trends, competitors, role models, technology, and leveraging existing assets and competencies.

Customer-Articulated Unmet Needs

Some unmet needs are visible to customers of an offering, who often are capable of articulating them if given an opportunity to do so. The trick is to access that information, to get customers to detect and communicate unmet needs. What user experience problems have emerged with the offering? What is frustrating them? How does it compare with the experiences of competing categories or subcategories? Are there problems with the total-use system in which the product is embedded, which might include other products and services? For example, egg substitutes are used in a breakfast system that involves other products and several processes including preparation, presentation, and clean-up. How can the product be improved? This kind of research helped Dow come up with Spiffits, a line of premoistened, disposable cleaning towels.

A word of caution. When interacting with customers, it is important to distinguish between the limitations of the category or subcategory and the dissatisfactions resulting from a brand's not living up to its promise. In discussing dissatisfactions and problems, the two can easily get intertwined. It is unmet needs associated with a category or subcategory that is the focus.

One direct approach is to simply talk to customers informally. When Lou Gerstner took over a struggling IBM in the early 1990s, he used his first one hundred days to conduct "operation bear hug," in which he and his top two hundred reports talked to three customers each and wrote up the interviews. That base of information led IBM to make some fundamental strategy decisions—namely to keep the company together, to enhance and leverage the IBM brand, and to deliver a systems value proposition that had become an unmet need because customers wanted to solve problems rather than buy computers.

Another source insight into unmet needs can come from everyday customer feedback mechanisms represented by the firm's Web site, 800 numbers, and active social media sites. The trick is to mine this data so that they illuminate unmet needs, and then examine the size and trends of those unmet needs.

A structured approach, termed *problem research*, quantifies the unmet needs. A list of potential problems with the product or service is generated. The problems are then prioritized by asking a group of one to two hundred respondents to rate each problem as to whether (1) the problem is important, (2) the problem occurs frequently, and (3) a solution exists. a problem score is obtained by combining these ratings. A problem research study of dog food found that buyers felt dog food smelled bad, cost too much, and was not available in different sizes for different dogs. Subsequently, products responsive to these criticisms emerged. Another study led an airline to modify its cabins to provide more leg room.

Another approach is to look to customers who have requirements that stretch the boundaries of the current offerings. Intel, for example, began designing microprocessors as a result of a need of a Japanese customer who was making a calculator. The innovation this project generated became a huge growth platform that powered Intel for decades. HP for many years used the "next bench" model, by which an engineering colleague would articulate an unmet need and existing instruments would not be adequate for the job. The result would be a new instrumentation product that solved the problem.

Eric von Hippel, a researcher at MIT who studies customers as sources of service innovations, suggests that lead users provide a particularly fertile ground for discovering unmet needs and new product concepts.[6] Lead users are those who face needs months or years before the bulk of the marketplace. A person who is very into nutrition, for example, would be a lead user with respect to health food. Lead users in regard to office automation would be firms that stand to profit from technological advancement. Lead users are positioned to benefit significantly from an offering responsive to their needs.

Ethnographic Research

Sometimes customers may not be aware of their unmet needs. They may be so accustomed to the implicit limitations of existing equipment that they have simply accepted the problems that go with them. Henry Ford famously said that if you asked customers what they needed prior to the introduction of the automobile they would have replied, "A faster horse." They had no way of anticipating the option of a functioning car. Also, customers are not always a good source for some kinds of unmet needs, especially those involving emotional and self-expressive benefits. The attractiveness of a rugged SUV, for example, did not really result from its functional benefits but customers were not willing or even able to describe self-expressive benefits such as being a rugged outdoors family (that in actually rarely goes camping in any wilderness).

It is therefore helpful to understand customers in depth in order to detect unmet needs that may not be visible to them, and then to apply creativity to imagine what might be possible. Ethnographic research can provide these needed customer insights and a platform to generate creative responsive offerings.

Ethnographic or anthropological or immersive research involves directly observing customers in as many contexts as possible. By accurately observing not only how the product or service is used but also *why* it is being used, companies can better understand the customer's needs and motivations and generate actionable insights. For example, the financial data company Thomson Corporation in order to improve or extend its services regularly studies from twenty-five to fifty customers by examining their behavior from three minutes prior to using its data to three minutes after.[7] One such study, which found that analysts working for the Thomson customers were inputting the data into spreadsheets, led to a new service in which the data-entry step was eliminated.

Ethnographic research can be done with cameras when it is too intrusive or inefficient to observe directly. Kimberly-Clark used motion-activated cameras to catch diaper changing and therefore to generate hundreds of instances that could be examined in slow motion. This research led to insights about the relationship of diaper fit to the problem of dealing with active baby legs.

Ethnographic research works:[8]

- As a result of one ethnographic study's finding that people experience frustration in cleaning the bathroom, P&G developed Magic Reach, a device with a long handle and swivel head.

- P&G's Downey Single Rinse came out of a close-up view of the water availability problem in rural Mexico, when water becomes extremely precious an extra rinse cycle became a high cost luxury.

- Observations of contractors and home renovators in action resulted in the development of the OXO hammer (with a fiberglass core to reduce vibration and a rubber bumper on top to avoid leaving marks when removing nails) as part of a line of professional-grade tools.

- Sirius followed forty-five people for a week, studying music listened to, magazines read, and TV shows watched. Insights into the habits of these people led them to develop a portable satellite-radio player that can load up to fifty hours of music for later playback.

- GE found through ethnographic research that buyers of plastic fiber for fire-retardant jackets were more concerned with performance than price. That led to a completely different business model.

- Marriott had a multifunctional team of seven people (including a designer and architect) spend six weeks hanging out with guests in hotel lobbies, cafés, and bars. As a result, Marriot redesigned lobbies and adjacent areas to be more suitable for transacting business. The new environment had brighter lights and social zones with a mix of small tables, larger tables, and semiprivate spaces.

- Prophet spoke to women in their homes about their under-
  wear drawers. The resulting insights about women's dissatisfactions contributed to the development of Maidenform's
  One Fabulous Fit bra.

Although this research approach has been around for nearly a
century, it has taken on new life in the last few years, not only in
packaged-goods firms like P&G and consumer software firms like
Intuit but also in business-to-business (B2B) firms like Intel and
GE. P&G has institutionalized ethnographic research with programs to have executives and other employees to live with
consumers (Living it), shop with them (Shop-alongs), and work
behind the counters of retailers (Working it). Nearly all P&G
executives have had at least one such experience, and many
participate in these programs regularly. One finding is that in
addition to supplying actionable insights this consumer contact
has improved employee job satisfaction.[9] Shop-alongs helped
Safeway understand shopper confusion and the whole shopper experience and influenced the development of its Lifestyle
stores in which the lighting, fixtures, and presentation have
been designed to support the selling of solutions rather than
items, salads rather than heads of lettuce.

Conducting ethnographic research is not easy, it goes beyond
the prescription to live with or shop with customers. There is
skill involved that some have mastered more than others but
that can be enhanced for anyone. The anthropologist Grant
McCracken talks about two key skills. The first is the ability to
notice the unusual, what cannot be easily explained ("I wonder
what that is").[10] Noticing involves both observing and explain-
ing. Ongoing hypothesis development is a vital part of the process. If a design engineer consults the Internet, for example, is
it because he or she is searching for a role model or because he
or she just needs a break? The second skill is empathy, the ability to feel what another is feeling. When Lafley, who became
CEO of P&G in 2001 and who was a believer and practitioner

of ethnographic research, is talking to a Mexican customer as he did, for instance, empathy helps create the insight that skin-care products deliver entertainment as well as functional benefits. The skin-care products become something to talk about, a point of interest within their lifestyle. McCracken believes that empathy can be learned or at least improved by gaining experience and by practicing. It is not entirely innate.

Ethnographic research often benefits from the use of teams of people. P&G, for example, sends out pairs of people into customers' homes. One person can take notes and the other can pursue observation and conversation. The conversation needs to be inquisitive and adaptable. The endpoint is rarely in view. After the interviews, the team gathers and distills the experience, looking for nuggets of insight. This stage can take a long time and be exhausting. It may involve some brainstorming efforts in order to tease out the insights and turn them into actionable ideas.

Observation

Innovation can come from simple observation. It doesn't need a formal research project. Just observe customers, dealers, colleagues, or random people. Look for the unusual. Ask why or why not.

You can observe yourself, your family, and friends. Make a list of what bugs you or others. Quicken's founder got the idea for Quicken financial software after observing his wife's frustration in keeping track of their finances and realizing that graphical interface could be made to look like a checkbook reducing the barrier to using a computer-based system. A twenty-six-year-old recovering from a ski accident and looking for exercise did some snowshoeing and was amazed at how awkward, bulky, and inefficient they were. As a result he designed the high-tech snowshoes we see today and created a new industry, growing his business to over $10 million.[11]

Observation needs to be taken to the next level, to be pursued. Some of the transformational innovations were based on lucky happenstance—someone not only observed but had the insight to see the implications of what he or she saw. A mistake in production around 1880 led to a soap that floated. This soap became Ivory and was the base product for P&G. Someone recognized that there were symbolic and functional benefits in a floating soap and did not simply correct the problem and move on. Ivory came to mean mildness and purity, a significant claim in a day of harsh soaps. Its floating quality became a point of differentiation that lasted for many decades. P&G's SK-II skin-care line originated when older workers in a sake brewery were observed to have young and smooth hands. That observation led to a line of high-end skin-care products that created a rather intense following. The key is to be able to capitalize on luck by recognizing the potential of a fortuitous event and being prepared to develop and test the resulting concept.

Finding New, Unintended Applications

How are customers actually using the offering? Are some uses very different than intended? If so, is there a core group that might have a similar need? Would it represent a very different value proposition? Ethnographic research can illuminate applications, but applications also can be discovered by providing customers with a means—perhaps a survey research instrument—to communicate how they are using the product or service. The key is to be curious and connected in some way to customers.

A classic example is Arm & Hammer baking soda, which dates from 1846 and was long used for baking but also for baths and the cleaning of teeth. In 1972 it was discovered that customers were using baking soda in their refrigerators to freshen the air and protect foods from odors. By advertising the application, the firm created a whole new business that turned a

sleepy brand into a high-growth one. The percentage of households that reported having used the product in this application
went from 1 percent to 57 percent in just fourteen months.
Arm & Hammer used the odor-protection property to expand
the brand to include products for deodorizing sinks, freezers, cat-
litter boxes, and carpets. There were other deodorizer brands,
of course, but only one baking soda solution. During the last
decade the firm added a special container for refrigerators and
an Arm & Hammer baking soda shaker.

Nalgene was a firm founded in 1949 to make polyethylene
laboratory equipment, such as bottles, filters units, and storage
tanks. In the early 1970s some of the scientists started using
one of the bottles to carry water on camping trips. An executive, observing how useful it was to a boy scout camping exhibi-
tion, decided to go commercial with it, and Nalgene Outdoor
Products came to life. It was a sleepy business until the con-
troversy around plastic water bottles emerged. The fact that
Americans discard 38 billion plastic water bottles a year, which
it takes 17 million barrels of oil to produce and which are not
biodegradable, started to become visible.[12] Nalgene bottles provided one answer, suggesting a new application for its products
that promised to dwarf the outdoor focus. One lesson is that
although a sleepy business may not be attractive, its presence
gives it the option of participating in relevant trends. Recall
the Fiber One cereal brand that became a real asset when the
value of fiber consumption became visible.

Customer Partnering in Concept Generation

Customers can be effective partners in the development of
breakthrough concepts by going beyond identifying needs to
actually proposing solutions, which can then be transferred
into offerings. LEGO, for example, uses its customer base to
develop, customize, and test new products. Over a hundred
users helped create LEGO Mindstorms, a kit that combines

LEGO construction and robotic technology. Many more LEGO enthusiasts are involved in the development of LEGO castle and city models.

An effective and efficient way to access customers is to use the Internet to engage them in a dialogue. Dell, for example, has a Web site called Ideastorm on which customers can post ideas and observe and "vote" on the ideas of others. Customers also see Dell's reactions, which can include such responses as "under review" or "partially implemented." Among the suggestions were to have backlit keyboards, to support free software like Linux, to design quieter computers, and to have more USB ports. Starbucks, with its My Starbucks Idea site, is among many firms attempting to do something similar.

A risk with customer-driven idea sites is that there can be a surge around an idea that is impractical or unwise, putting the company on the defensive. But these sites have the potential of leveraging many perspectives to generate ideas that can result in real energy and innovation. They can also help to determine if the time is right to introduce an offering or if the idea needs more time.

A customer-oriented Web site can also be focused on testing and refining ideas. The Wells Fargo Labs site exposes customers to new ideas and technology and invites their comments. The Intuit Labs site similarly makes available to customers experimental software applications, mobile software, and small-business solutions and invites comments. Boeing got some 120,000 people to join Boeing's World Design Team, an Internet-based global forum in which ideas regarding the Dreamliner plane's design can flow during the design process. The audience attracted to these sites will be those customers who have a special interest in the topic and are able to understand and comment, an excellent sample profile.

With respect to the B2B firm, a classic way to gain sustainable differentiation is by working with customers to provide a systems solution to a broader problem rather than attempting to sell a product or service. In doing so, the value proposition becomes stronger and the ability of the competition to duplicate the offering is reduced. The idea is to partner with customers to include in the offering things like ordering, logistics, warehousing, and so on. Federal Express (FedEx), for example, worked with clients to provide a warehouse service that stores products that are needed immediately and even handles returns. P&G has worked with Walmart and other retailers to create efficiencies in logistics, warehousing, and ordering that provide a barrier to those that would compete with their low-price value proposition.

Noncustomer Needs

Customers know the category or subcategory, have experience with it, and are thus in a good position to identify unmet needs. But noncustomers of the category or subcategory have untapped potential. They represent virgin territory, a source of new growth. Why are noncustomers not buying? What is holding them back? What is the purchase barrier? Is it some missing feature that they would need for their applications? Or is it that the category is simply too complex, expensive, or advanced for their needs? Why phone cards and not mobile phones? Why frozen dinners and not a shelf staple like Hamburger Helper?

Shimano, the bike components manufacturer, was in the enviable position of having the highest reputation and credibility for supplying top-end bikers who were into upgrading their equipment. The problem was that bike ownership was not growing. To find out why, Shimano talked to some of the 160 million Americans who did not ride. These people generally had fond memories of childhood biking but believed the sport had become too complicated, expensive, and even intimidating. To respond, Shimano developed and defined the experience of a "coasting" bike—wide seats, reachable ground, backward-kick braking, upright handle bars, and no controls. The gear box, hidden and controlled by a microprocessor, automatically shifts between three gears. Fueled in part by the Shimano Coaster and by an increased desire to commute with bikes, coaster bikes started to take off. In 2009 a magazine for coaster riders, *Kickstand*, came out, giving the subcategory a signal that it had emerged.

Often, particularly in emerging economies, the problem is price: there is a gap between what is affordable and the cost of what is available. Nokia in researching consumers in India found that even a simplified phone cost too much.[13] However, by packaging the phone with a flashlight, an alarm clock, and a radio, the price of the combination, though high, was much closer to being acceptable. There were other problems: the dust that affected reliability, the humidity that resulted in slippery hands, the glare of bright sunlight that made the screen hard to read were addressed with a phone that was dustproof, had a better grip, and featured a polarized screen. Retailers would not carry phones, so Nokia developed a network of people willing to sell its phones from small stands. By 2007 something like 100,000 retail outlets were selling Nokia phones. This all came from identifying and addressing the barriers to buying.

Market Trends

Thomson Corporation in 1997 was a Toronto media company that owned some fifty-five daily newspapers that were doing well.[14] CEO Richard Harrington, however, observed several trends in the environment that caused him to move the firm away from newspapers. He could see that the Internet was going to undercut classified advertising and that cable television and the Internet were going to steal readers. Despite the fact that the company was profitable, he made the rather dramatic decision to disinvest from newspapers and to move the firm into delivering information and services online to the law, education, health-care, and finance industries. As a result of that decision, Thomson was thriving nine years later, whereas other newspaper-based firms were struggling. The decision was based on projecting existing environmental trends and acting on them.

A customer trend can be a driver of a category or subcategory. The expression "Find a parade and get in front of it" has some applicability here. That was part of the strategy of Whole Foods Market with organic products: it was able to capitalize on the surge of interest in organics. What market forces will influence the winning value propositions and choice of target markets? What trends will create new unmet needs or make the existing ones more visible? What is the white space around the trend, unexplored markets? There was a trend toward less fat consumption but no firm had found a way to deliver creamy taste in the ice cream arena until Dreyer's unveiled its Slow Churned ice cream.

It is even better if an offering can access multiple trends, because this will create higher barriers to competitors. Annie Chun capitalized on four trends with a line of packaged Asian food that delivered Asian flavors, healthy eating, natural ingredients, and the convenience of at-home meals. In a crowded marketplace, this combination coupled with interesting menus provide a unique subcategory.

Firms have a strong tendency to fail to understand important trends or predict future events. One reason is that executives are focused on execution and have little attention span left for "might be." Another is that there is a natural perceptual bias toward ignoring or distorting information that conflicts with the strategic model of the day. Still another is the support of "groupthink" within the organization—it is awkward to point out that basic assumptions may be wrong. Finally, it is just difficult.

How can a firm do better at detecting and leveraging trends? A few guidelines.

First, have organizational tentacles stretched throughout the relevant environment looking for weak as well as strong signals.

External scanning should be elevated to be a strategic discipline supported by an internal information system. A working intranet should be the cornerstone. Be curious.

Second, create discovery mechanisms. Texas Instruments holds a "sea of ideas" meeting each week to recognize emerging needs and innovation at the fringe of its business. One such meeting led to the development of a low-power chip for mobile phones.

Third, look to secondary as well as primary effects. Johnson & Johnson has a strategy process termed Frameworks that looks at regulations, insurance coverage, and competitive moves and considers their implications. New products and subcategories can often be expected to have indirect impact on behavior and products. The iPod has had a host of indirect effects. For example, iPod-driven speakers have affected music listening and speaker products.

Global Reverse Innovation

Global reverse innovation aims to develop simpler, less-expensive products for emerging markets like India and China and then adapt them to developed markets like the United States or Europe. Also termed *frugal innovation*, the idea is to start over to create a design that will supply the function but at a fraction of the cost. The conventional global approach to business development, in contrast, develops sophisticated products for developed countries and markets stripped-down versions for the emerging markets, a tactic that is logical, efficient, and increasingly unsuccessful.

There are two rationales for participating in global reverse innovation. First, the only way to get traction in emerging markets is to innovate for them. Adapting products does not work. A stripped down, small car is not what the Indian economy needs—it requires instead a radically different car like the Nano described in Chapter Four designed for the Indian market.

Tata Chemicals, for example, created a water filter system based on purification using plentiful rice husks that sells for $24 and expects to sell one hundred million units a year.[15] Such a product was not an adaptation but was conceived and developed in the context of the Indian market.

Second, the reality is that firms are going to market inexpensive products, tailored to emerging markets, in the United States and similar markets. It is a question of which firms. Will Chinese firms, such as Haier in appliances, or Indian firms, such as Tata in automobiles, dominate, or will firms from developed countries also participate? There is no question that there are markets for simple, very low priced offerings in developed markets. People are becoming more sensitive to price because they face more income constraints. A U.K. retailer observed that "the frivolous is now unacceptable and the frugal is 'cool.'"[16] And this retrenchment period is forecast to last for a long time.

In 2009 GE announced they would spend $3 billion over six years to create more than one hundred health-care innovations that would "substantially lower costs, increase access, and improve quality."[17] One role model is a cheap, portable, PC-based ultrasound machine developed by a local team in China for rural Chinese clinics. Initially selling at around $30,000, it provided an entry for GE, who had previously been marketing equipment that was $100,000 and up. A redesign in 2007 dropped the price to $15,000, and sales took off not only in China but in the United States. It is now used by U.S. ambulance squads; in emergency rooms; and even in operating rooms, where it helps place catheters for anesthesia.

Open Innovation

Creativity is all about making connections, sometimes among seemingly disparate sources or perspectives. Products, technologies, or even ideas found among people or firms outside the organization potentially represent huge additions to the creative efforts of the firm. P&G with its Connect and Develop (C&D) programs, which started in 2001 under the auspices of the then-new CEO A. J. Lafley, provides a model.[18] The objective of C&D is to make P&G an open organization with broad networks that will ultimately generate one-half of the firm's flow of new products. The program has some seventy-five technology entrepreneurs around the world who have connected with a host of innovative sources in universities, think tanks, and other firms. They not only look for products that have evidence of being worthwhile but also research market needs and suggest innovation directions. They are supported by innovation centers simulating home and store environments that can be used to test ideas. These efforts are supplemented by such Internet-based engines as the InnoCentive, which links "seekers" (companies with problems) and "solvers" (experts with solutions). and a P&G-supported company, YourEncore.com, that taps the expertise of retirees from P&G and other firms.

After seven years the C&D program was generating some two product concepts per week and had spawned some two hundred products. They include the following:

- *Olay Regenerist*, which reached $250 million in annual sales after four years, which was based on an ingredient for wound healing developed by Sederma, a small French company.
- *Swiffer Duster*, which was sourced from Unicharm, a Japanese firm that competes with P&G in the diaper and feminine-care categories. P&G even used the advertising and positioning ideas of Unicharm.
- *Mr. Clean Magic Eraser*. A C&D team noticed a household sponge product sold in Japan that was very effective as a spot eraser. The underlying technology was licensed from the German chemical company BASF and introduced in the United States under the Mr. Clean brand.

- *Nice 'n Easy Root Touch-Up.* A design firm developed a root touch-up brush for Nice 'n Easy by adapting a proprietary brush technology from P&G's Clairol group that was previously used on men's facial hair. Nice 'n Easy Root Touch-Up was named by the Marie Claire magazine as one of twenty-five products that changed women's lives.[19]

In an effort to create outside perspectives, Prophet's innovation practice, mentioned earlier, uses a human library inspired by a project of the city library in Malmo, Sweden, which allowed visitors to check out living people for forty-five-minute conversations. People are selected as human library "books" because they bring a tangential perspective or context to the topic at hand. For example, a firm targeting females spoke to a hair stylist to understand the elements that compose femininity and learn about trends the stylist was seeing. A private bank interested in client partnership learned about establishing trust from a professional ballroom dancer. A director of a high-end restaurant discussed with a specialist from an upscale clothing brand how to increase premium perceptions in offerings that are being commoditized by price-oriented competitors. The use of a human library is not designed to generate a solution or even ideas but rather to provide new perspectives from which to start.

Looking to Role Models

It can be fruitful to look outside the industry for firms that have addressed issues successfully that have some similar characteristics to those facing your firm. For example, Boeing in developing the Dreamliner looked to Walmart's inventory tracking system for ideas about handling passenger luggage, because lost luggage is a major issue for airlines, and to Disney to understand more about customer service that can delight customers.

As noted at the outset, ideas are rarely new—it is a matter of reframing and repackaging them. Henry Ford, for example, did not really invent the assembly line.[20] He actually gathered together and adapted what he learned from a set of role models. He got the idea for the assembly line from Chicago's meatpacking industry and combined it with the concepts of interchangeable parts, introduced in 1801 by Eli Whitney for assembling pistols, and the continuous-flow production that was used in the tobacco industry in 1882.

The challenge is to observe how other firms have solved an analogous problem and then making the connection. Marks & Spencer, the U.K. food store, realized that its sandwich business involved an inordinately large amount of labor to spread butter.[21] The head of the unit charged with making sandwiches observed a silk-screen process used by another supplier to print patterns on bed sheets. It turned out the process worked for applying butter onto bread, and the result was a distinct edge in an important and growing business. An old idea in a new context.

Competitor Analysis—Looking for Openings

Competitors are frequently the source of new ideas when they create categories or subcategories that are vulnerable to the entry of substantially more appealing offerings. Many of the Apple innovations were in this category. The idea is to take over the new category or subcategory or create a new one by leapfrogging competitors. Which competitors are having success in promising markets—those with increasing demand and possibly a buzz? How can the benefits offered by the competitive brands be surpassed with a qualitatively improved product? What competitors have entered healthy or potentially healthy arenas and are struggling? How can the limitations or deficiencies of the competitors be overcome?

It is remarkable how many successful new offerings that drove new categories or subcategories were directly enabled by simply improving on competitors' offerings. Sometimes the competitor was simply premature in that the technology was not there yet. Apple, Zara, Zappos, and Prius all were beneficiaries of timely advances in computers that helped them overcome technical challenges. Subway exploited the unhealthy menus of its competitors and showed with Jared's vivid story how fast food could be healthier.

Nintendo, the most successful brand in the 2000s according to the annual BrandJapan tracking study (it went being ranked in Japan from 135 in 2005 to number 1 in 2008 and 2009), had a competitor-driven strategy. Sony's Playstation and Microsoft's XBox both emphasized performance graphics, the key to the success of action games aimed at young males. Instead of playing the performance game, Nintendo chose to deemphasize technology and to instead focus on player involvement and on expanding the use profile from young males to the whole family. The key for this group was a wide array of easy-to-use, involving games that would move beyond the action genre and even include some learning vehicles. One goal was to have the mother a participant and an advocate rather than a cynic and opponent. Another was to involve the whole family so the games would not simply represent the boy's retreats. Nintendo's competitors had left open a wide white space.

Sometimes the very strength of competitors can stimulate options. The strength of Kirin in lager beer was turned against them when Asahi came out with its "not lager, not older, not traditional" Super Dry entry. Similarly, the success of the station wagon concept and its clear functional approach was a help to Chrysler as they established the minivan as an alternative.

Technology-Stimulated Concepts

A development in technology can stimulate a concept. In that case the challenge is to create or simulate a latent, unrecognized, unmet need. There was no unmet need for dry beer in Japan until Asahi Super Dry was invented and Asahi, through the product and the brand-building activities, created a new subcategory. The same was true with Kirin Ichiban and IKEA.

There was a $1.2 billion encyclopedia industry in 1991, with Encyclopedia Britannica fighting with WorldBook to sell $1,000 sets. Two years later Microsoft introduced Encarta, the somewhat inferior Funk & Wagnalls encyclopedia but on a compact disc for $100, and within three years had captured nearly 20 percent of a market that had shrunk to $600 million. The door-to-door sales forces of the legacy firms turned from an asset to a liability. Encyclopedias on a disk was a technology-enabled new subcategory. The key was recognizing the potential application of a new technology, perhaps aided by a creative-thinking exercise. Microsoft closed Encarta in 2009, but during nearly two decades it had a nice run.

Often a new technology is developed for a use that is very different from its ultimate role in creating a new business arena. The challenge is to recognize promising developments and continually test them for applications outside their initial scope. As noted earlier, the main Intel business driver from the early to mid-1980s through the 1990s was the microprocessor, which was developed when a Japanese company asked Intel to design the innards for a calculator they were planning. The potential commercial applications of the technology did not at first seem promising but it was intriguing enough that a decision was made to gain the rights to it. When IBM chose Intel's 8086 in 1981 to power its personal computer, an event unanticipated with the microprocessor bet was made, the microprocessor train really took off. Flash memory, big business for Intel in the 1990s, was first thought to have little potential until the belief caught hold that it might replace power-hungry disc drives. The ultimate winning application turned out, however, to be mobile computing. At least two of Intel's big products during the two decades of phenomenal growth, microprocessors and flash memory, were fueled by unexpected applications that emerged well after the technology was developed.

Timing is particularly important with technology-driven offerings. Premature offerings can fail, whereas just a few years later a very similar offering with the benefit of a technological advance will be a big winner. Apple experienced a premature launch with the Newton but got the timing right with several of its other products. The challenge is to stay close to technological developments and have the instinct to see when a barrier can be overcome with new advances. The market also has to be ready, especially if the technology is radical and requires a change from the familiar in customer habits.

Leveraging Assets and Competencies

A new category or subcategory, if it is to have value and legs, needs to be based on hard-to-duplicate assets and competencies. If existing assets and competencies can be leveraged, that means that they do not have to be developed but will be in place, perhaps with some adaptation. Most of the risk is therefore reduced. The process starts with an identification of exactly what the assets and competencies are—for example they could be drawn from marketing, distribution, manufacturing, design, R&D, or the brand. Mercedes-Benz, for example, launched a style division in 2010 to leverage its styling expertise to design helicopters, yachts, watches, interiors, and more.

Disney has a powerful brand that means family fun and memories and a host of subbrands around characters from Mickey onward, experiences at theme parks, and such movies as *The Lion King*. It also has operational excellence: the ability to execute as evidenced by theme park operations so exemplary that others use Disney as a role model. The brand assets and operational competencies combine to make a Disney cruise ship a highly differentiated entry that immediately forms a new cruise ship subcategory.

When a breakthrough technology is found, it often is not clear what applications will be the big winners. The aggressive course is to leverage the technology by exploring a wide range of applications. The Freeplay Group in Cape Town, South Africa, invents and sells devices that generate electricity when the user cranks the handle on a flashlight-like product containing a carbonized steel spring.[22] As the spring unwinds it produces electricity. This advance led them to a host of products that needed an energy source including a radio, a global positioning system, a land-mine detector, a water purifier, and a toy monster truck.

One way to leverage assets and competencies is to employ those found in one business unit to other business units. When that happens, the resulting offering will often have an advantage that is unique to the organization and thus easy to defend. 3M's Optical Systems Division, for example, makes computer displays that are more energy efficient, easier to read, and able to direct the light toward the user because they are based on insights and technology drawn from all over the firm. And P&G regularly explores whether a technology in one product arena can be used in another. For example, Crest Whitestrips was developed by combining the film technology from corporate R&D with bleach technology from the laundry organization and Crest's business knowledge of oral-care issues and distribution assets. Other firms without those competencies will find it hard to duplicate the offering.

Employing assets and competencies across organizational silos should be easy because such divisions are often down the hall from one another. However, silo barriers can be severe, and assertive programs and incentives may be needed even to share information. Unilever has the Genesis project, which encourages scientific breakthroughs useable across Unilever's product lines.[23] The role model is the yellow-tint-canceling whitener developed for Radiant detergent and Signal toothpaste.

Consider Category or Subcategory Definitions

Another approach to gaining ideas for new concepts is to observe how categories and subcategories are defined and determine if any of these definitions trigger a new concept. Most category and subcategory definitions involve a limited number of value propositions, such as adding a service to an offering, systems benefits, functional design, premium offerings, new-generation offerings, and offerings that share an interest such as baby care with their customers. Chapter Eight provides a description of eighteen of these defining value propositions.

Prioritizing the Analysis

The result of the concept-generation phase is not necessarily a concept that will be pursued to the market. Rather, the process might identify a concept that is promising but immature. Or an area that has potential might be identified but without a responsive concept in mind. There may be a promising trend, a potential technological development, an emerging application, or some other market dynamic that could become the core of a new category or subcategory if some of the dynamics were to grow or change form or if some of the barriers were removed. There could be an offering concept that is only an identification of a potential market opportunity. Whatever the nature of the dynamic, it could define an information need area, an area that will merit ongoing monitoring and analysis.

The problem is that there will be dozens of information need areas with associated strategic uncertainties, leading to an endless process of information gathering and analysis that can absorb resources indefinitely. A publishing company may be concerned about satellite TV, lifestyle patterns, educational trends, e-readers, social technology, geographic population shifts, and changing tastes in books. Any one of these issues involves a host of subfields and could easily spur limitless research. For example, investigating e-readers might involve a variety of suppliers, technologies, reader reactions, competitive strategies, and author experimentation. Unless distinct priorities are established, the total analysis can become unmanageable.

The challenge is to identify and prioritize the information need areas. Some will merit high-priority task forces whereas others should be assigned a low-key monitoring effort. The level of resources expended and the form of the monitoring and analysis effort will depend on the potential impact on strategy and its immediacy.

Impact. How likely is it for an offering to emerge from the information need area that will have a major impact on the business, not only financially but also in terms of the firm's assets, competencies, and strategies? For example, battery technology will have a significant impact on hybrid car makers or potential makers. An information need area could also involve potential threats. How likely is it that the market will change such that the firm's current offerings and strategies will become less relevant to a significant segment? For example, a microbrewery market surge could have an impact on mainstream beer firms in a major way.

Immediacy. The immediacy of an issue or strategic uncertainty is related to the probability that involved trends or events will occur within a planning horizon. An uncertainty area representing a very low probability of occurring in the immediate future will be of lesser interest. After a trend or event crystallizes, a firm needs to develop a reaction strategy, to develop a new offering or strategy. A key variable is the reaction time likely to be available in relation to the time required. If the available reaction time is inadequate, it becomes important to better anticipate emerging trends and events so that future strategies can be initiated sooner.

Figure 6.3 suggests an approach to prioritization. When both the immediacy and potential impact of the underlying trends and events are high, a dedicated, budgeted task force may be appropriate, as will be the development of reaction plans or strategies. If both the immediacy and impact are low, then a low

Figure 6.3 Prioritizing Information Need Areas

Immediacy

	Low	High
Impact High	Monitor and analyze; contingent strategies considered	Analyze in-depth; develop strategy
Impact Low	Monitor	Monitor and analyze

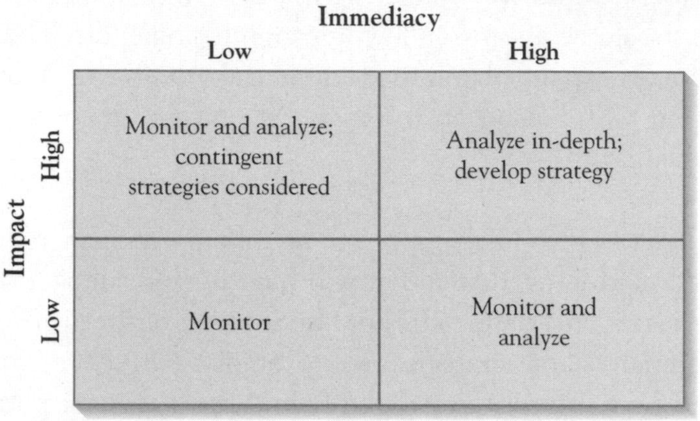

level of monitoring may suffice. If the impact is thought to be low but the immediacy is high, the area may merit a higher level of monitoring and analysis.

If the immediacy is low and the impact high, then the area may require monitoring and analysis in more depth, and contingent strategies may be considered but not necessarily developed and implemented. Events that are thought to be rare but can have a huge impact are often underestimated. Financial crises through history have happened because an event thought to be rare actually occurred. The identification of signals of an uptick in immediacy or a trend surging can help avoid being surprised. If the probablility is seen to increase, contingent strategies can then be put in place.

The goal of an approach to identify and prioritize information need areas should not be to build a library of facts. The process should be designed to avoid descriptive, ill-focused, and inefficient efforts. The focus should instead be on understanding market dynamics that have the potential to be creating new categories or subcategories. In that spirit, the process should be linked to current offerings, strategies, and potential opportunities and threats that surround them.

Key Takeaways

An organization can enhance the chances of creating a new offering that will transform the market by becoming proficient in creative thinking and by pursuing several idea-generating approaches, such as identifying customer-articulated unmet needs, conducting ethnographic research, observation, identifying unintended applications, customer partnering, asking why noncustomers don't buy, interpreting market trends, using global reverse innovation, employing open innovation, looking to role models, leapfrogging competitor offerings, seizing technology-driven opportunities, leveraging the firm's assets and competencies, and looking at the commonly used category and subcategory defining value propositions. Some concepts or trends not ready for market should be prioritized as in the basis of their impact and immediacy.

For Discussion

1. Create a list of the top five to ten unmet needs in your marketplace. Categorize them as to how feasible a responsive offering might be. What would be the size of the potential market?

2. What trends are emerging that would affect Best Buy? Apple? Zappos? Prioritize their associated information need areas.

3. What are some role models that might provide offering ideas to Muji? To Wheaties?

7

EVALUATION

A great company is more likely to die of indigestion
from too much opportunity than starvation from
too little.

— *David Packard, founder, HP*

Nobody has ever bet enough on a winning horse.
— *Richard Sasuly, author, horseracing authority*

A key to creating and implementing an offering that will
drive a new category or subcategory is an accurate evaluation of the prospects of a concept and the ability to pull it off.
The Segway case provides a good illustration of the difficulties
of both.

Segway's Human Transporter

Dean Kamen was a successful inventor mainly in the medical
device field. One of his inventions was a wheelchair, the iBot,
that could climb stairs. That technology provided the basis for
a far more exciting product, the Segway Human Transporter
(HT), introduced in 2001. An upright, two-wheeled people
mover with which the driver could accelerate or stop simply by
leaning forward or backward, it could travel up to 12 mph and
had a 17-mile range before needing recharging. Its core mechanism was termed *dynamic stabilization* and involved six gyro-
scopes, two tilt sensors, and a dual computer system capable of
adjusting the Segway one hundred times a second.

The prospects of the Segway were high in 2001. One of the major backers predicted publicly that it would reach $1 billion in sales faster than any other company and would be as important as the Internet. Steve Jobs predicted it would have as great an impact as the personal computer.[1] Kamen himself predicted that it "will be to the car what the car was to the horse and buggy"[2] and built a large factory that had the capacity to turn out nearly 500,000 units per year.[3] The firm was valued at $600 million. Sales were expected to be between 50,000 and 100,000 units during the first thirteen months and to build from there, but, instead, sales during the first seven years were under 30,000 units.[4]

Why?

It was not because the Segway failed to get attention. The publicity for this unique product was amazing. It was featured on network shows and in major magazines. It was even built into the plot of popular TV shows like Frazier. Celebrities used it. There are few products that received more PR attention than the Segway. A *New Yorker* cover, for example, showed Osama bin Laden traversing the Afghan countryside with an all-terrain version of the Segway. Because the product was so unique and attuned to environmental concerns about saving energy, it delivered significant self-expressive benefits. There was an event organized by Segway owners in Chicago in 2003 called the SegwayFest to celebrate the Segway lifestyle.

Nor was it because the firm could not deliver or because the product did not work. There were few reports of quality or performance problems. There were some design issues in the early versions that were solved but nothing that inhibited the sales.

The problem was that the unmet need was overestimated and the product limitations were underestimated. The prime target initially was those employees who would benefit from a device that would compete with walking—three times the speed with less effort. With respect to postal workers, less than 5 percent of them actually walked, and those who tried the

Segway disliked the fact that they could not adjust mail between stops because two hands were needed to operate the device. Plus there was no provision for an umbrella if it rained. Police and security professionals were concerned about the range and sales to this group was far below expectations. Alternatives like mountain bikes were cheaper and did not run out of fuel. Other workers who might have been prospects found that the new alternative was too much of a change from their existing habits and processes.

There were a host of customer acceptance issues. Sales to the general public were offered through Amazon in 2002. One issue was that some four hours of training were recommended, which was difficult to provide with Amazon's direct channel. Another was the fact that some states and cities did not allow the Segway to operate on sidewalks with the argument that it would be dangerous to walkers, especially those with disabilities, whereas other localities imposed a speed limit of 8 mph. The unit's 80-pound weight was also an issue, but a bigger liability was the limited range in terms of distance traveled before a recharge. There was a lack of a critical mass to make the usage experience widespread and the social endorsement visible. Finally, the value to those who were unused to such a strange vehicle was not obvious. Sales never reached the tipping point.

There were marketing issues as well. The firm had trouble keeping top executives. In particular, the top sales slot was unfilled at a time when distribution was the key to success. There may have been some strategic mistakes as well. Holding off on consumer sales and then relying on Amazon may have been an error. If Segway had partnered with a firm that had on-the-ground retail presence, such as a car dealer or a major retailer like Costco or Home Depot or Sears, they might have created some user proof points.

The Segway firm did not give up. They introduced a golf transport HT in 2004 and a second-generation product line in 2005 with LeanSteer, whereby the unit could be steered by leaning. It expanded its reach to some sixty countries. It developed a Segway social online networking site whereby owners could compare notes and experiences. They still have no competition for their product and are considering extension to four-wheel vehicles in cooperation with GM. But there is little question that the optimistic prospects did not materialize.

Not to be discouraged, Kamen's next venture is to produce a box fueled by burning cow manure to purify water.[5] If the device, with inexpensive, reliable parts designed by Kamen's firms, can get distribution it would potentially reduce sharply the number of deaths caused by impure water now estimated to be in the neighborhood of five million people per year. Kamen did learn one lesson from the Segway. In the future he plans to get a large firm to handle the production and distribution of the product.

What are the learnings here? Where did the evaluation go wrong? First, market research needed to have more depth. The overestimation of the market for postal and security workers could have been reduced, perhaps with ethnographic research or a more systematic field test. Second, distribution is a key link to any new offering and, in retrospect, chains that could demonstrate, train, and service were necessary. Third, the talent deficiency in marketing was a contributing factor in the disappointing sales. The role of talent is too often underestimated. Finally, there is a downside of exuberance and widespread publicity. If an evaluation had led the way to a modest plan spread out over a decade, the Segway, with its performance, quality, and publicity, might have been recorded as a clear winner.

Evaluation: Picking the Winners

There will always be too many concept ideas if the organization is open to them and way too many if the organization actively creates them. Because there are limits on any organization's resources and tolerance for risk, it becomes critical to prune them back with discipline and identify those that have the most potential to be game changers. Part of the turnaround at Apple when Steve Jobs returned in 1997 and also at P&G when A. G. Lafley became CEO in 2000 was a disciplined decision to focus on the most promising new offerings and markets and to stop trying to pursue so many.

One of the reasons why such a high percentage of new offerings, especially radically new offerings, fail is that they do not receive the commitment needed to support the final development, the needed improvements, and the marketing required for success. When resources are spread over too many projects, most if not all are inadequately funded and the failure percentage goes up. Focus is a key for sure.

Pruning, however, puts an increased burden on evaluation. Getting evaluation right becomes more important than ever. The risk, of course, is not only in funding disappointments but in erroneously or prematurely terminating those ideas with potential. These mistakes, which are usually hidden or forgotten, may be the most costly of all.

The risk of backing an idea that is faulty or premature or one that cannot be implemented by a firm because of a culture misfit or the absence of key assets or competencies can be stronomical. AT&T reportedly lost more that $50 billion in the 1990s trying to get into three businesses that turned out to be debacles: computers with NCR, mobile telephones with McCaw Cellular, and cable broadband with TCE and MediaOne.[6] Intel lost some $1 billion on a foray into the Web-hosting business. The evaluation process should be professional and objective and should minimize the chances of missing the great ones and hitting on the disasters.

Basically the firm needs to ask three questions, shown in Figure 7.1:

- Is there a market?
- Can we compete and win?
- Will a market leadership position endure?

Figure 7.1 Three Dimensions of Evaluation

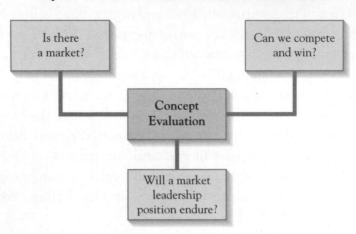

Each question is tough. Executives evaluating options need to make predictions about complex and dynamic trends; uncertain innovations some of which are not even in evidence; the impact of organizational limitations; customer responses to new offerings, which can be radically different from current offerings, and the reaction of competitors to the new category or subcategory.

Is There a Market—Is the Opportunity Real?

Is there really a substantial or transformational innovation that will change what people buy and create new categories or subcategories? The ability to distinguish between incremental and substantial or transformational innovation is at the heart of the matter. And will there be enough customers in the new category or subcategory to make it worth the investment required? What are the top-line growth prospects for the category or subcategory? Is it a fad or something more enduring? Will it grow into something substantial, or will it always be a niche?

Forecasting the market is critical. There needs to be a worthwhile market. If not, it will not make sense to invest. An analysis of the many market failures experienced at P&G, including some very prominent disappointments, revealed that one of the main reasons for these was that the market turned out to be too small.[7]

A forecast dramatically affected the fortunes of two aircraft companies.[8] In the mid-1990s Boeing and Airbus undertook a joint market research study to estimate the market for a super-jumbo jet that would be larger than Boeing's hugely successful 747 Jumbo, which at that time had sold over 1,000 planes. In part as a result of the research, Airbus estimated the market to be over 1,000 and decided to invest in the A380, an investment that involved well over $10 billion. Boeing, however, estimated the demand at 250 and made a very different decision to invest $10 billion in the intermediate-size 787, a plane that sacrificed speed for efficient operation. Of course, both firms used other information sources in addition to the joint market research study, but they were looking at the same trends, same customers, and same environment.

This story illustrates how a market estimate can have a huge impact on strategic choices, which in turn can dictate not only a firm's success but the nature of its organization—its people, systems, and culture—moving forward. Another observation is that the same data, even gleaned from a common research study, can yield very different interpretations. Why? In part it can be that the two firms placed different weight on different scenarios—one, for example, believed in the efficiencies and growth of long-range routes of airlines like Singapore and Dubai, and the other saw more of the point-to-point future represented by Southwest and the European regional carriers. In part it can also be caused by a confirmation bias. Airbus, watching Boeing have success with the 747, may have had "fuselage envy." Further, such key members as France in the country consortium behind Airbus may have had some biases due to a belief that they might benefit with more work with the larger plane. Boeing might have seen the problems with a large plane and could also have had a smaller plane in the planning stage. As a result, information could be filtered and interpreted by both parties in order to support their preferred strategies.

Evaluating Trends

The goal is to evaluate an offering and its associated category or subcategory. However, because offerings will be motivated in part by a marketplace or societal trend, the evaluation of a trend should have a role in the overall evaluation process. Is it real or a fad that will fade or even collapse? Will it persist or even surge? It is crucial to evaluate correctly trends that are expected to drive growth for a new offering and its associated category and subcategory.

It can be damaging to miss an important trend. Schwinn, the classic name in bicycles, proclaimed mountain biking a fad in 1985 with disastrous results for its market position and, ultimately, its corporate health.

It can be more damaging to assume a trend is strong when it is weak or nonexistent. A "mirage" trend might last long enough to attract investment that could have been productively used elsewhere.

Some key questions:

What is driving the trend? The source of power and energy of a trend is a key predictor of its strength. A trend, as opposed to a fad, will have a solid foundation with legs. Trends are more likely to be driven by demographics (rather than pop culture), values (rather than fashion), lifestyle (rather than a trendy crowd), or technology (rather than media).[9] There is thus substance behind the trend that is enduring while a fad will have little substance behind it. If there is a confluence of two forces, such as technology and lifestyle, the trend will be more stable. Consider for example the forces behind the Twitter and Facebook surges. Faith Popcorn observes that fads are about products, whereas trends are about what drives consumers to buy products. She also suggests that trends (which are big and broad, lasting an average of ten years) cannot be created or changed, only observed.[10]

Do early sales growth represent an overhyped bubble? Too much growth too fast can be a signal that what is observed is a fad, especially if it is based on fashion or unproven technology. A classic fad was the colorful Crocs rubber shoes that became ubiquitous and caused the firm's stock to soar to $75 in October 2007 only to fall to $1.20 eighteen months later when the fad collapsed.[11] Crocs may survive by offering other designs, but the signature product could not maintain its position. The initial success of the Yugo was based on hype and not substance and its collapse should have been predictable.

How accessible is the trend in the mainstream market? Many strong appealing trends start have real strength but are constrained to a niche market for the foreseeable future. Others will break out into the mainstream and have much more impact. It is important to understand what determines if the offering will evolve into a mainstream market or whether there are factors that inhibit that breakout. What is the role of ingrained habits, excessive price levels, or difficulty of use, for example?

Is the trend based on talk or action? Just because someone says it three times does not make it true. Peter Drucker opined that a change is something that people do, whereas a fad is something people talk about.[12] The implication is that a trend demands substance and action supported by data rather than simply an idea that captures the imagination.

Does it find expression across categories or industries? If so it could qualify as a mega-trend, as do sustainability, digital technology, and healthy eating. Such trends started with small segments but have broken out so dramatically that they touch many if not most business operations. Mega-trends are particularly risky to ignore or avoid. However, they also can be hard to interpret because they often take on different forms in different contexts. Further, they attract competitors, making it particularly important to have an offering and category or sub-category that are highly differentiated.

Is the trend based on projected, future innovations? The difficulty of forecasting the success of futuristic products is graphically illustrated by an analysis of more than ninety forecasts of significant new products, markets, and technologies that appeared in *BusinessWeek, Fortune*, and the *Wall Street Journal* from 1960 to 1979.[13] Forecast growth failed to materialize in about 55 percent of the cases cited. Among the reasons were overvaluation of technologies (for example, three-dimensional color TV and tooth-decay vaccines); consumer demand (for example, two-way cable TV, quadraphonic stereos, and dehydrated food); a failure to consider the cost barrier (for example, the SST supersonic transport, a aircraft designed to exceed the speed of sound and moving sidewalks); or political problems (for example, marine mining). The forecasts for roll-your-own cigarettes, small cigars, Scotch whiskey, and CB radios suffered from shifts in consumer needs and preferences.

Yes, But . . .

Some trends are real but can be exaggerated if they are not put into perspective. For example:

Yes, Internet access and usage are growing rapidly, *but* . . .

> A significant proportion of the population still sees no need for the Internet, and some are outright hostile toward technology.

Yes, people can and will price shop on the Internet, *but* . . .

> Many are loyal to single sites and do not use price comparison services.

Yes, there is a strong trend toward healthy eating and exercise, *but* . . .

> Indulgent food items like upscale chocolates, super-premium ice cream, and high-fat burgers still make up a substantial and sometimes growing niche.

Yes, cell phones are a platform for multimedia marketing programs, *but* . . .

> In 2009 nearly half of U.S. mobile customers used their phones only to make calls and do not use them for messaging or Internet access.

Predictions of a checkless society, where paper checks would no longer be needed, was off by at least five decades.

Even if the trend is real, it might not be a basis for the success of the new category or subcategory. Is it a real force behind the new category or subcategory, or is it tangential? Zipcar was helped by the urban lifestyle; Healthy Choice by the healthy-living trends; Muji by the natural, back-to-nature trend; Whole Foods Market by the natural and organic trends; and Subway by the obesity-driven weight-reduction trends. All were responsive to real trends. The Segway was not supported by the green trend because that was not central to the perceptions of the people mover.

The Rosy Picture Bias

One danger in evaluating new offerings is the rosy picture bias—the assumption that customers will be as excited and impressed with the new offering as are the champions who have focused for months and maybe years on its attributes and potential upside. There has been a well-honed logical argument that the advances are transformational, that it will create a new category or subcategory. It can be difficult to put aside this almost obsessive optimism and take the perspective of the customer, who is flooded with conflicting messages and faced with tough budget allocation decisions. This customer may have a tough time getting excited about an innovation or even paying attention to it, as the Segway case study illustrates.

There are professional as well as psychological reasons for an offering champion to believe. For one thing, the innovation may be closely associated with the career of a person or group inside the organization. A success would accelerate careers, and a failure, even a premature exit, might hold them back. In addition to professional momentum is the personal psychic momentum. Championing an innovation is simply stimulating and fun, whereas running an existing business can, in contrast, seem boring. Perhaps more important, the development of a trans-formational new offering can become part of the champion's identity, and success represents personal as well as professional fulfillment.

As a result of an intensive need by the champion and the associated team for an offering to go forward and to succeed, information is filtered. Information that supports the offer-ing gets through, and that not supporting gets distorted or minimized—confirmation bias in action. And hard decisions get postponed or become less objective than they should be. It is just the nature of people and organizations. Of course, a disciplined, objective evaluation process can reduce the risk, but it will always be there.

As a result, the value proposition may be overestimated or it might even be something of a mirage. The vision of one-stop financial service, for example, had much less value to customers than was hoped when it was first tried in the early 1980s and again two decades later. Customers wanted competence and out-standing service from all financial service suppliers and whether they came from the same organization was relatively unimpor-tant. Yet, those conceiving of the concept could only see the on-paper advantages and ignored both the implementation dif-ficulties and the lack of customer interest.

The Gloomy Picture Bias

The risks of killing a project with high potential on the basis of erroneous or false judgments can be much more costly than giv-ing the green light to one that will fail. The possibility for a large business platform may be lost by a bad "no-go" decision. Further, executives who spend resources on failures are held accountable, but incidents in which executives allow opportunities to pass through their hands are forgotten. For example, although the unwise expenditures at GM of then-CEO Roger Smith on robot-ics and IT were visible, the less-visible decision to kill the electric car or the failure to respond to the Chrysler minivan may have been just as bad. The gloomy picture bias can be based on a pessimistic projection of the firm's ability to improve the offering through innovation, resolve perceived flaws, find the right application, or find the right market. A discomfort with a radically different approach may also play a role.

A dramatic example of the risks of killing a development project is the story of P&G's Tide, the synthetic detergent introduced in 1946 that changed the way clothes were washed. The R&D effort took well over a decade, and during the last five years of development the effort was defunded entirely—it was killed. However, it did not die. The development proceeded under the radar because one scientist was committed to making it happen. Only in 1945, when the product was made to work in a lab setting, was top management informed. To their credit they then realized its transformational potential, reversed course, and made the extraordinary decision to make a huge factory investment. They cut some two years off the normal test market process in order to gain time on competitors. If the review process five years earlier had worked, P&G might today still be a soap company.

Sometimes a flaw is incorrectly assumed to be fatal. Mint.com, for example, the personal finance service, had trouble getting funding because the judgment was made that no one would provide personal financial information to an independent Web site. However, that judgment turned out to be wrong. The firm argued that the service was not vulnerable to moving money by unauthorized people because it was designed to be a read-only system. They could honestly claim that the site's security had never once had been compromised, despite sponsored efforts to do just that. The firm found further ways to communicate data safety by using such third-party brands as VeriSign and Hackersafe.

As the Tide example illustrates, there is a real risk of giving up on a concept prematurely because the concept under review is flawed. The possibility that further refinement and improvement can change the equation is easy to dismiss. There are plenty of examples in the automobile industry of flawed products from Toyota in the 1960s to Hyundai in the 1990s, and more that were scorned and could have been killed by an evaluation process but instead survived and with improvements became market leaders.

Estimates of market size can rely too much on an existing market that consists of flawed products. Digital readers, termed *e-readers*, were around for a decade but had never gotten traction, in part because accessing books was difficult and the units were clunky. Then in November 2007 Amazon launched the Kindle with its Whispernet system for fast-downloading books, thirty hours of battery life, a book-like reading experience, and a market buzz. The Kindle sold over one million units in just over a year and made sales of prior products irrelevant as points of reference.

A concept can be killed because the right application is not identified and forecasts are based on the wrong premise. Intel's experience with the development of the 80286 microprocessor illustrates that finding the right application can be illusive especially when the supporting technologies are in flux. During the develop phase that began in 1978, fifty possible applications were identified.[14] The personal computer, the ultimate application that became the basis for the Intel business for decades, did not make the list of fifty. This failure was in part due to an understandable inability to forecast the development of the host of supporting technologies and software programs that eventually made the PC a runaway success. A lesson is that nurturing technological breakthroughs can be worthwhile, even when their ultimate applications are uncertain.

A new offering can also give strong fail signals because the firm has directed it at the wrong market. Joint Juice is a firm founded by an orthopedic surgeon who had the breakthrough idea of making glucosamine, effective in reducing joint pain, available in a liquid form.[15] The initial target market, young to middle-aged athletes, led to a series of choices involving product content, packaging, distribution, and advertising built around professional athletes. The problem was that the real market was an older demographic, people who wanted lower-calorie, less-expensive products and who were accessed through a different channel. The effort aimed at the wrong market almost caused the venture to fail.

There can be a basic reluctance to step beyond the conventional way of doing things. An offering with a totally new perspective might be dismissed out of hand. There is a true story about a high jumper good enough to be on the Oregon State University track team who had an unusual style. The coaches insisted that he learn the conventional "straddle roll" way, but his progress declined to the point that they gave up and let him jump his way. A few years later, as a senior, he won an Olympic gold medal using his "Fosbury Flop," and within five years after that his novel method was the norm and the world record was advanced 5 percent.[16] There were hundreds of promising tennis players with games that were destroyed because they were forced by coaches to hit one-handed backhands until Chis Evert and Jimmy Conners made the two-handed backhand, now the norm, acceptable. So when a novel approach comes out of a brainstorming session, remember the Fosbury Flop and the two-handed backhand.

The "Market's Too Small" Problem

A market needs to be substantial enough to support a business. A niche too narrow may have substantial and sustainable differentiation but will not be viable, in part because its operating and marketing costs become too high. However, avoiding small markets carries its own risk. A combination of niche markets can create a substantial business. In an era of micromarketing, much of the action is in smaller niche segments. If a firm avoids these, they can lock themselves out of much of the vitality and profitability of a business area.

Furthermore, most substantial business areas are small at the outset, sometimes for many years, before they become significant. Avoiding the small market can thus mean that a firm must later overcome the first-mover advantage of others or miss out entirely. Coke resisted bottled water and other beverages for many years, in part because such products were too small in the context of corporate Coke, a decision that was in retrospect a big mistake. Microsoft Office has smothered embryonic ventures at Microsoft, because its huge sales base made many new ideas seem trivial. As a result, many high-tech innovations came from other companies despite Microsoft's huge cadre of exceptional engineers. Frito-Lay, with a policy of avoiding any offering incapable of generating large sales levels within a few years, has limited its ability to innovate and test the waters with ideas.

A key issue is often whether a niche market, perhaps one with a high level of customer connection and sustainable differentiation, can be scaled into a broad market base. Such a move is difficult because the brand and the new category or subcategory that it represents often lose what made them special as it goes mainstream. But some brands have done just that, such as Nike, Starbucks, and SoBe, although there are many others like Snapple and Gucci that have tried and run into problems. To do so successfully requires a personality and set of benefits that the brand can retain as it is scaled. It is not easy, for sure.

The potential market may be large, but the actual market may still be too small because of barriers to its realization. There might be an economic barrier. For example, the demand for computers exists in many underdeveloped countries, but a lack of funds and the absence of suitable technology inhibit buying. Or the demand might simply take longer to materialize because the technology is not ready, as in the case of batteries for electric cars, or because customers are slow to change. Demand for electronic banking, for example, took many years longer than expected to materialize. There may be an inhibiting factor that prevents the value position from translating into behavior. For example, people like the idea of reducing fat or salt in food but are not willing to sacrifice taste. Or the value proposition may not be believable. A detergent product that cleaned better with half the product and had no messy foam was rejected in Mexico because customers thought that less product and the absence of foam meant less clean, a belief that could not be overcome.

Testing and Learning

An evaluation of any new concept should include exposing it to prospective customers. They can be asked to evaluate it in a group setting, in a survey, in a laboratory, in a simulated home or store, in trial user experiences, or in test markets. A ongoing test-and-learn program can guide the process of refining the offering as well as testing the concept. Taste tests played an important role in validating the potential of such food products as Asahi Super Dry, Kirin Ichiban, Wheaties Fuel, Dreyer's Slow Churned, and Healthy Choice. If the products can't win at that level, then more work is needed.

The feedback from potential customers is helpful but is not definitive, in part because how the offering is presented has an impact on customers' opinions. The offering may not be fully developed, and the concept will probably not be surrounded by marketing programs. As a result, respondents might not recognize or fully appreciate the value proposition and also might raise limitations and objections that would be less visible in a more realistic setting.

The reverse can also be true in that an offering may seem attractive in a limited context. New Coke, one of the most disastrous new products of modern time, was launched based on successful blind taste tests. New Coke did well without a label. The trouble was that in the marketplace the product had a brand attached to it. When the "real" Coke brand was identified, new Coke went from a winner to a loser in the taste tests.

Customers have a hard time evaluating novel products like the Segway. Even when the concept is understandable, research shows that respondents are less likely to follow through and actually purchase novel products than offerings that are less of a departure from existing products and that have more easily understood benefits. Feedback that is useful for a novel product will generally be from early adopters and opinion leaders, those who have an interest and feel for new concepts, or will be based on actual trial usage from a pilot test.

Starting with a small market footprint is a step beyond using a test market. It means that the firm is using a market presence initially to validate and refine. The firm enhances what works and replaces what does not. Many retail brands, such as Muji, Zara, Best Buy, and Whole Foods Market, evolved dramatically during the first years of their existence as their founders experimented with different ideas and types of presentation. Others from packaged goods firms to service companies deliberately started with small parts of their respective markets in order to test and refine both the offering and its position. In fact, there are few breakthrough innovations that do not evolve over time, and managing that process can be important to success.

Knowing the Value Proposition

There are a host of successful new offerings that defined new categories or subcategories but that were not subject to any formal customer testing. Steve Jobs is famous for not testing any ideas, including the iPod, iPhone, and iPad. He simply has a clear concept of the value proposition based on his knowledge of what is possible, what competitors have, and what the market wants. Ted Turner never tested the CNN concept but for several years just knew that an all-news network with national cable distribution would fly. He knew that people liked news and would value not having to wait for the evening news or newspaper.

Having confidence in the value proposition often accompanies or is based on an in-depth knowledge of the target segment. Retailers like Muji and Whole Foods Market each had an intimate feel for the target audience and understood the values-driven motivation and the energy behind it. Enterprise Rent-A-Car had a deep comprehension of what problems its target customers, drivers with cars being repaired and their insurance companies, were facing. Asahi also had a feel for its target segment, the young, modern, Western-oriented customer looking for an alternative to their "fathers'" beer.

An intimate knowledge of competitors and their limitations can also lead to confidence in the value proposition. Mint.com, introduced above, is a free, Web-based financial management service for budgeting, preparing taxes, managing investments, and keeping checkbooks balanced. It was stimulated by the limitations of the competition, MSN Money and Quicken.[17] Both competitors required you to categorize your expenditures, a very time-consuming process because their categorization programs were very inaccurate. In addition, their programs involved a painful installation process after which you had to input the data. Mint.com, in contrast, has an accurate categorization program, is much easier to set up by being Web based, and is free because it creates revenue by referring users to financial services.

Can We Compete and Win?

A fatal flaw is to overestimate the ability of the firm to actually create a reliable, performing offering and to bring it to market. The risk of failing on this dimension is particularly severe when the firm ventures beyond its core business. This leads to several questions about the offering. Does it fit the strategy of the firm? Is there synergy with the existing core business operations? Will the firm support the effort? And even with firm support, is it feasible for any firm to create the offering and bring it to market.

Does It Fit the Strategy?

If the new offering fits the current strategy of the firm, the comfort level will be high. The strategy could in fact spawn the offering initiative. An alternative energy offering, for example, would fit the strategic direction for GE, which emphasize businesses directed at energy creation or conservation. Kirin needed a rejoinder to Asahi Super Dry and the plan was to generate Kirin Ichiban or something like it. Or the offering could be unplanned but consistent with the strategy. It could use the same assets and competencies or address the same markets. Thus it would take little to stretch the plan to include the new offering.

The acceptance bar is raised when the product or offering is outside of the strategy and represents not a stretch but an addition to it. When Intel went into microprocessors, for example, the capabilities were not adequate—it needed to add new design capabilities around the logic of the complex microprocessors. Thus the decision to accept the new direction became more than simply adjusting to a new offering that was opening up a subcategory in an established business. In effect Intel had to create a new strategy and accept the reality that it needed to nourish new capabilities.

One of the most important decisions that top management can make is whether or not to commit to an offering that is off-strategy because the costs, risks, and payoffs can all be significant. Such a decision can suck resources and divert attention from the core strategy and even place it in jeopardy. Of course, it can also create a new platform for growth that might become important, even critical, in the future. There is another possibility. It can precipitate a change in strategy because the firm has reached what Andy Grove of Intel called an "inflection point," driven by a major change in the competitive environment that has made the existing strategy unpromising.[18] The decision by Intel to leave the memory business in 1984 when it became commoditized was one such inflection point.

How can a firm determine if it is facing an inflection point? Grove gives some suggestions. First, observe when the identity of the most feared competitor changes.[19] If you had one bullet, which competitor would you use it on? Are you changing the direction of the gun? Second, look at data rather than emotions, because fading businesses have a lot of emotional momentum. What do the data show about sales, prices, market share patterns, and profits? Third, consider "strategy dissonance," which occurs when the actions of managers in the trenches do not flow from the strategy but drift in other directions.

Does It Create Synergy?

A new offering aspiring to create a new category or subcategory will be more attractive and have a lower bar to acceptance by the firm if it can share assets and competencies with existing business units. If a new offering can use an existing distribution system or leverage a brand asset, a portion of the execution risk will be reduced and it may have a competitive edge that might be meaningful if not decisive. Further, the new offering could enhance assets and competencies. If, for example, a brand is used in the new offering, it could gain energy and the reinforcement of its associations.

Amazon's Kindle, for example, provides a host of synergies. Amazon is the leading bookseller. In that context, digital books should become a threat. Instead, by taking a leadership position, Amazon participated in the digital book market by creating a huge business selling digital books as well as marketing Kindles. In doing so it provided some much-appreciated energy for the Amazon brand, reinforcing its image as the go-to place for books.

When the new business is far afield from familiar markets, the firm will have to develop new and unfamiliar assets, competencies, and strategies. Segway, for example, lacked distribution, and its unsuccessful efforts to create such an asset were instrumental in its disappointing sales. Further, synergy can turn negative when the new offering detracts from or cannibalizes an existing brand or business, or when it takes needed resources from the core business. Recall the automobile firms in the 1980s that diverted resources away from their core businesses and, as a result, dug holes from which it was hard to recover.

Home Depot, founded in 1978, has been successful as a home improvement outlet with broad selection and a well-trained staff of dedicated do-it-yourselfers. In 1991 they decided to capture the upscale home decoration market with a chain of EXPO Design Centers. There was little synergy, given that the new venture involved a different market, products set of capabilities, and brand. After struggling for nearly twenty years, they shut it down in 2009. It took an economic downturn to force the tough decision.

A lack of fit does make success less likely, but it also makes success valuable because the firm could end up stronger and in the possession of new capabilities and a broader brand and customer base. Virgin's success in airlines when it was a pop record company, with its distinctive strategy and personality, created a host of strategic options for it.

Will the Firm Support the Effort?

For a new offering to succeed, the firm needs to commit and provide the resources, risk tolerance, and guidance to support the effort. This requires will as well as resources, especially when there are bumps in the road that require some innovation. Some firms have deep pockets but short arms—when the going gets tough the resources disappear. There can be a fine line between making a rational assessment that a concept is not going to be successful enough to merit ongoing investment and the tendency to pull the plug at the first sign of difficulty.

A firm's commitment will depend on the availability of investment resources, the competing alternatives within the firm, the political power of those wanting to access the resources, and the process used to allocate the resources. Chapter Eleven will discuss the need to have an objective, firm-wide allocation process that will identify which initiatives and business units should be funded and defunded and will neutralize the economic and political power of large business units.

A key issue is often whether first-mover advantages, which can include scale economies, preempted locations or positions, and a loyal customer base, will exist. That in turn will often hinge on whether the offering will have a broad market or be restricted to a niche market and whether the level of commitment will be enough to achieve the position of early market leader. If there is a potential first-mover advantage, it is particularly important for the firm to fund the new offering adequately enough to capitalize on the opportunity.

Can the Offering be Created?

Can the offering be created by the firm? By any firm? Is it even feasible? Putting nuclear energy plants in the ocean might, for example, present construction barriers and innovation would be unlikely to overcome. It is true that a concept should not be killed just because it has flaws or limitations that require some innovations. However, the firm needs to make a realistic appraisal of the probability of succeeding with the needed innovation and its resulting cost. If the probably is low or the cost is high relative to the payoff, the concept should be put aside.

Even if any problems are resolvable, there may be uncertainties around whether the organization can deliver. The strategy may require assets and capabilities that are currently inadequate or do not exist, and programs to develop or upgrade these may turn out to be unrealistic. Allied partners to fill the gap may be difficult to find or to work with. The right kinds of people, systems, culture, and structure may be incompatible with the current organization. For instance, the success of the digital animation company Pixar depended on a unique blend of culture and people that encouraged team would not have worked in most film organizations.

Can the Offering be Brought to Market?

Even if the firm can develop the offering, can it bring it to market successfully? A host of tasks need to be accomplished for this to happen. The new category or subcategory needs to gain visibility and be clearly defined, developed, and communicated. The new offering brand needs to acquire credibility within the new category or subcategory, an effective distribution channel, and a loyal customer base. The firm needs a guiding plan with a business vision for the offering, the brand, and the category and subcategory complete with a go-to-market strategy. Not easy for sure.

Even if the firm accomplishes the brand-building tasks, the market can be fickle. Segway with its transporter and P&G with Olestra both did a lot of things right, but the market did not accept either offering when the firms could not overcome product limitations. Sony developed by some measure the best VCR format VCR player, its beta technology, but failed to convince the market, eventually losing to the VHS format. A firm needs to factor the probability of a disappointing result into the decision to support a concept.

Does the Offering Have Legs?

Perhaps the biggest risk for a new offering is the possibility that competitors will enter with a comparable or even a superior offering. There are several dimensions to the evaluation of the threat of competitor entree, including the attraction of a growth context, the internal strategies of competitor firms, and the barriers to entry.

Attraction of a Growth Context

There is a tendency for a firm to assume that competitors do not see the same opportunity, in part because competitive strategic intelligence is hard to come by and in part because a firm's focus is internal not external. There are many tough issues and uncertainties involving a new concept that suck up team energy. However, if the target market looks like it will enjoy attractive growth, there is a serious risk of too many competitors' being attracted by the same analysis using the same inputs.

Overcrowding is a reality in virtually all hyped markets, from railroads to airplanes, radio stations and equipment, televisions sets, personal computers, and e-commerce. At one point in the Internet bubble there were at least one thousand travel-related sites and thirty health and beauty sites. The sales volume is usually insufficient to support all competitors. A key question is, Will the number and competence of competitors that may be attracted create overcapacity and price competition that will turn the marketplace hostile?

The following conditions make overcrowding more likely:

- The market and its growth rate have high visibility, especially to firms in adjacent markets.
- Very high forecasts and actual sales growth in the early stages are seen as evidence confirming high market growth.
- The initial barriers to success such as distribution availability or brand loyalty are not visible or are discounted, and there is little to dampen enthusiasm, which may be spread by journalists, the venture capital industry, and many others.
- Some potential entrants have low visibility, and their intentions are unknown or uncertain.

Competitor Strategies

An analysis of competitors should identify the candidates most likely to enter—those with the needed assets and competencies in place. But there will also be those that find strategies to bypass an apparent asset. For example, a firm may choose to market through the Internet, thereby neutralizing a need to access a fixed distribution channel.

A concern is whether a fast-follower firm will be able build on the learnings of the early market leader and neutralize the first-mover advantage. Much of the innovation and the results of a test-and-learn process may be visible. Thus the competitor can save a lot of investment in time and resources, they can focus on how to extend or improve. The ultimate risk is that a firm will establish a position in a healthy growth market and a competitor will enter late with a product that is demonstrably superior or that has an inherent cost advantage. That has happened in many industries, such as consumer electronics, in which Japanese and Korean companies entered the U.S. market late and were able to capture leadership positions with a persistent strategy of low price and product improvements over time. Ironically, some of these same consumer electronics firms entered China and became early market leaders only to see their positions lost to fast-follower Chinese firms.

A key issue is whether a competitor has the motivation or resources available to enter the new market arena. If there are strategic problems or opportunities that compete for funds, they may forego the opportunity even though it is attractive and within their capability. It is often a matter of timing. If by luck or insight a firm can take a strategic initiative in a new category or subcategory when a competitor is occupied elsewhere, the phase with little competition will be more certain and last longer. The tendency is to ignore or minimize competitor actions when making strategic decisions but they can play a key role in the ultimate success of the strategy.

Recall the case of the Chrysler minivan. It had some fifteen years without a serious challenger and ultimately sold about 12.5 million units by 2009. Competitors all made the conscious decision to avoid putting the necessary investment in the minivan area. GM was investing in robotics, Ford in trucks and the Taurus, and both in diversification. Both were also making profits on station wagons, enjoying the illusion that that profit flow would continue from that source, and did not want to be the cause of its demise. The Japanese were reacting to restrictions on imports by creating more margin per car, entering the high end with the Lexus, Infinity, and Acura. Minivans in each case just did not make the cut, and this fact more than Chrysler's ability to create a good design, innovate over time, and develop a loyal base created the fifteen-year window.

Barriers to Entry

A key element of analyzing competitor response is determining whether the new offering can come with barriers to competition sufficient to make the new business area worthwhile for some length of time. Barriers can involve a host of assets and competencies. They can be based on technology, distribution, product design, marketing insight and programs, brand, and more. The brand is often the key because although the product or service can be copied, the brand cannot. Potential barriers are the topic of the Chapter Nine.

Beyond Go or No-Go—A Portfolio of Concepts

An evaluation should not be restricted to a go or no-go decision whereby the firm commits to either bringing the concept to market or killing it for all time. A go decision should rather mean that the concept advances to the next phase along a path that is perhaps defined by development, laboratory testing, field testing, and market introduction. The idea is to reduce the risk. Too many resources made available at the outset can lead to waste, perhaps in the form of ill-advised expenditures on a defective design. Venture capital firms have learned that keeping the entrepreneurial group lean with interim funding is prudent.

A no-go decision, conversely, can result in the premature killing of a good concept. The issue is timing. It may be that the market or the technology is simply not there yet but may become ready as the market evolves or the technology improves. That was the case for MP3 players before the iPod and for hybrid cars before the Prius. The organization should have an evaluation process that allows a promising idea to be monitored and to receive some ongoing investment around understanding or resolving troublesome issues rather than being unfunded and forgotten. The goal is not to provide a reason to avoid tough decisions but a way to handle the dynamics that underlie concepts with real potential.

Recall how information need areas identified by a promising trend, technology, application, segment, or other driver of a potential new category or subcategory can be prioritized by assessing their immediacy and their impact on the business, as discussed in Chapter Six. For a concept that has promise but is not ready, the prudent course is to associate it with an information need area and have a team actively analyze or simply monitor it over time.

A business should have a portfolio of concepts at various levels of development, in recognition of the reality that there will be a series of decisions as the concepts advance toward market introductions and that each will result in attrition. In addition to managing the attrition, a concept portfolio will best employ organizational assets that then can be spread over different phases. If too many projects are clumped in a single phase such as market introduction, the marketing team may be stretched and the R&D team might be short of projects.

Key Takeaways

Evaluation is based on three questions. The first, Is there a market? hinges on evaluating the strength of underlying trends, understanding the rosy picture and gloomy picture biases, determining if small or niche markets can go mainstream, employing a test-and-learn strategy on an ongoing basis, and knowing the value proposition. The second, Can we compete? asks whether the firm is capable of supporting the concept, which will depend in part on whether it fits the firm's strategy and creates synergy and whether the firm has the assets and competencies to deliver the offering and bring it to the market. The third question, Does it have legs? involves determining if overcrowding is likely, predicting competitor strategies, and evaluating the barriers to entry.

For Discussion

Pick two concepts, one that is embryonic and one that is more refined, and address the following questions for each.

1. Answer the three evaluation questions:

    Is there a market?

    Can we compete and win?

    Will the leadership position endure?

2. What are the two or three key issues and areas of uncertainty that will determine whether the concept is a success?

8

DEFINING AND MANAGING THE CATEGORY OR SUBCATEGORY

Results are gained by exploiting opportunities, not
by solving problems.

—*Peter Drucker*

The best way to predict the future is to invent it.

—*Alan Kay*

Creating a new category or subcategory is a path to generating a winning brand relevance position in which competitors fail to qualify or are marginalized. The key to the strategy is to influence the definition and positioning of the category or subcategory and to actively manage it over time perhaps having it evolve based on an ongoing innovation stream and marketing effort. If that can be done successfully, there will be a better chance that competitors will be excluded not only in the short term but also over time. Saleforce.com and Seibel are excellent examples of innovative firms that have created a sharp, distinct positioning of their categories with clear descriptive labels (analogous to brands) and then managed the category perceptions over an extended time period. In doing so, they put potential competitors at an extreme disadvantage.

Salesforce.com

Marc Benioff, an Oracle alum who created salesforce.com in 1999, is credited with launching and leading a whole new software category that is called *software as a service* (SaaS), often referred to as *cloud computing* because the software resides not in a firm's computers but in the Internet or "clouds."[1] Enterprise software, which is used by enterprises or organizations as opposed to individuals, whether sold by Oracle, Microsoft, IBM, or others, historically had to be installed into a firm's computers, customized to an application, maintained over time, and periodically upgraded. All of these tasks were disruptive to the firm and extremely costly in terms of people and money. A major enterprise software program could take from six to eighteen months to install and often require expensive upgrading of the IT infrastructures—not to mention ongoing maintenance and software upgrading costs.

Benioff's idea was to maintain and upgrade software on an external site and "rent" it to firms as SaaS on a per-person, per-month subscription basis. He thought that it would be possible to do for enterprise software what Amazon had done for retailing, making it easy, even fun to use, and always at a person's fingertips. Like Amazon, it would be available on demand 24/7 to anyone authorized to access it. Because the infrastructure would be shared by many users, the price of upgrading and operating the external software could be much cheaper than the alternative.

Benioff, who as an Oracle executive saw up close the costs and problems associated with enterprise software as it was conventionally sold and used, actually was toying with this idea for three or so years and looking for the right application. Sales-force-automation (SFA) software, which customers used to manage their sales force from lead flow to sales contracts to customer relationships, seemed right because it was widely used with established vendors, most notably Seibel Systems described in the sidebar on page 231. SFA shared with other enterprise software programs significant cost, hassles, and risks, so there was room for another way. With the value proposition of SFA already established in the conventional software world, salesforce.com could then focus on creating the new cloud-computing category.

There were significant development problems. Creating a system that would be easy to use with a straightforward interface, scalable so that millions could use it, and at the same time reliable and secure enough to overcome a client's fear of losing control of mission-critical software was formidable. In fact, the idea was a dream at the beginning—there was no software substance behind it, only a belief that it could be done. Of course, salesforce.com did not have to invent everything. In particular, they relied on Oracle's database and Sun's Java programming language. Nevertheless it was imperative that the right development people be attracted with the right objectives, namely to make it fast, simple, right the first time, and fast (worth mentioning twice). The last objective may have been stimulated by Google's third guiding principle—"Fast is better than slow."

A key task was to convince customers used to controlling their software and data that the new system would be secure and reliable. The security issue was lessened because of customer's experience with others who had hosted e-mail and other sensitive services. Further, the multi-tenancy metaphor helped: people who shared an apartment building, for example, could lock their own doors and still have access to common facilities. But reliability was another matter, despite the fact that internal systems also had reliability issues. Even with assurances of multiple backup data sites around the world and an emerging record of users, people were uncomfortable initially about relying on the clouds.

In late 2005 the salesforce.com Web site went down, the reliability issue became visible, and the whole essence of salesforce .com was jeopardized. One outcome of the crisis was a decision to become completely transparent with a "trust site" (http://trust .salesforce.com) that describes how data is safeguarded, provides information of malicious threats, posts notice of planned maintenance, offers information on new security technology and practices, and gives real-time systems performance information including transaction volume and speed. Users could see the uptime statistics, which was running at 99.99 percent in 2009. Salesforce.com evolved to have a broad range of applications, including those involving customer relationship management (CRM) as described in the Seibel sidebar. However, there was a demand for applications much broader in scope and variety than salesforce.com could possibly deliver. So in 2005 salesforce.com, an operating platform for the Internet, was launched. It offered a way for everyone, including customers and developers, to create applications online by using a salesforce.com as a platform as a service (PaaS). Morgan Stanley, for example, used it to build a recruiting platform, and others used it to create accounting programs all linked into the salesforce.com platform, which made the relationship with salesforce.com even closer. The platform liberated a host of developer activities. To make its products more readily available, salesforce.com created AppExchange, a marketplace for solutions where software makers can make available applications they develop. *BusinessWeek* called it the "eBay for business software."[2] In 2008 there were over eight hundred applications from over 450 partners on AppExchange.

Salesforce.com was positioned as a feisty underdog competitor trying to introduce a new way of computing, "cloud competing," to the firms using such conventional enterprise computing software as that of Siebel Systems that were not cloud based. Such an underdog personality, which creates energy and reinforces brand position, was used to great advantage by Apple, Virgin Airlines, and many other brands. Toward that end, salesforce.com did several stunts to make the point. During a huge Siebel Users Group conference at the Moscone Center in San Francisco in February 2000, salesforce.com hired people to picket the hall with signs reading "No software" and "Software is obsolete." Fake TV reporters provided more hype. One ad showed the contrast between a vintage biplane (Siebel) and a modern jet fighter (salesforce.com) and others associating the "cloud" with "incredibly easy" (see Figure 8.1). Of course salesforce.com was just delivering software in a different manner, but

Siebel Systems

In 1993, six years before salesforce.com started, Tom Siebel, another Oracle alum, started Siebel Systems, which became the force behind the new category CRM, and in the process changed what software customers were buying from components to systems.

The CRM concept was to offer an integrated suite of programs all involved in managing customer contacts in the realms of customer acquisition, customer feedback, call centers, consulting, product support, customer service, and accounting services plus the supporting information database. A key element of its success in becoming the CRM exemplar was its ability to link to over seven hundred alliance companies dealing with a wide variety of enterprise support data and software, which meant that a Siebel customer would be connected to a broad software and data system. Another was advances in computer and software technology that occurred during the 1990s and really enabled its CRM product. Siebel turned a fragmented, component-centered software industry containing some four hundred firms in 1993 into an integrated systems solutions offerings. Siebel saw sales going from $8 million in 1996 to over $1 billion in 2000. It controlled 45 percent of the market in 2002, and in 2006 was bought by Oracle for $5.6 billion. It was an industry-changing idea well executed.

A side note. Tom Siebel liked Benioff's idea of cloud computing and offered to implement it. However, he was interested only in the small-firm market that Siebel Systems was underserving and did not want it to disrupt his primary large-firm clientele. So Benioff went his own way. An all-too-familiar result, the leading, successful firm was reluctant to embrace an innovation that might cut into a profitable business.

the "end of software" message made the point graphically that it represented a new generation of software. The story of a small combative company taking on the industry giant was intriguing to the major media like *Wall Street Journal* and *Forbes* and it helped salesforce.com get prominent coverage.

Benioff, a colorful executive taken to Hawaiian shirts and yoga, also had a new take on social programs. Influenced by an Indian guru with whom he interacted during a sabbatical in the mid-1990s, he resolved to create a firm that would

Figure 8.1 Salesforce.com Advertisement

integrate social programs into the business. The answer was the 1/1/1 program. Salesforce.com invested 1 percent of equity and profits into social programs. Because of its Internet experience, one of its programs focused on bringing the Internet to underfunded schools and showing them how to use it. Further,

1 percent of employees' time (actually six days per year) was made available to social programs and causes. Finally, 1 percent of the salesforce.com installations were for not-for-profit organizations to help them become more effective and efficient. In Benioff's view the 1/1/1 program not only does good but also helps the brand and provides employees with a larger purpose.

What impact does participation in these social programs have on customers not just for salesforce.com but for any firm that makes social consciousness a part of their values? Some customers will ignore or be unaware of them. Many others will regard the firm's social consciousness as a positive with the potential to affect their brand preference decisions. Some others, however, will include participation in effective social programs as part of the definition of a category and will exclude brands from consideration that do not have at least a minimal effort on that dimension. The size and intensity of this group will determine whether supporting social programs does affect the very definition of the category.

Salesforce.com played an active role in positioning a new category. In doing so they told the story about cloud computing and SaaS subscription service as a new generation of software and how it should be used in enterprise computing. The new generation was portrayed as the underdog, just as was the brand, surrounded by an aura of inevitability. In defining the new category, salesforce.com became an exemplar, which tied its brand to the new way of looking at and using software. Salesforce.com was more than a category, of course. It was an organization with values, a suite of applications, and some strong subbrands as well.

Salesforce.com hit $1 billion in its first decade and became the leader in cloud computing in terms of sales and customers with over sixty-five thousand customers and over one million subscribers. Salesforce.com, also a thought leader, made every effort to stay in the forefront, to be perceived as an industry leader and the exemplar of cloud computing. They held "launch events" every six to eight weeks to introduce something new, such as an acquisition, partnership, or product, and to talk about the future direction of the industry and its role in that future.

As noted in Chapter One, when creating a new category or subcategory, marketing strategists have a new responsibility in addition to managing their brand. They need to define and actively manage the category or subcategory, a task that is usually assumed away. However, in dynamic markets the category and subcategory definitions are very much in play and the challenge is to be the driver of the dynamic. We turn first to the category or subcategory definition, which provides the platform for its management. In doing so, a set of eighteen dimensions that have been used to defined categories or subcategories will be discussed and illustrated in order to provide a baseline feel for the definitional challenge. Finally, some comments and suggestions will be introduced about how categories and subcategories can be managed including how the underlying substantial and transformational innovations can be leveraged.

Defining a New Category or Subcategory

Managing a category or subcategory, like managing a brand, starts with a definitional task in which the priority aspirational associations, usually one to five in number, are identified. This defining set often is selected from a larger aspiration association set. As noted in Chapter One, the priority association set should differentiate the category or subcategory from alternatives, appeal to customers, deliver functional and, if possible, self-expressive and emotional benefits, and drive choice decisions. It should define the category or subcategory so that the boundaries are as clear as possible, especially if the category or subcategory lacks a label. In doing so, there should be an emphasis that favors the brand to be a relevant option and provides barriers to other brands that may aspire to gain relevance.

Although the association set that defines the new category or subcategory may have five or so dimensions, there may be one or two that are new and unique and really are the drivers. So when Westin developed the Heavenly Bed, a new hotel sub-category was formed that included premium hotels and good locations but it was the sleeping experience and the aesthetic and comfort of the bed that were the distinctive elements. Similarly the "W" hotel chain has several dimensions but it is the sharply contemporary design and user profile that is unique.

From this set of defining associations, a smaller group of associations, possibly a single one, will be used to position the category or subcategory. The associations reflecting the substantial or transformational innovation driving the definition of the category or subcategory will nearly always be prominently involved. Positioning, recall from Chapter One, guides the short-term communication and can differ by segment. So the Prius could emphasize economy for the functionally oriented segment and self-expressive benefits for the "green" segment.

To illustrate category or subcategory definitions based on a set of associations, consider some of the new categories or subcategories that we have seen so far. Some are defined by clear exemplars and may not have well-established labels. Others have labels or descriptors and may or may not have well-accepted exemplars. The existence of a label is significant because if it gets traction it can be influential in shaping the category or subcategory.

Exemplar-Driven Categories or Subcategories

- Prius—hybrid sedans, hybrid technology and hybrid synergy drive, expression of green values, gas economy, appealing design

- Best Buy—customer-friendly consumer electronics retailers, salespeople as informative advisers, wide selection, green and recycling programs, geek squad

- Enterprise-Rent-A-Car—car rental companies for accident repair, pervasive locations, "We deliver," service-oriented, connected to insurance companies

- Whole Foods Market—natural, organic, systems to support delivery of natural and organic food, passion about healthy eating, sustainability

- Muji retailers—simple and functional, natural, sustainable, value offerings, close to nature, nonprestige

- Dreyer's Slow Churn—ice cream, low fat, creamy, varieties

- SnackWell's—no fat, cookies, crackers, healthy indulgence

- Salesforce.com—cloud computing, feisty underdog, sales force support software, social programs

Label or Descriptor Designative Categories or Subcategories that May or May Not have Exemplars

- Car sharing—urban lifestyle, save money, green values, convenience

- Minivans—Roomy interior, feels like a car, family life style and activities

- Fast fashion—trendy, new fashions weekly, very low prices, young

- High fiber—high fiber, active, healthy

- Healthy frozen dinners—steaming technology, interesting recipes, healthy ingredients

- Healthy fast food sandwiches—low fat, weight loss, convenient, nutrition conscious

- Diesel sedans—good gas mileage, clean driving, environ-mentally sensitive drivers
- 4-wheel-drive SUVs—stylish, comfortable, good gas mile-age, outdoor lifestyle

Selecting the core or priority associations is thus a crucial step in managing the new category or subcategory. What are the key associations? What are the salient features and benefits? Should it have a personality? What distinguishes it from other categories or subcategories? What is the link to the customer? What are the emotional, self-expressive, and social benefits delivered? What one, two, or five characteristics define the cat-egory or subcategory?

There follows a discussion of a dozen and a half or so poten-tial associations or dimensions, summarized in Figure 8.2, on which new categories or subcategories have frequently been defined. There are others as well, but the successful new offer-ings usually have some combination of items from this set. And in most cases, it is a combination of associations. It is rare for a strong new offering from a firm that aspires to create a category or subcategory to be based on a single association.

Having a list of widely used category and subcategory association-based definitions can also help those attempting to develop a new offering. As suggested in Chapter Six, this set of options can provide one starting point. Each can be evaluated as to its potential in the context at hand. Some will not be appropriate, whereas others might be promising and still others very promising. In any case it can stimulate ideas for new concepts.

The first group in Figure 8.2 relates to the functional ben-efits driving a value proposition. The second group extends beyond functional benefits to include factors that drive a cus-tomer relationship, addressing such dimensions as personality, shared interests and values, passion, or social programs. Each

Figure 8.2 Defining Categories or Subcategories

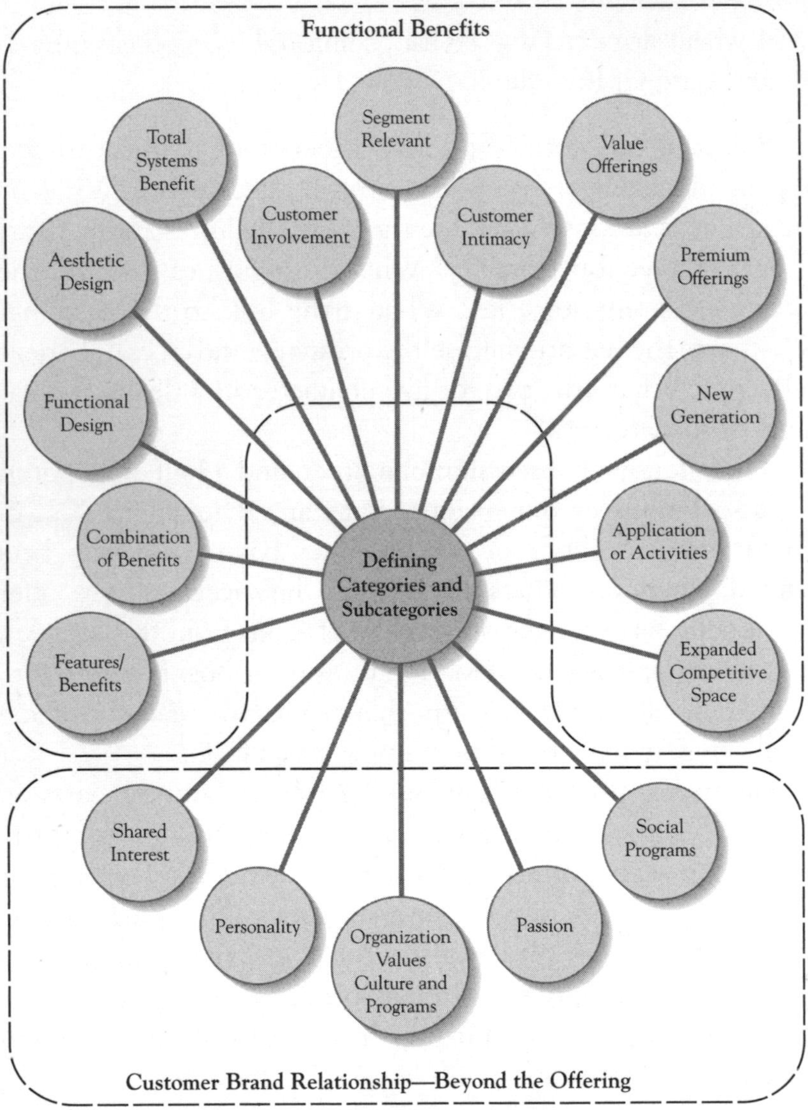

Functional Benefits

Total Systems Benefit

Segment Relevant

Value Offerings

Customer Involvement

Customer Intimacy

Aesthetic Design

Premium Offerings

Functional Design

New Generation

Combination of Benefits

Application or Activities

Features/ Benefits

Expanded Competitive Space

Defining Categories and Subcategories

Shared Interest

Social Programs

Personality

Passion

Organization Values Culture and Programs

Customer Brand Relationship—Beyond the Offering

group provides a potential "must have" part of a category or sub-category definition. Without one of these specific associations tied to a category or subcategory, a brand will not be considered, will not be relevant.

It must be emphasized that although this set of defining associations applies to a category or subcategory, these characteristics can be and have all been applied to brands as well. And when there is an exemplar brand, the category or subcategory will merge into that brand's vision or position. But we are here concerned with defining a category or subcategory and not a brand.

Functional Benefits Delivered by the Offering

Every new category or subcategory needs to have a value proposition. This value proposition will almost always provide a functional benefit that can define or contribute to the definition of a category or subcategory. If a brand lacks that benefit, it is not in the category or subcategory and is not considered. Volvo has long owned the benefit of safety by designing its cars and positioning its brand so that its has extremely strong credibility on that dimension. For some, Volvo is the exemplar for the subcategory of "safer cars." Heinz has ketchup that pours slowly because it is so thick and rich and for some defines a subcategory of thick, premium ketchup. Among the functional benefits that can define a category or subcategory are features or benefits, a combination of benefits, a functional design, an aesthetically pleasing design, having a systems-based solution, being customer-involving, tailored for specific segments, providing customer intimacy, being value or premium, a new-generation offering, new applications or activities, and an expanded competitive space.

Features or Benefits

A feature or benefit can be so compelling that it defines a new category or subcategory and part of the market will not purchase brands that lack that feature or benefit. British Airlines for many years was the only major airline to offer business-class passengers more comfortable sleeping space and therefore defined a subcategory for some business travelers; such travelers would not consider brands that were not comparable on that dimension. Westin's Heavenly Bed did the same for its hotel chain by creating the premium bed subcategory. General Mills' Fiber One or Nabisco's SnackWell's each is defined by one salient attribute—high fiber and nonfat—important enough to affect the purchasing decision.

The attribute can represent something new to the category. Dannon, a firm with roots in Europe since 1919 that started U.S. operations in 1942, was a yogurt company positioned as a health-food provider. In 1950 the yogurt world changed when Dannon put jam in the bottom of the cup. The offering added a distinctly new and valued benefit and defined a new subcategory to which the existing brands were not relevant, at least for a time. In doing so, it created energy and vastly expanded the potential customer base.

A defining attribute can come from or involve another company. Nike Plus is a running shoe with a built-in chip that connects to an iPod music player and allows users to track and share their training data. In the first three years, Nike Plus runners logged some one hundred million miles, and Nike increased its running shoe dominance from 48 percent to 61 percent, in part by tapping into the iPod energy and audience and in part by finding the concept that resonated, a "training assistance" running shoe. Not incidentally, Nike at the same time reinforced its message of bringing inspiration and innovation to every athlete. The fact that Nike reached out beyond its own organization not only for product technology but for the go-to-market branded partnership is instructive. Too many firms are insular in their perspectives.

The problem is that having a very strong position on one benefit may imply a deficiency on another. This issue is endemic among the value entries, those brands that introduce a subcategory based on a lower price point. The natural implication is that they will have a quality, reliability, and feature deficiency. The experience of Toyota in the 1970s and more recently Hyundai shows that it is possible to overcome this assumption, but it can take a long time. In the meantime, the subcategory will struggle, and the ability of competitors to exploit the perceived deficiency lingers. The problem is not restricted to value entries. Volvo has owned safety but has struggled over the years to be perceived as having a stylish design that someone would be proud to drive.

Combining Benefits

A new subcategory can be defined by a combination of benefits. An acceptable brand would then need to have a set of benefits. Many of P&G's transformational innovations resulted from its ability to combine attributes often sourced from different business units. There is, for example, Tide Free for Coldwater HE (high efficiency) Liquid Laundry Detergent that delivers three benefits. It works in cold water for high-efficiency washing machines and is free of dyes and perfumes. As mentioned in the last chapter, Annie Chun offered packaged dinners that were Asian, convenient, interesting, natural, and high quality, creating a subcategory defined by multiple benefits.

Subcategories defined by multiple benefits have also driven the toothpaste market. Crest added cavity protection to quality cleaning action in the 1950s, which led to a subcategory that provided a strong market position for decades. In 1997 the market had become so fragmented, with a host of additional benefits plus flavors and packaging forms, that choice had become complex and frustrating. Colgate's Total formed another subcategory by combining a set of benefits into one. In particular, it provided cleaning, long-lasting breath protection, and antibacterial ingredients controlling a wide range of bacteria that are active between brushings. This new subcategory allowed Total to surge past Crest.

Multiple benefits could be driven by a cobrand. The Ford Explorer Eddie Bauer Edition, launched in 1983, has sold well over one million vehicles by offering a combination of benefits, becoming an exemplar for a subcategory of SUVs. The vehicle has the features and qualities of the Ford Explorer, and in addition the Eddie Bauer brand serves to communicate the vehicle's leather-appointed comfort and styling and reinforces the outdoor activity association to which the Explorer brand aspires.

The Right Functional Design

Can an offering be delivered in a different form that does not involve a new technology but is qualitatively different from what came before? The Plymouth Voyager, for example, one of the subjects of Chapter Four, provided a very different product from the station wagon it replaced both visually and functionally. Functionally, it offered much more internal room plus a way to access that room that was far better than in the station wagon. The Yamaha Disklavier, described in more detail in Chapter Nine, moreover, is a piano that can be played with a digital memory and was different functionally from its predecessor the player piano. The Kindle wireless reading device, Listerine PocketPaks breath strips, the Segway people transporter, and Crest's Spinbrush all delivered benefits in new and different ways that served to define new categories or subcategories.

Packaging innovation can provide a defining attribute. Yoplait's Go-Gurt, the yogurt in a tube that kids slurp up, created a new business with a different target market, value proposition, and competitors from those of conventional yogurt containers. It created a major market share shift, and Yoplait overtook Dannon as a result. Further, the L'eggs stocking package, a white plastic chicken-egg-shaped containers, coupled with its dedicated displays and availability in new channels such as supermarkets, completely turned the stocking industry on its head and created a subcategory when it was introduced in 1970. Finally, the Hershey

Kiss, a simple packaging innovation, provided a subcategory that Hershey enjoyed for decades.

Appealing Aesthetic Design

An offering can break away from a functional tradition and create a category or subcategory based on aesthetics, providing substantial self-expressive and emotional benefits. Jaguar has long pursued this strategy and is somewhat unique among competitors that look all too similar, as if they all use the same wind tunnel and ended up with identical car shapes. W Hotels have a unique look and feel (which extends to its rooms) that appeals to fashion-forward travelers. The translucent Apple iMac showed that even computers could have design flair, and the Apple product stream that ensued showed that design could be an ongoing value proposition. Steve Jobs has been quoted as saying, "Design is the soul of a manmade creation."[3] Ugly and distinctive can also work. The lovable Volkswagen Beetle became a part of the pop culture, developed a cult-like following, and sold over twenty-one million cars from the mid-1950s to the mid-1970s.

Pursuing a design option requires the firm to really have a passion for design and to support a home for a creative design team. Creating such a culture and infrastructure is a key to success for firms like Jaguar, W Hotels, and Apple, as well as other such design-driven firms as Disney and Ralph Lauren. Because achieving a home for design can be difficult, another route is to create an alliance with a design firm or associations with independent designers, which allows access to best-of-breed designers when needed. Outsourcing is not easy to manage but it can succeed with proper management.

Making the design credible and visible is another challenge. The used of branded personality designers allowed Target to break through its utilitarian image and create a subcategory of discount stores with designer lines of clothing and other items. The well-known designer Isaac Mizrahi in 2004 launched an affordable Target line of sweaters, blouses, pants, skirts, dresses, shoes, and purses that was well received. The renowned architect Michael Graves developed for Target a collection of cookware and other dining products.

From Components to Systems

A classic way to change the market is to move from components to systems. The idea is to look at the system in which the product or service is embedded and to expand perceptions horizontally. The move to a system-driven offering is large, pervasive, and growing as customers are increasingly demanding a system solution and one-firm accountability. Competitors selling ad hoc products, even though these might be superior, are increasingly at a disadvantage or even irrelevant. Sears offers a one-stop place to deliver home improvement projects. The Kindle book reader from Amazon is linked into the Amazon infrastructure so that the ordering and downloading of books is easy and takes seconds. If the Kindle were on its own it would not be compelling and would be very vulnerable.

Software firms have regularly combined component programs. We have already seen how Siebel was the creator of CMR, the integrated suite of customer-contact programs, and how salesforce.com started with a suite of programs dedicated to salesforce management. Microsoft in 1992 combined Word, Excel, and PowerPoint into an integrated system branded as Office, a move that dramatically changed what customers bought and made the major competitors less relevant and ultimately fade. Fifteen years later Microsoft tailored its Office suite to different segments when they offered several versions—standard, small business, professional, and developer—in a move that closed the door to others who might try to use a niche approach to become relevant.

KLM Cargo's offering was becoming a low-margin business.[4] In response, KLM initiated its Fresh Partners initiative to provide a systems solutions to customers, importers, and retailers who were experiencing spoilage issues and were frustrated because it was never clear who in the logistics chain was responsible. Under its Fresh Partners programs, KLM provided an unbroken "cool chain" from the producer to the point of delivery, with three levels of service—fresh regular, fresh cool, and fresh supercool—with end-to-end responsibility (whereby products are guaranteed to have a specific temperature from truck to warehouse to plane to warehouse to truck to the retailer). Firms importing orchids from Thailand and salmon from Norway were among those using the service.

Business-to-business firms have augmented their offerings and created differentiation by adding services and value to the logistical system. FedEx, for example, pioneered the tracking of packages and the integration of its computer systems with those of customers so that its business customers could control and manage the shipping function. Cemex, a concrete company, realized that its customers had a lot of money riding on predictable delivery because concrete was highly perishable.[5] As a result, Cemex created capabilities using digital systems that allowed drivers to adjust in real time to traffic patterns and changing customer timetables. It can now deliver its product within minutes and process changed orders on the fly. It addressed an unmet need, and the totally new business model that resulted has led to Cemex's going from a regional player to being the third-largest concrete company in the world, serving thirty countries.

Being Customer Involving

Most categories and subcategories have offerings that interact with customers in a passive way. However, there can be an opportunity to create a category or subcategory in which the customers become active participants, involvement that becomes a part of the defining effort.

A retailer normally services a customer. But, at a do-your-own frozen yogurt deserts retailer, you operate the machines yourself, using as much of each flavor as you want. Then you can put on any combination of some fifty or so toppings, including hot fudge. Your choice, you are in charge. No more being satisfied with a fixed size and a choice of a single topping and waiting for a server to make those decisions. Local pioneers are dominating local markets and have carved a growth subcategory out of a rather stagnate category.

Kettle Foods nearly doubled its market share in the premium potato chip category in five years, approaching the 20-percent level in 2010 with a highly differentiated subcategory offering defined by its all-natural processes, by its over-the-top sustainability commitment, and by its customer involvement in generating quirky flavors. It all started when Kettle asked customers to choose among five flavors using a "crave-o-meter" scale. The response was so enthusiastic that Kettle developed a program for getting customer input on possible flavors that has resulted in dozens of new products including Fully Loaded Baked Potato and Spicy Thai. The program has given energy and authenticity to the line that simple factory-generated line extensions could not have done. It has defined a subcategory based on how the product is made, the flavors, and the sustainability commitment.

Nintendo, introduced in the last chapter, launched the Wii in 2006, the ultimate involving offering. Using the Wii remote, which detects movement in three dimensions, the user can dance, box, play a guitar, and on and on. A user can even play tennis or baseball and compete against someone across the world. The Wii's sales reached nearly thirty million units in 2008, two years after its introduction—nearly as much as Sony's PS3 and Microsoft's Xbox combined (33.4 million units).

Offerings Tailored to Segments

A common evolution is for a category to fragment into subcategories as it matures in order to reach customers who are underserved or not served at all. This process represents a significant opportunity for the firm that can identify the unmet need, recognize its potential, and determine that there is a way to create a compelling offering.

The market for energy bars pioneered by PowerBar ultimately fragmented into a variety of subcategories. Initially positioned as energy sources for athletes engaged in demanding activities like running marathons, these bars were focused primarily on males, and the core product was large and sticky. Women, especially those not engaged in demanding high-performance sports, were not attracted to the product or the positioning. As a result, a competitor to PowerBar, the firm making the Cliff Bar, came out with a bar for women, the Luna Bar, which had a taste, texture, and ingredients tailored for women. Luna created a new subcategory. PowerBar after a year of research responded by attempting to create a better women's energy bar. It was the Pria bar, which was smaller and had fewer calories than the Luna Bar and thus was even more attractive to women. Although Luna had the market to themselves for over a year, the Pria bar succeeded in redefining the subcategory for some.

The key to finding a niche is to avoid the trap of focusing only on the heavy user, the large sweet spot in the market. Look instead at underserved segments, those for which the current offerings represent a compromise or that avoid the offering altogether because it is deficient or even repellent. That was the key for Nintendo—it looked beyond the young, male, heavy-user group.

A niche specialist strategy, in addition to capturing a market, can lead to a strong brand and a well-defined category or subcategory. A focused firm will have more credibility than a firm that makes a wide array of products, as demonstrated by Shouldice Hospital, whose doctors only perform hernia surgeries; Williams-Sonoma in cooking; Raymond Corporation in offering lift trucks; and the In-N-Out Burger chain in making no-compromise hamburgers. If you are really interested in the best, you will go to a firm that specializes in and has a passion for the business. In addition, the bond between the loyal user and the brand will tend to be greater when the brand is focused and the people are seen to have passion for their product. The reunions of Shouldice Hospital patients and the passion of Harley-Davidson customers would not happen without these firms' focus strategies.

Customer Intimacy

All firms place an emphasis on the customer. A few, however, create an intimacy that connects the offering to the customer on a more involving and passionate level and serves to define a subcategory. For these firms, customer intimacy is a strategic option. Some local hardware stores create this feeling of intimacy, supported by amenities like hot popcorn and personalized service that allow them to prosper while competing with "big boxes" such as Home Depot or Walmart. Nordstrom has generated a customer link by offering personalized service and a shopping experience that often delights rather than merely satisfies. The Apple store provides the energy of the Apple products but also a dramatic ambiance and sense of expertise around complex products that create an experience-based relationship. The Ritz-Carleton provides an extra level of personalized service supported by a culture, training, and reward system.

Starbucks' vision of a "third place" (after home and office) where people feel comfortable and secure represents an experience that many customers view as a high point in their day. Once a relationship is established, customer expectations also develop. So Starbucks has to be concerned about jeopardizing this relationship by adding coffee and food items only in a way that enhances rather than detract from its authenticity.

Intimacy can be created by shared interests. Etsy created a site that enables craft makers to expose their products to prospective buyers. It capitalizes on a yearning for authentic, homemade, unique goods that are not out of a production line in China. The site provides not only a market for goods but a community home, a place where a person can exchange ideas, form go-to-market teams, announce events, and attend forums. As people join, the benefit grows.

Dramatically Lower Price Point

A significant number of new subcategories are those represented by firms that entered the market with markedly lower prices, prices often made possible by offerings that are simpler with fewer features, involve reduced quality, or have been sourced where costs are low. Clayton Christensen, a noted Harvard strategy researcher, has studied this phenomenon with his colleagues.[6] One finding is that there are two sources of customers. One source is existing customers who don't need or want a full-featured, high-quality variant and welcome the simpler, cheaper version even with compromised quality. The other is new customers who believed the other offerings too expensive and consider the new, low-cost offerings to be justifiable purchases.

There are many examples of firms that followed the model and attracted customers that had been inhibited from buying because of price. Tata's Nano is a classic example of a brand offering that reduced costs on all fronts. The single-use camera provided a new market, just as the Kodak Brownie did a century earlier. Southwest Airlines started its operation in the early 1970s by targeting not only customers looking for a value airline but also people who could be lured from their automobiles, a segment that was ignored by the established airlines of the day. Vanguard's low-cost index funds attracted new buyers into the industry. The clothing retailers Ross and T. J. Maxx exploited production overages to allow some customer access to name brand goods they had avoided. The noncustomers, in this case facing a price barrier, have typically been ignored by the established firms who, again, tend to focus their efforts on the current heavy users, the most profitable customers.

Premium Offerings

The polar opposite of creating a value subcategory is to create a premium or super-premium subcategory. Everyone is attracted to the best. Further, being part of the top subcategory automatically means that the quality and experience are superior, and customers receive emotional and self-expressive benefits knowing that they are buying and using the best.

Singapore Airlines introduced a passenger class that was a significant step above first class by configuring the huge A380 planes to have twelve suites that deliver unprecedented luxury with meals designed by famous chefs. Suntory took leadership in the upper-premium malt category by creating a pilsner beer using European aromatic hops from the Czech Republic. Its advertising features "Ah, a blissful aftertaste" and "The aroma, richness, and aftertaste of a gold-medal-winning beer." Van Houten has a super-premium chocolate with a patented coca formula that has delivered "velvety feeling" for over 180 years. Armani has a members lounge in the Armani Ginza Tower that proves a true luxury getaway and a place to conduct business in a rarefied atmosphere. The ultimate in exclusivity.

There can be a premium subcategory within a value category. Starbucks introduced Via, a soluble coffee aimed at the huge market for such a product, in which Nestlé's Taster's Choice (termed Nescafé outside the United States) is a dominant brand. The connection with Starbucks provides the credibility that Via could indeed be a prototypical premium brand, residing above the existing offerings. P&G's Olay brand brought department store skin-care benefits to the mass marketplace. Greyhound launched Bolt Bus in 2006, a bus aimed at young, professional travelers with leather seats, ample leg room, free Wi-Fi, and seatback electrical plugs. The goal was to create a premium bus category that would remove the stigma on busses as inferior modes of transportation.

Branding is often the key component in establishing a premium subcategory because it is the brand that represents the necessary credibility and supports the delivery of social and self-expressive benefits.

New-Generation Offerings

An attractive position for a new category or subcategory is that of the new-generation offering that represents a breakthrough innovation, representing an option that makes the existing brands and offerings either obsolete or demonstrably inferior. A new-generation offering has the advantage of being potentially newsworthy, worth talking about, and having a credibility, a reason why its claims are true.

One challenge facing firms with a new-generation offering is to convince customers that the risk of buying into a new approach is either minimal or controlled by programs and procedures. As the breakthrough difference is emphasized, the perceived difficulty of overcoming the associated change and risk is also increased. Salesforce.com provided a new generation of software delivery and promised much, but they did have to address the perceived security and reliability risks that were associated with cloud computing.

Another challenge—communicating a new generation in a cluttered media environment—is illustrated by Sharp and Samsung, both of which had new-generation TV sets. Samsung, one of the leaders in flat-screen TVs since 1999, came out in 2007 with a new-generation light-emitting diode (LED) television, the Luxia TV. The Luxia has an array of LED lights behind the screen, resulting in superior contrast and brightness, a longer screen life, lower power consumption, and a thinner housing that is used to justify a 50 percent to 100 percent price premium. In 2010 Sharp introduced what promised to be another new generation with its addition of a fourth color, yellow, to a technology that had heretofore relied on three colors. The technology, branded as Quadpixel and placed in Sharp's Aquos Quantron TVs, displays more than a trillion colors, many more than in current models. Because the Sharp advance was easier to communicate with the fourth color and a strong set of technology brands, namely Quadpixel and Aquos, it was more feasible for it to position its product as new generation than it was for Samsung with its weaker Luxia brand and its complex story. The challenge is to create the perception of a new generation rather than of an incremental improvement—the difference between gaining a brand preference edge and creating a new subcategory.

The smart or lucky brands create a series of offering generations. Intel during the 1980s and 1990s had a new generation out about every three or four years. The challenge for Intel was determining how to brand the new technology. There turned out to be degrees of newness. Those offerings that were clearly breakthroughs with corresponding impact would get their own names. So there were the 86 Series, Pentium, Celeron, Xeon, and Itanium. Others were labeled as variants, such as Pentium DX, Pentium 4F, and Pentium Extreme.

A New Application or Activity

The creation of an activity-based category or subcategory can expand the market and provide credibility and relevance for the driving brand. In addition an application or activity can often enhance customer involvement and confer self-expressive and emotional benefits. Competitor brands that are not relevant to the application or activity may not make the consideration set.

Consider the following cases in which a subcategory was defined by an application or activity. Crayola has fine-quality crayons and other drawing instruments for children. However, it reframed the value proposition of its brand and its target category to be about colorful fun and creativity in the lives of children, providing vehicles for visual expression. Very different from an art category. Orville Redenbacher attempted to make microwave popcorn part of bringing a theater experience to watching movies at home. Lindsay Olives attempted to change its category from olives to a social experience that is more fun, flavorful, and interesting with olives than with alternatives like carrots and celery. Bayer helped define a new subcategory baby aspirin taken regularly to ward off heart attacks—with its Bayer 81 mg—and tap into the emotion around avoiding heart attacks.

An Expanded Competitive Space

A firm can sometimes expand the scope of the category or subcategory to include noncustomers who would value their offering and include competitors that would be in a severe disadvantage. Recall the classic case of Southwest Airlines who created a new category when they started service between Houston, Dallas, and San Antonio and proclaimed that it was competing with cars, which introduced totally new dimensions in the category such as travel time and effort. recall also the case of DiGiorno frozen pizza, discussed in Chapter Two, which framed the competitive space to include delivered pizza. With a tagline "It's not delivery, it's DiGiorno," the brand went from having a modest price disadvantage to a huge price advantage.

The Clorox brand Brita is a water-filtering product with a limited customer base of those who want better tap water. However, it has expanded its category to include those who buy and use bottled water and contribute to enormous energy usage and disposal problems. The concept is to use a Brita filter and a reusable container instead of bottled water. The customer will not only save significant money but also, more important, will have a positive effect on the environment. Brita users will not contribute to the some thirty-eight billion bottles that end up in landfills each year. Brita has sponsored the FilterForGood.com Web site, which discusses the cost to society of disposable bottles and the advantages of filtered water.

Customer-Brand Relationship–Beyond the Offering

The preceding routes to defining a category or subcategory all involve the functional benefits of an offering in some way. That is a familiar and logical approach. However, the brand and the category or subcategory it drives can also be defined in whole or in part by aspects of the brand-customer relationship that go beyond the offering itself. These include common interests, personality, shared passion, organizational associations, energy, and corporate social programs. None of these affect the offering, but they do affect the relationship between the customer and the brand and are much harder to duplicate than the functional benefits an offering delivers. Competitors can become irrelevant because they lack these elements and, as a result, may fail to appear to share the customer's values, to be interested in customers, to be innovative, or even in delivering high quality.

Shared Interests

An offering can be embedded in a larger activity or goal that is more meaningful to customers than the offering itself. If a brand can demonstrate that it is also interested and involved in that activity or goal, then this common interest can form the basis of a relationship and can change what people buy. Customers could decide to buy from brands and firms that demonstrate a common interest and exclude those that do not. A rationale could be that a brand sharing a common interest will create and deliver better offerings because they have better knowledge and care more but there is also the factor that people like others with shared interests.

Pampers has repositioned its brand's category to be associated with baby care in addition to being a disposable diaper brand. Their Web site is the centerpiece of the brand's focus. Its sections, which include pregnancy, new baby, baby development, baby toddler, preschool, me and family, all have a menu of topics. For example, under baby development there are 57 articles, 230 forums, and 23 play-and-learn activities. This tactic raises Pampers above the product feature shouting noise. The fact that Pampers is so knowledgeable and involved in the larger context of baby care means that it is more interesting than a product-preoccupied firm, and it also means that whatever products it supplies are going to be right for the baby.

Hobart is a manufacturer of appliances for the food-service sector, including restaurants and institutions. A quality and reliability leader, Hobart decided to stop communicating the latest product features of their mixers, ovens, and other appliances and, instead, to become a thought leader in regard to such customer problems as finding, training, and retaining good workers; keeping food safe; providing enticing dining experiences; eliminating costs; and employee pilferage. One element was a customer magazine called *Sage: Seasoned Advice for the Food Industry Professional*. At industry trade shows, the Hobart booth had an "idea center" at which people could approach industry experts for sound advice. Hobart also offered over one hundred technical papers on its Web site and shared insights through speeches at key industry shows. Even its advertising was redirected from products to issues. This program changed the way customers looked at the appliance category and propelled Hobart into a leadership role that lasted well over a decade until they were bought and integrated into a larger firm.

Kaiser, an integrated medical insurance and medical delivery system with some thirty-two hospitals and fourteen thousand physicians, completely repositioned their brand and the subcategory in which they reside from a focus on health care to health. Research found that health care was associated with bureaucracy, insurance, sickness, lack of control, and profit and greed. In contrast, health was linked to control, fitness, wellness, happiness, empowerment, and goal setting. As a result, pictures of empathetic doctors delivering health care to appreciative patients were replaced by scenes of members controlling their own health by exercising, accessing preventive health programs, and using "My Health Manager," a secure online way access health records, contact physicians, monitor program participation, and so on. The image numbers, flat for so long, went up, even those numbers pertaining to the quality of physicians.

A category can change in emphasis from products to lifestyle. Zipcar, described in Chapter Four, defines a modern urban lifestyle of which its rental fleet of cars is a part. Muji, from Chapter Three, is another brand that defines a lifestyle as represented by its functional products, its values, its campgrounds, its environmental programs, and its rejection of the glitz and materialism of the times.

Personality

A category or subcategory can have a personality just as can a brand. Such a personality can be distinctive, enduring, identifiable, and often rich in texture. If a brand lacks that personality, it would be excluded from consideration. The personality often, but not always, is created by the exemplar.

In cases discussed, we have seen examples of personality categories or subcategories. Asahi Super Dry was a personality brand—western, young, and modern—in sharp contrast to Kirin, which was the classic "your father's brand." The personality became part of the subcategory of dry beer. Customers were buying the personality as much as the functional benefits. Zara has a fashion forward and trendy personality that delivers self-expressive benefits. Some will only consider stores that deliver those self-expressive benefits, other competitors can start to look passé. Saturn was perceived as being unpretentious, hardworking, and a value seeker and that personality helped define the new subcategory. Segway as a brand and people movers as a category has a personality reflecting people who will try new things, people who are not tied to the past. The important point is that categories or subcategories these brands represent have taken on personalities as well that have implications for the relationships between customer and categories or subcategories.

Passion

Some brands go beyond personality to have palpable passion for their offerings and categories or subcategories. When that passion becomes visible and important to the customer or potential customer, it can become part of the definition of the category or subcategory and difficult to copy. A brand to be relevant must have it. Whole Foods Market, for example, is passionate about healthy food, especially food that is natural and organic. In contrast, the average supermarket is interested in warehousing, layout, checkout, stocking shelves, and so on, but comes across as disinterested in food. Apple is passionate about design and ease of use, always delivering self-expressive benefits. The Apple user is not a corporate type, but rather is creative, even artistic, and is willing to chart an independent course. Muji is passionate about its values—moderation, self-restraint, and being close to nature.

Not only do customers value the brand's passion and energy and the associated self-expressive benefits, but also ascribe to the brand a commitment to deliver innovation and an over-the-top experience. In effect, the brand becomes a role model in terms of living the values that the customer holds dear. This is surely the case with the customers of Whole Foods Market, Apple, and Muji.

Organizational Associations

A category or subcategory could include only those brands supported by organizations that have certain characteristics. When that happens, competitors face another relevance bar. Offerings described in terms of attributes and benefits are often easily copied. In contrast, it is difficult to copy an organization, which will be uniquely defined by its values, culture, people, strategy, and programs. Further, an organization, unlike its offering, is enduring. It is not always in a state of continuous and confusing change. The challenge is to get the customer to buy an organization with certain characteristics instead of an offering.

There are many organizational characteristics that can influence category or subcategory definitions, but the major ones that drive category and subcategory dimensions include being global (Visa), innovative (3M), quality driven (Cadillac), customer driven (Nordstrom), involved in community or social issues (Avon), having the right values (Muji) or concerned about the environment (Toyota). These are generally relevant to customers. Perhaps as important, they are usually more resistant to competitive claims than product-attribute associations.

Corporate Social Programs

Corporate social programs and efforts toward sustainable operations can serve as definers of a category or subcategory. There is usually a worthwhile segment motivated to be loyal to the social brand that will exclude brands from consideration and that do not qualify if there are options that do. The Body Shop, for example, built up a following through its visible endorsement of Third world ecology and workforces. Ben & Jerry's has supported environmental causes in a colorful way that has enhanced the company's image among like-thinking customers. Frito-Lay's SunChips has created a defining point of differentiation with its visible use of solar power and compostable packaging.

The Ronald McDonald House and the Avon Breast Cancer Crusade, further, provide unmistakable expressions of organizational values. Finally, the "HP way" involves a commitment to employees, customers, suppliers, and the community to which people can relate.

There are three ways that social and environmental programs can affect a brand and provide a reason to exclude competitor brands. First, many people fundamentally want to have a relationship with good people who can be trusted and believe that social programs reflect a firm's values. Kettle Foods and salesforce.com both have visible programs that create respect and admiration. There is a large and growing segment that will support firms that become relevant with respect to social and environmental programs.

Second, a strong and visible social or environmental program can deliver to customers self-expressive benefits, particularly for the core group of customers who have strong feelings about these issues. Certainly, many drivers of Toyota's Prius achieve significant self-expressive benefits. In fact, the glamorous CEO of the Body Shop in Japan drives a Prius as a statement about both herself and her firm. With Prius as the flagship of dozens of environmental programs, Toyota has taken the leadership position with respect to the visibility of social programs in both Japan and North America.

Third, a social program can add energy and make a boring brand interesting. Purina Pet Rescue, a program that has saved some 300,000 pets since it was established in 2005, is more interesting and involving than pet food.

The bottom line is that a firm's involvement in social programs affects sales and loyalty. In a global 2009 survey of some six thousand people in ten countries, well over 50 percent of people surveyed said that their support of social causes affects their purchasing habits. Further, 83 percent said that they are willing to change their consumption habits if it will help make the world better. Of course, actions will be less dramatic than opinions, but the fact that these numbers are large and are growing is impressive and suggests that visible programs can affect how people define as relevant options. Further, the many responsive new products that are finding success indicate that there is a real opportunity behind the numbers.[7]

Categories and Subcategories: Complex and Dynamic

Although there are exceptions, in most cases the definition of a product category or subcategory, like that of a brand, is multidimensional and complex. Consider offerings like TIVO, Segway, Apple's iPhone, Muji, or Enterprise Rent-A-Car. In each case there are many elements of the brand and the new category or subcategory that it is driving. When such complexity is present, it can be a serious mistake to attempt to focus on one element or insist that the concept be distilled into a single thought. The essence of the ongoing point of differentiation might be missed. Further, trying to simplify a product category or subcategory can result in missing a key defining ingredient.

A multidimensional category or subcategory definition is therefore desirable. It is often easy for a competitor to overcome or neutralize a brand that has defined a category or subcategory with a single benefit. More difficult is to overcome is a complex, multidimensional concept because the challenger brand will likely be deficient if there are several dimensions acting as hurdles to overcome.

Another observation is that the definition of a category or subcategory will change over time. Those brands that are successful at discouraging others from entering will usually continuously innovate. Their offerings will be moving targets. Apple's iPod, for example, was followed by a half-dozen products that raised the bar for imitators.

Managing the Category or Subcategory

Defining the category or subcategory, identifying the priority aspirational associations, and creating a positioning strategy represent only the first step. The category or subcategory needs to be actively managed to succeed in the marketplace. Similar to building a brand, there is a need to build visibility, communicate the aspirational associations to the marketplace, create loyalty, and employ innovation to make the category or subcategory dynamic. There are some observations and suggestions that reflect two aspects of the challenge that are unique: there is a category or subcategory involved instead of a brand and it is driven by a substantial or transformational innovation.

Build the Culture to Support Execution

Execution, execution, execution. The best ideas not executed well and consistently will fail. The first challenge is to execute early. That means that the right assets, competencies, people, processes, and organization need to be assembled. The early adopters need to be satisfied. There should not be deficiencies and erratic delivery.

The second challenge, to maintain execution excellence over a long time period, is sometimes more difficult. The key is to enunciate, develop, and nurture a culture and values that will support execution. Zappos, Muji, H&M, IKEA, and Enterprise all had strong cultures with active and effective methods to keep them strong and fresh. The culture issue is particularly difficult when a business is part of a larger firm. The intense culture at Saturn eventually was undercut with the GM priorities and values. Healthy Choice had a strong culture for a time but corporate priorities at ConAgra eroded it until a revitalization brought it back.

Become the Exemplar

When possible, the brand should strive to become the exemplar of the category or subcategory, the brand that represents it in the minds of the customers. When the brand gains exemplar status, the brand strategy and its associated brand building will play the role of building the category or subcategory and developing its associations.

Another important attribute of an exemplar is that it will naturally develop not only a connection to the new category or subcategory but also credibility and authenticity. A challenge for any brand when a new category or subcategory emerges is to gain relevance. Being an exemplar means that relevance hurdles will almost certainly be overcome. Without the exemplar status, creating a link and credibility can be an uphill struggle.

How can a brand become an exemplar? Some guidelines were discussed in Chapter Two. First, be thought leaders and innovators. Don't stand still. Innovation, improvement, and change will make the category or subcategory dynamic, the brand more interesting, and the role of the exemplar more valued. Disneyland is the exemplar of theme parks and it is always innovating. Second, be the early market leader in terms of sales and market share. It is hard to be an exemplar and to leverage that role without market share leadership. Third, and most important, advance the category or subcategory and not the brand. If the category wins the brand will win.

When a brand is an exemplar, the category will be built under the auspices of the brand. It is the brand's resources, programs, and platform that will be telling the category or subcategory story. That means that much of the effort will be focusing on describing the category or subcategory characteristics, describing their advantages, and promoting loyalty not to the brand but to the category or subcategory over other categories or subcategories. The objective of brand building will be to encourage customers to buy gluten-free cake mixes rather than buying Betty Crocker. Of course, Betty Crocker is the only brand making gluten-free cake mixes.

Devoting much or all of the brand building away from the brand toward a category or subcategory can be hard to justify because it only indirectly creates top-line sales. Further, investments in building categories or subcategories have the potential to create sales for competitors that are able to achieve some level of relevance.

However, as noted in Chapter One, a category or subcategory can be inherently more interesting, more credible, and often more meaningful to a customer than a brand. Owning a performance ski can be a statement delivering meaningful self-expressive benefits independent of the brand. Riding first class may be more important than riding first class on a particular airline.

Stimulate Buzz

A new category or subcategory will involve a substantial or transformational innovation. That often means that it is worth talking about, even newsworthy. So the Segway got enormous free publicity as did Disklavier and the Zipcar. The offerings involved a value proposition that seemed to be meaningful, needed, and novel. There is an opportunity to leverage this reaction into talk if not buzz, the ultimate brand builder.

Being talked about is powerful in the era of social media. One person with a tweeter comment about a new category or subcategory can be quickly multiplied. A single person with a few hundred followers can literally reach millions in a few weeks if the followers of followers of followers and so on pass the message on. Some of those followers will have very large followings and be capable of influencing as well as reaching many others. The key is to get the conversation started with the right intriguing message to the right people.

One way to get the conversation started is with a story about such topics as these:

- *Dramatic features or benefits.* The Tato Nana with its break-through priced of $2,000 has a host of stories surrounding the effort.
- *The people behind the idea and how they brought it to life.* The story of Zappos, the Prius, Saturn, and Google all had development human-interest stories.
- *How the technology developed.* The story of Ivory soap, which was found through a production mistake and P&G's SK-II that was found because women in sake factories had great skin, are compelling stories that reinforce a key association.
- *Interesting applications.* Stories can be based on applications. How is Segway or the minivan used?
- A *culture that underlies the innovation.* The domestic 24/7 call center at Zappos that reflects its accessibility culture or Nano's single windshield wiper illustrating the "cost plus function" culture.

Surrounding the brand with excitement, energy, and visibility has a downside. As in the case of Yugo and Segway, it can create the appearance that the potential of the new arena is actually greater than it is. An in the case of Amazon's Kindle, it can also attract competitors who are looking for growth opportunities in the hopes of themselves gaining a relevance advantage. The optimum in some contexts is to have visibility that is targeted to a segment not now in the mainstream. That is what Enterprise did. By focusing on insurance companies and those needing a replace for a vehicle being repaired, they were under the radar for many years. Zappos also had limited visibility because it emphasized existing online customers and relied on word-of-mouth rather than mainstream media in order to build a huge business.

Create Advocates

A substantial or transformational innovation also has the potential to gain some early adopters who are not only attracted to the offering but also have some ownership due to the fact that they "discovered" it or at least were among the first to recognize its potential. These intensely loyal believers and followers who become advocates can be powerful both in the short term and in the long run. The Chrysler wagon was such a welcome contributor to the lifestyle of families that they named it the Magic wagon and talked about it.

To create advocates, it is necessary to get trial use, to get potential loyalists to try the offering. Retailers such as Muji, Ikea, Starbucks, Zara, H&M, Best Buy, and Whole Foods Market can demonstrate their value proposition and personality directly in the locality in which they have presence. Others can create demonstration opportunities. The Disklavier, for example, was available in various venues for people to see and try out.

To fully leverage advocates, it is worthwhile to support them and their activities. The design competition at Muji involves not only the participants but also those involved in the Muji culture. Some firms successfully nurture social networks. From the Saturn dealer BBQs to the Apple user groups, to the Internet-based social groups, there is an opportunity to provide energy and activity to the advocate group.

Manage Innovation

The category or subcategory, if successful, will be a target for competitors who will aspire to gain credibility. If the category or subcategory is static, the task becomes more feasible and the likelihood that competitors will become relevant or that they will even exceed expectations by adding a feature or benefit or extending the performance levels increases.

The challenge is to continue to innovate. If the brand achieves the status of an exemplar, it is natural to create ongoing innovations attached to the brand that can become part of the defined dimensions of the category or subcategory. That will make the category or subcategory a moving target and make it harder for a competitor to become relevant. As the definition evolves driven by brand innovations, the relevance challenge will increase.

Chrysler did exactly that by continuously innovating over time. Every two or three years there were significant innovations that raised the bar for competing firms. The driver side sliding door, for example, changed the category parameters. Westin followed the Heavenly Bed with the Heavenly shower and accessories like soap and shampoo, which also raised the bar.

Key Takeaways

In creating a new category or subcategory, marketing strategists need to position the category or subcategory as well as the brand. It needs to be labeled or described, and its image needs to be actively managed. Business strategists often overlook this critical function.

A firm can position a category or subcategory based on functional benefits driving a value proposition, such as by augmenting the offerings with features or benefits, a combination of benefits, functional design, and aesthetic design; providing systems-based offerings or customer-involving offerings; targeting segments; fostering customer intimacy; creating value, premium, or new-generation offerings; aligning the offerings with new applications or activities; and expanding the competitive space. It can also be based on a customer relationship with a category or subcategory that extends beyond functional benefits to such dimensions as shared interests, personality, passion, or social programs. Each provides a potential "must have" part of a category or subcategory's definition.

Managing a category or subcategory needs to use substantial or transformational innovation. There is a need to build a culture to support execution, to use the brand as an exemplar if possible to build the category or subcategory, to create advocates and stimulate buzz, and to manage innovation to create a moving target.

For Discussion

1. Look at offerings in a firm's product portfolio. How is the category or subcategory defined? What brands are exemplars? What brands are marginal—on the fringe of the category? What brands with products that qualify are not relevant? Why?

2. Pick a category, such as cars or snack foods. What new entries have created subcategories? How were those subcategories defined?

9

CREATING BARRIERS

Sustaining the Differentiation

Always pursue a strategy that your competitors
can't copy.

—*Jim McNerney, CEO of Boeing*

When I don't know whether to fight or not,
I always fight.

—*Lord Nelson*

The key to enduring success is to create barriers to competitors.
The creation of a new category or subcategory can generate
a marketplace in which the competitors are irrelevant and not
considered or they are weakened. The question is for how long.
The answer is the barriers created. The Yamaha Disklavier story
is not only a good subcategory story but also illustrates the
nature of barriers. As you read the story look for the different
barriers that Yamaha built. In addition to those based on technological innovations, there were an impressive set of other barriers as well.

Yamaha Disklavier

The player piano was in place in the very late 1800s, after a
host of inventions over decades and advances in materials came
together.[1] Actually, the punched holes in the player piano rolls
could be traced back to the automation of the textile mills and
were the forerunners of the punched-card data input of the early

computers. Technological progress builds. The timing for the player piano was finally right. The concept, which was improved over time, hit its peak in the mid-1920s. In its best year, 1924, when over 300,000 pianos were sold, the player piano was the center of home entertainment and held over 50 percent of the piano market. Then phonograph records, the radio, and finally the depression virtually killed the industry only six years after its zenith.

Over fifty years later, Yamaha Pianos brought back the player piano concept but in a digital form. The Yamaha Disklavier created a new subcategory when it was introduced in 1988. It functioned and played just like comparable Yamaha pianos, except that it also included a digital control system located outside the piano that could record and then replay the performances of top artists as well as beginners. In 1992, in the first of several significant upgrades, the electronics were installed inside the piano to provide a fully integrated product. The Disklavier was a transformational innovation.

Like the player piano, the Disklavier completely changed the industry, in part by allowing those who lack the time or talent to learn to play to have Sergei Rachmaninoff, George Gershwin, or Elton John playing in their homes. A restaurant, hotel, lounge, or retailer could have a quality performance in place without hiring someone to play. Whenever that occurred, Yamaha got priceless exposure for its piano. A library of discs, the Yamaha PianoSoft Library, lets users play recorded versions of the best artists' live performances. Most recently, users have the option of getting live feeds off the Internet via Disklavier Radio and can also download songs from the Disklavier Music Store.

The Disklavier offers considerable benefits for the professional. A composer or arranger can explore variations of an execution by altering the key or tempo of the piece when using the instrument's playback function. A vocalist or instrumentalist can have the accompanist's role recorded so it will be available for practice sessions with adjustable tempo—no longer does practice require a live accompanist.

A teacher can also benefit from the record and playback feature, especially with the slow-down option. Replaying student efforts can be used to demonstrate technique or to help display errors or deficiencies in play. A link to background music can serve to make scale drills more useful and enjoyable for the student. Further, practice with one hand can be more meaningful if the music from the other hand is being played by the Disklavier. A record of a student's early efforts can provide a baseline against which to demonstrate future improvement. Also, the most recent models allow users to connect two pianos in different locations. A teacher on one end and a student at the other can see and hear each other play. As a result, it becomes feasible for top artists to remotely teach students around the world. Further, piano competitions are held featuring contestants playing on Disklaviers in remote locations.

Like the original player piano, the Disklavier was based on dozens of innovations over decades and would not have been possible without advances in computers and related equipment. Timing was important, but so were instinct and commitment.

Researchers at Japan's University of Okayama developed a rough prototype in 1979. Yamaha saw the potential and became first its partner and soon thereafter the developer of the concept. There were, in addition to technical issues, the fact that some important intellectual property (IP) rights protected by patents were owned by other firms. Terry Lewis of Yamaha Corporation of America impressed with the concept, decided in 1986 to commit to it even without support from others at Yamaha. In a critical step, he acquired some of the key IP rights from a company that had no plans or ability to exploit the patents they held. Later he hired an inventor named Wayne Stahnke in order to obtain access to the rest of the needed rights and to get his help in bringing the product to fruition. The result was the 1992 version of the Disklavier, the Mark II.

Lewis, who championed and managed the Disklavier for over two decades, had a lot going for him as he made the commitment decision, mobilized support from the firm, and led the product through the early years. First, Yamaha had the capability needed to create a product and support a business. It had a top name in piano quality, a strong U.S. dealership distribution, and an in-house R&D presence in consumer electronics. Second, the piano operations of Yamaha, like the whole piano industry, had been in the doldrums, had little energy, and was financially disappointing. Piano lessons for kids had too much competition. Home entertainment had moved on. The Disklavier with all its applications had the potential to revitalize Yamaha as well as the whole piano industry. Third, even though the conditions were very different, the player piano's legacy provided a success proof point that made projections believable.

There was another important consideration. The Disklavier would not cannibalize the sales of Yamaha conventional acoustic pianos but, rather, would create incremental business. That fact was crucial in overcoming internal resistance to the initiative. The Disklavier has without question expanded the market. Over half of its home buyers do not play the piano, suggesting that the player piano's legacy is an important driver of purchase decisions. Nearly two-thirds of the buyers already had a piano. The target market—upscale, older nonmusicians—is very different from that of the acoustic piano, which is geared to young families.

Yamaha has continuously improved the product over the years, and as a result has been the dominant leader. The firm was awarded the Musical Merchandise Review "Dealer's Choice" product of the year by a trade group every year from 2000 to 2007. In 2000 the Disklavier did over $100 million, which represented 15 percent of the total piano industry volume that year. By some accounts its share of the acoustic piano market continued throughout the next decade to be around 50 percent, with

Figure 9.1 Yamaha Disklavier

the second place brand far behind. Their closest competition did not make pianos but, rather, made retrofit systems that added the digital capability to existing pianos.

Yamaha developed several significant barriers to competition. The first is the Yamaha brand. Yamaha, through its piano heritage, its presence on concert stages, and its ongoing leadership, has credibility in anything piano. Thus the consumer risk issues of quality and reliability that would be associated with such a complex product as the Disklavier are largely mitigated. And customers know that Yamaha would not allow the piano's electronic functions to compromise the piano's acoustic core. The brand means more than quality and performance. For some, its heritage as a concert piano reinforced by the recorded performances provides self-expressive benefits. For others, memories of learning to play on a Yamaha provides nostalgic emotional benefits.

A second is the Yamaha distribution channel, which provides a presence in the community, a go-to place to try and buy the product, a service support system that reassures customers, and, most important, a flow of customers. It is not easy to compete with a superior distribution system.

The third barrier was Yamaha's in-house proficiency in digital electronics, which meant that they could design an integrated product within one organization with the same culture, values, and goals. The electronics R&D team provides ideas and capabilities and also access to innovations throughout the digital world. This is the firm that introduced the PortaSound Portable Keyboards, the Clavinova Digital Piano, the DX7 Synthesizer, and the Virtual Acoustic Synthesis technology, all breakthrough products. The stream of new-generation Disklaviers created by the Yamaha R&D staff has made the brand a moving target for sure. No other piano firm has any remotely similar capability. The competitors making retrofit products lack the access to the piano side of the equation, and because they work with many manufacturers they can not be as focused and intimate with the piano design.

Finally the Yamaha has scale economies in design, manufacturing, logistics, and marketing. Because the cost of these activities can be spread over a large base, budgets can be larger. Yamaha can justify a large R&D staff; a dedicated production line; efficient warehousing and shipping; healthy dealers; and national marketing programs, such as user education, that are economically difficult for others.

Creating Barriers to Competition

The goal of creating a new category or subcategory is to have a phase in which competition is nonexistent or greatly reduced, leading to an attractive profit stream that is above normal levels and market momentum leading to a significant market position. This first phase can last months, years, or decades. It is potentially followed by a second phase in which competition is introduced but the market position still allows the pursuit of a healthy business, a business that the firm can potentially leverage to create still other new categories or subcategories.

The success and longevity of the first phase will be based on the barriers that isolate a brand from competitors for a time or at least put competitors at a disadvantage. Accomplishing that task can be difficult because in many cases potential competitors have the capability of matching any new category or subcategory and copying any decisive point of differentiation. The strategy is to make that matching strategy so expensive or the prospective rewards so reduced that these potential competitors choose not to invest in attempting to become relevant in the new category or subcategory, at least for a time. Another strategy is to create offerings and strategies for which the response time for potential competitors is extensive, providing a window to solidify a market position.

There are four different types of barriers, as summarized in Figure 9.2. The first is an investment barrier making it technically or economically unattractive or even infeasible for a competitor to develop an offering. The second is to own the compelling benefit or sets of benefits that are driving the category or subcategory. The third is to have a customer relationship beyond functional benefits of the offering based on such dimensions as common interests, personality, passion about the category or

Figure 9.2 Creating Barriers to Competition

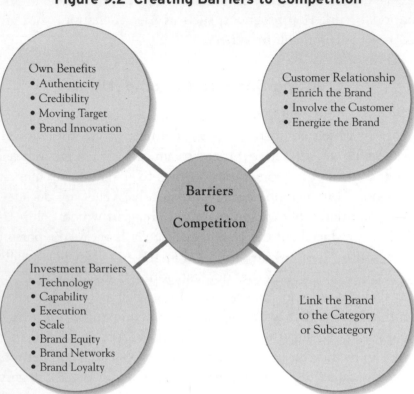

subcategory, or corporate social programs, which will also serve to define what brands will be considered and which will be excluded. The fourth is to have a strong link to the category or subcategory perhaps by being an exemplar so that the brand will dominate the consideration set.

Investment Barriers

A competitor will have to make an investment and justify that investment with an ROI analysis. A substantial investment can inhibit response. Such an investment not only affects prospective ROI negatively but also increases the risk, taking resources away from alternative investment opportunities. An investment barrier can be based on proprietary technology or capability, execution, the scale of operation, brand equity, brand networks, or brand loyalty.

Proprietary Technology or Capability

The strongest competitive barrier is having an innovation based on strongly protected intellectual property or patents. P&G's Olestra and Pringles, the Yamaha Disklavier, and Dreyer's Slow Churned Ice Cream were all based on many years of research and testing and had patent protection. It would be extremely costly, if feasible, for a competitor to follow them in any reasonable time frame. An accumulation of incremental innovations can also provide a formidable barrier. Toyota's Prius and Tata's Nano were based on a host of technological advances, some more significant than others, that made matching them a difficult task.

The sheer size of the investment level can be a barrier because it represents resources that could be used elsewhere. Developing Kirin Ichiban, for example, was an expensive process to which others were not willing or able to respond, and the Ichiban brand has not had a direct competitor. CNN and ESPN enjoyed many years of competitor-free life, in part because the investment to set up and staff a new channel is enormous and because sharing the audience reduces the potential. The development of a product such as a hybrid, minivan, or minicar can be a huge drain on time, money, and people resources.

Executing the Idea—The Capability to Deliver

If there is one key to sustainable differentiation, it is the capability to execute the idea, to deliver on the promise. The lack of such a capability is frequently the reason why well-conceived offerings with attractive value propositions fail—the implementation is not there. The ability to execute is often underrated. Even great strategies badly exccuted will fail.

Delivering an offering consistently against expectations over time often requires organizational commitment, assets, and competencies that can be significant barriers. IKEA's design and sourcing capabilities are crucial in their ability to deliver to expectations.

Execution needs to be supported by the right culture and values because they provide the motivation to deliver over time. Zappos with its Wow! experience focus and Muji with its culture and vision both inspire the organization to maintain its executional excellence.

The details of making a new product or delivering a new service may be known, but that does not mean that they can be duplicated. Nordstrom created a service offering and brand around its ability to deliver a high level of customer service in its department stores. Its success prompted others to pursue a doomed effort to copy. Competitors were missing or deficient on one or more key elements of the strategy such as the commission reward system, people who were trained to roam the whole store with clients, a staff empowered to deal with customer issues (the one rule at Nordstrom about dealing with customers is that there are no rules), a culture and values that put customer satisfaction first, and a heritage of stories about how customers were delighted. The classic story about how a customer got a refund for a used tire even though Nordstrom's did not sell tires may not be true, but it makes the point that it takes a special kind of organization to operate the Nordstrom's way.

Scale of Operation

A first-mover advantage can generate an early market share position. The market share leaders will enjoy scale advantages. All fixed costs, such as those pertaining to plant, systems, staff, advertising, promotion, and sponsorships, will be spread over a larger sales base. The result can be a decidedly lower cost structure, the cumulative effect of which builds over time. Scale can also trigger an experience effect: as an organization accumulates experience in building a product or delivering a service, its effectiveness will increase and its costs will decline because of the learning involved.

Local scale is particularly important in retailing. When a retailer like IKEA, Zara, Amazon, McDonald's, Walmart, Whole Foods Market, Starbucks, or Subway develops a large local footprint quickly, they create competitive barriers. There will be economies in logistics; warehousing; back office support; management; advertising; and, maybe most notable, brand recognition and perceptions. Competitors will at a minimum be at a disadvantage in attempting to enter. They will face an uphill fight because the cost of operations will be higher for them and they will find the best locations preempted.

If first-mover advantages will lead to worthwhile scale effects, the firm should expand aggressively at the outset so it achieves scale and the associated advantages quickly and so that the window of opportunity for competitors will be short-lived. Expanding aggressively is easy to talk about but hard to do because there will be organizational resistance in the face of the danger that the "winner" judgment is wrong or that competitors may counter. But when Asahi with its Super Dry and Chrysler with its minivan did make stretch investments in plant at the outset they enabled the early sales success that was critical to becoming dominant in their subcategories.

Sometimes there are network effects whereby the functional benefits grow as the user base grows. The functional benefits of eBay, for example, are based on the fact that there are many, many users. As a result, a seller will find more buyers for goods and buyers will find more goods to buy or bid on. It has been estimated that in the average market the market share pattern is 60 percent for the leading firm, 30 percent for the number-two firm, and 5 percent for the third-place firm. In a market with network effects, the largest firm may have 95 percent of the market, and creating a critical mass becomes very difficult for competitors.

Brand Equity

Brand equity often represents the strongest barrier. The brand that first gets traction for the new subcategory, the early market leader, has more freedom to create brand associations, less clutter in which to operate, and the potential to define the new category or subcategory in a way that links to the brand and emphasizes the innovations the brand owns. The result can be a strong brand with visibility and energy that has preempted the most effective positioning strategy.

The strength of the brand, indeed the success of the offering, will depend in part on the brand strategy. Should it be a stand-alone new brand? An endorsed brand? Or should the firm use an existing master brand with a new subbrand?

A new brand developed to support an offering that defines a new category or subcategory is able to signal "new" and to develop a benefit story and a personality without inhibitions. For an offering that hopes to transform the marketplace, such as Muji, Zipcar, or the Segway, a new brand with a blank sheet of paper is desirable or even necessary. A new brand is needed when there are resources to build the brand, when the story is so new and compelling that it can break through the clutter, and when there is no established brand that fits the offering.

However, an established brand used as a master brand can mean that the brand-building effort will be less expensive and more feasible, and the resulting brand strength is likely to be higher. The established master brand provides credibility and visibility. Asahi Super Dry, Kirin Ichiban, and the Plymouth Voyager minivan would probably not have been successful without the master brands Asahi, Kirin, and Plymouth, respectively.

Another option is to create a new brand but one endorsed by an established brand. Consider the role of the endorser brand for General Mills' Fiber One, Toyota's Prius, Apple's iPod, and PowerBar's Pria. In each case the endorser added credibility to what otherwise would be an unknown brand from an unknown firm.

If a master brand would make a difference in establishing the new category or subcategory, especially in crowded contexts, a radical step is to source a brand from another firm to be either the master brand or a cobrand. P&G developed an advance in plastic food wrap and considered going to market under the Impress name. However, a sober analysis suggested that the pay-off would be long and uncertain. Instead, they went to the cat-egory leader Glad, owned by Clorox, and suggested that this technology and other P&G innovations be marketed under the Glad brand. They formed a joint venture, in which P&G held 20 percent, that included the new Glad Press 'n Seal wrap and Glad ForceFlex (a stretchable, stronger trash bag also developed by P&G). The resulting new subcategories were protected by brand and distribution strength that would never have been possible as a P&G venture.

Whether a new brand, an endorsed brand, or a subbrand is used, the optimal result is for the brand to become an exemplar defining and simultaneously linking to the new category or sub-category. An exemplar brand can create enormous barriers to and sources of frustration for competitors. Much of competitors' own brand-building work will often end up helping the new category or subcategory and thus the exemplar. Google, like classic exemplars Kleenex, Xerox, V-8, Crayola, Band-Aid, Jell-O, and Birkenstock, has created decided barriers to competitors by being such a strong exemplar that their brand. The ultimate exemplar signal is when the brand became the label for the cat-egory or subcategory as in the phrase "Google it."

Brand Networks

If a firm can create networks around its brand, the tasks for competitors will become more complex and difficult. Apple has long benefited from a supporting network that would be hard to duplicate because it largely is controlled by the participants and because it is nurtured by the brand and the products. There has always been an Apple user's group with a life of its own. When the iPod, iPhone, and iPad emerged, each had a large and active network of application writers who were creating and sharing ideas to extend the product. They also had a new-generation Apple user's group that used the social media to create cohesive, meaningful augmentations to the products and brands.

The big idea is that a brand is at the center of a network of users, programs, products, influencers, dealers, and others. If a firm can create nodes outside the brand, activate those nodes, and link them to the brand, the brand will become stronger and more energized. So Avon is linked to community groups and cancer research organizations through its Walk for Breast Cancer. Salesforce.com has a host of firms writing software to be used on its platform and a network of firms involved with its social programs. Pampers is linked to organizations involved in raising babies and keeping them healthy. In each case the brand has been augmented. And competitors now have to compete not only with the branding effort but with the brand network, a much harder task.

Brand Loyalty

The customers who become loyal to the brand early on are usually the easiest to sell because they have a need, are interested, and may even be risk takers. If these customers are unavailable or are expensive to attract, competitors will find building their own bases expensive. Loyalty can be based on a compelling attribute, an attractive brand personality, or a set of values that resonate. However, it can also be created by brand switching costs, such as the learning costs in the case of software products. And there are the underestimated but powerful drivers of loyalty to products ranging from candy to cars to hotels—habit and familiarity.

The firm usually needs to make a decision between an aggressive effort to build sales and a more deliberate one that would reduce investment and risk in addition to allowing for offering improvement. The more aggressive option, particularly when others are only too willing and able to copy innovations, is the one that will leverage all forms of loyalty in the future. The more bodies there are connected to the brand, the greater the power of all the drivers of loyalty. If, however, the offering is evolving and natural barriers to competitors exist, a go-slow approach may be appropriate.

Because of the long-term strategic importance of loyalty, it is worthwhile to develop programs to enhance and protect it. The most basic need is to simply deliver on the brand promise, but there is much that a firm can do in addition. A loyalty program, for example, may be used to support a natural customer affinity. A new serve-yourself frozen yogurt store, for example, can cement local enthusiasm with a loyalty card that allows a customer to earn free deserts and, additionally, provides a tangible link to the brand. Another tool is to manage customer touchpoints, times when the customer interacts with the brand, to make sure the experience reinforces the loyalty. Particularly important touchpoints occur when customer problems arise, because these represent contexts in which the relationship can be strengthened or placed at risk. The advent of social technology means that the extremes of customer satisfaction have the potential to be multiplied manifold. Dramatic incidences of dissatisfaction, in particular, can get traction in the social media space and explode.

Owning a Compelling Benefit or Benefits

Many of the new categories or subcategories are defined by compelling benefits that attract customers and provide the basis for subsequent loyalty. How do you own a compelling benefit beyond owning a technology or capability? Four routes are to develop an aura of authenticity, to become a moving target, to develop visible credibility, and to find a branded differentiator.

Delivering Authenticity

A brand that claims authenticity and can paint competitors as opportunistic copiers will have created a significant barrier. People are inclined to be loyal to an authentic brand and even resent a brand that attempts to copy or, worse, is phony and attempts to be an original. Asahi Super Dry beer, as discussed in Chapter One, was an incredible success in 1986. Kirin Draft Dry, which appeared fewer than two years later, was a comparable product but failed because it was a transparent effort to copy the success of an underdog brand that had broken out of the Kirin lager beer world. It was clear that a firm that had prided itself on offering the best lager did not really have its heart in the dry beer space, and Kirin Draft Dry failed the authenticity test big time. The fact that Asahi, with associations of Western, young, and cool, delivered more than crisp taste made Kirin's task more difficult because gaining "authentic taste" was not enough.

Authentic means genuine, original, and trustworthy. A genuine offering is one that can be counted on to deliver to expectations on all dimensions. It will not disappoint. Original means that it is not a copy or fake. It may not have been the pioneer, but it was the first to get the offering right. Trustworthy indicates that the organization or person behind the offering exhibits an interest and sincerity in—if not a passion for—creating a genuine product or service.

Getting and retaining authenticity ultimately means delivering on the entire value proposition, never compromising. That starts with having high standards and developing the people, culture, and systems to deliver against those standards. The firm behind a "real brand" will not compromise. The most trusted names in a 2010 survey were Amazon, FedEx, Downey, Huggies, and Tide, all brands that deliver on their promises consistently.[2]

There was once a beer named Schlitz that was, with Budweiser, the market leader. The Schlitz product's brewing process was compromised in order to reduce costs. As a result the beer turned flat while on the shelf, and the brand lost everything. Even returning to the original formula and showing live taste tests during the Super Bowl were not enough. The problem that Schlitz could not overcome was the raw fact that the organization cared more about cost and profits than it did about its product, brand, and customers. When you have to talk about a quality claim, it becomes suspect. An authentic brand doesn't have to directly point to quality, it is assumed.

Brands with authenticity usually have an organization behind them with a heritage, values, and programs that create confidence that the promise means something. These organizational qualities will drive an image of authenticity. Google's guiding principles, mentioned in Chapter Eight, have resulted in a customer interface that is clean, fast, and functional. Recall that Muji has a values and lifestyle story that is so strong that authenticity becomes a given. Jet Blue values safety, caring, fun, integrity, and passion, and that shows through.[3]

Research from Australia in 2009 revealed that heritage is a driver of authenticity.[4] If there is a relevant and engaging story behind the brand, its perceived authenticity will be stronger. The story of Henry Ford's concept of a car for everyone, accounts of over-the-top service at Ritz-Carlton, the "cloud" vision at salesforce.com, the story of Jared at Subway—all buttress the authenticity of their brands.

When the brand carries the name of the founder, the story behind the brand becomes more tangible. Ben & Jerry's ice cream, Oreck Vacuum Cleaners, and Ted Turner's Teds Montana Grill all have had active spokesmen who have carried the message of each brand's goals and vision. Others, such as L. L. Bean, Orville Redenbacher, Eddie Bauer, Peet's Coffee, and Newman's Own, carry the founders' names and stories even though the founders are not around. Still others, such as Victoria's Secret, have mythical founders that still carry a story.

Authenticity can also be based on the heritage of the offering's place of origin. Authenticity is likely to be ascribed to Russian vodka, a Swiss watch, French perfume, Danish cheese, a Japanese consumer electronics product, Argentine beef, or Singapore Airlines. Or authenticity could come from a regional or local association. Ben & Jerry's from Vermont, Tom's of

Maine, Sam Adams from Boston, Gallo wines from California, and Robert Mondavi wine from Napa County are just a few examples. In each case the association with a region bolsters the authenticity, and others without that association have a higher hurdle to overcome.

Developing Visible Credibility

The firm needs to be seen as capable of delivering behind the compelling benefit or benefits. Credibility can come from a good track record in the marketplace. Even more impressive, however, is when assets, competencies, and strategies are visible to customers. These represent real substance and can be hard to copy. Kirin convincingly was able to show that it owned a complex and expensive production process for Kirin Ichiban. Saturn was able to showcase its Springhill plant, the workers, and its dealer showrooms to demonstrate the quality and the culture of the firm. Best Buy has the very visible Geek Squad, and Dryer's has the Slow Churned technology.

Visible operations that support a value proposition can also provide credibility. When a customer learns about the distinctive operations of Zara and H&M that allowed each to deliver fresh fashions into stores, its claims of having a fresh assortment every week gains some substance. Dell became the dominant direct seller of computers for a decade with its build-to-order system that allowed the firm to offer the latest technology while still having low costs and a high level of customer contact. The delivery system reinforced customer's decisions to buy direct from Dell. FedEx created an operations-driven innovation that allowed them to track packages, a benefit so novel and compelling that it defined a subcategory.

Becoming a Moving Target

When a brand has a significant innovation that provides a benefit or benefits that get market traction, a competitor will likely either copy it or find a way to neutralize it with another innovation. When the new offering and the category or subcategory it represents are dynamic, the brand is a moving rather than a stationary target. Gillette has been an innovation machine by creating subcategories, and then improving or replacing them. From The Trac II in 1971, the first two-blade razor, the market has seen Altra, Sensor, Mach3, Venus, and Fusion, plus a host of innovations under subbrands such as Trac II Plus, Sensor Excel, Mach3 Turbo, Venus Embrace, and Fusion ProGlide, with a "snow plow guard" that prevents hydroplaning and a new ergonomic grip. Gillette is the essence of a moving target.

Continuous innovation presents challenges to brands attempting to gain relevance. There were a half-dozen variations of the iPod including the nano, the shuffle, and the touch which made it hard for competitors to find a point of vulnerability based on a specialized application or segment. The Prius each year has contained significant advances that mean that competitors working on cars even three or more years in the future will still have the wind in their faces. P&G has made Tide detergent and its feminine hygiene products a moving target with an ongoing series of innovations all designed to address the key consumer wants of comfort, protection, and femininity.

Finding a Branded Differentiator

The challenge is to own a benefit as long as possible to avoid having it drift into the noise surrounding the category or subcategory. One answer is to brand it—to create a branded differentiator—because a firm can own a brand. Other retailers can duplicate or even improve on the Best Buy services, but they will not have a Geek Squad or its personality and associations because Best Buy owns that brand.

A *branded differentiator*, summarized in Figure 9.3, is a feature, ingredient or technology, service, or program that creates a meaningful point of differentiation for a branded offering over an extended time period that is branded and actively managed.

Figure 9.3 Branded Differentiators

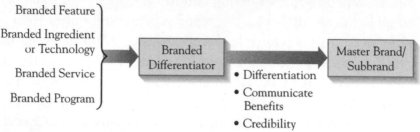

A branded differentiator will be either a feature, ingredient or technology, service, or program affecting the offering usually providing a graphic way to signal superior performance. General Motors' OnStar system, for example, is a branded feature that provides automatic notification of airbag deployment to roadside assistance agencies, stolen vehicle location, emergency services, remote door unlocking, remote diagnostics, and concierge services. Sara Lee's EarthGrains brands use the branded ingredient Eco-Grain, a new type of wheat that supports sustainable farming practices.[5] Sharp branded the four-color TV technology of Aquos as Quadpixel. Enterprise's ARMS system provides a branded service to insurance companies that allows them to manage the delivery of rental cars to their customers.

A branded differentiator needs to be meaningful in that it really matters to customers and represent a point of differentiation. For example, the Westin hotel chain created in 1999 the Heavenly Bed, introduced in Chapter One, a custom-designed mattress set (by Simmons) with 900 coils, a cozy down blanket adapted for climate, a comforter with a crisp duvet, high-quality sheets, and five goosedown pillows. The Heavenly Bed became a branded differentiator in a crowded category in which differentiation is a challenge. The Heavenly Bed was meaningful in that it was truly a better bed and addressed the heart of a hotel's promise—to provide a good night's sleep. It also had a significant impact. During the first year of its life, those Westin hotel sites that featured the Heavenly Bed had a 5 percent increase in customer satisfaction; a noticeable increase in perceptions of cleanliness, room decor, and maintenance; and increased occupancy.

A branded differentiator also needs to warrant active management over time and justify brand-building efforts. It should be a moving target. The Heavenly Bed has received that treatment with an active and growing set of brand-building programs. The reception of the bed was so strong that Westin starting selling it; in 2004 it sold some 3,500 beds, and the bed was ultimately placed in Nordstrom's stores. Imagine, selling a hotel bed. Think of the buzz. The concept has been extended to the Heavenly Bath, which features dual shower heads plus soap and towels. There is even a Heavenly dog bed. All the Heavenly products can be bought online at the Westin At Home Store.

A valued feature, ingredient or technology, service, or program will serve to differentiate a product whether or not it is branded. So why brand it? In addition to being a source of ownership of a benefit, a branded differentiator can also add credibility and legitimacy to a claim. The brand specifically says that the benefit was worth branding, that it is meaningful. A remarkable study of branded attributes showed the ability of a brand to add credibility. Carpenter, Glazer, and Nakamoto, three prominent academic researchers, found that the inclusion of a branded attribute (such as "Alpine class" fill for a down jacket, "authentic Milanese" for pasta, and "studio designed" for compact disc players) dramatically affected customer preference toward premium-priced brands. Respondents were able to justify the higher price because of the branded attributes even though they had no idea why the attributes were superior.[6]

A branded differentiator can also make communication easier. A branded feature, such as Oral B's Action Cup, in which a unique, round brush head surrounds each tooth for a tooth-by-tooth clean, provides a way to crystallize feature details, making the feature easier both to understand and to remember. Best Buy's Geek Squad brand not only helps communicate what they do but also their energy and personality, who they are. In general, a branded service can help capture the essence and scope of a concept that otherwise could be multidimensional and complex and directed to an audience that simply does not care enough to make an effort to understand.

Amazon developed a powerful feature, the ability to recommend such products as books or DVDs based on a customer's interests as reflected by his or her purchase history and the purchase history of those who bought similar offerings. But they never branded it. How tragic is that? As a result, the feature became basically a commodity that is an expected feature of many e-commerce sites. If Amazon had branded it and then actively managed that brand, improving the feature over time, it would have become a lasting point of differentiation that today would be invaluable. They missed a golden opportunity. They did not make that same mistake with One-Click, which allows the user to buy by hitting the One-Click button, a branded service that plays a key role in defining Amazon in what has become a messy marketplace. Nor did they do so when their Kindle users downloaded their digital books using the Amazon Whispernet, a brand that represents the fast, easy-to-use book download service provided by Amazon to support its Kindle book offerings.

Relationship with Customers

A competitor can copy or neutralize a functional benefit. However, it is usually not so easy to copy other aspects of a brand, aspects that create a customer relationship that goes beyond functionality, that is driving the definition of a new category or subcategory.

Enriching the Brand

One key is to make the brand and the category and subcategory it is defining about more than delivering functional benefits.

If the brand can become an exemplar and surround itself and its category or subcategory with a rich set of associations it will be more difficult to match or surpass. With more associations to match, it is harder for a competitor to gain credibility as a player in the new category or subcategory. Competitors are more likely to find themselves with a deficiency, which means they would fail to be relevant. When the deficiency is based not on functionality but on some combination of common interests, personality, passion for the category or subcategory, organizational attributes, or corporate social programs, it becomes very frustrating for the competitor. If you build a better mousetrap or one just as good at a lower price, shouldn't the customer buy? Not necessarily.

When the brand is capable of becoming an exemplar of the category, competitors will have to match or surpass the total brand and not just the functional dimension. Brand complexity can then work to the advantage of the exemplar. Prius, iPod, iPhone, Zara, Muji, Zappos, Subway, Whole Foods Market, Zipcar, Wheaties Fuel, Healthy Choice, Southwestern Airlines, and ESPN all defined a category or subcategory with the set of associations developed for them as exemplar brands. Brand richness and complexity make the exemplar status even more powerful.

The ways that a brand and its category and subcategory can be enriched beyond functional benefits that include shared interests, brand personality, and organizational associations, all of which were described in Chapter Eight. An authentic interest shared by customers and the brand such as Pampers and baby care, Hobart and food-service kitchen issues, and Kaiser and healthy living provide a barrier to competitors. A brand and its category or subcategory can be given a personality, such as occurred with Asahi Dry Beer, Zara, Saturn, and Segway, which can represent social and self-expressive benefits. Organizational associations such as being global, innovative, quality driven, customer driven, involved in social issues, or having green values can be difficult to match.

Involving the Customer

Offerings that expand their scope to involve the customer in ways that go beyond the functional benefits of the product or service can also provide barriers to competitors. The Betty Crocker Mixer Web site, for example, invites members to talk to experts and connect with others. Bikers can post pictures of their most recent ride on the Harley-Davidson Web site. BMW has race-tracks where you can drive its cars. In each case the brand creates and deepens the relationship, and customer loyalty becomes more intense and competitors become less relevant.

P&G's skin-care product SK-II, as noted earlier, was first developed when it was observed that older women workers in a sake brewery had young and smooth skin. That observation led to the ingredient branded as Pitera. But P&G went beyond the product to create a total holistic consumer experience with a skin-care regimen, beauty counseling, and an exceptional in-store experience. In department stores there is a sophisticated SK-II beauty-imaging computer system to assess and monitor the skin's condition—the lines, wrinkles, texture, and spots. Specialists provide personalized recommendations and maintain a relationship with their clients—even sending flowers on special occasions. The result is a half-billion-dollar business and women who spend up to five thousand dollars a year on the products. It might be feasible to create a competitive product, but duplicating the experience would be difficult.

Social media has taken involvement to a new level.[7] If a brand can connect to a community, that connection can reinforce the brand's authenticity. Owners of the small and quirky Smart Car, for example, have formed a social network of some eleven thousand with around two hundred subcommunities, some of which organize local events. The community was so loyal that it protected the brand by countering a rumor that there was a transmission problem.

If a brand lacks a driven passionate following, it needs an interest, shared activity, or cause that fits the brand to form the locus of a community. Sharpie, a drawing instrument, formed a community of mostly designers around creativity. One idea was to have an autograph wall at the backstage of a country music festival and opening up to the public one afternoon. Columbia, the outdoor clothing firm, uses Meetup, an online social platform that gets people together offline in local gatherings, to sponsor outdoor and hiking groups. A common cause, further, can mobilize a community. Dove has a community redefining society's conception of female beauty. Nissan is building a community around zero emissions vehicles to support the new Leaf model.

Some clear guidelines around social media are emerging. First, the proper brand role is to support, nurture, partner, and enable. Control just does not work. Second, the community needs to be perceived as intriguing, useful, or an extension of a lifestyle or interest. It cannot be a thinly disguised brand-building effort. Third, communities need to be authentic, focused on a real need like sharing knowledge or a real passion. There has to be a reason to participate.

Energizing the Brand

To maintain strong barriers it is important to create an energy leadership position, to make sure that it is competitors who seem tired. The best way to do that is to have a stream of innovations that are visible and keep the offering fresh. However, that is not always possible, and, even when it is, competitors might also appear to have innovations. In that case it may be time to find something with energy and connect it to the brand, creating and nurturing a branded energizer. Routes to creating energy and visibility will be discussed in Chapter Ten, which introduces the problem of maintaining relevance.

Link the Brand to the Category or Subcategory

The brand needs to be linked to the new category or subcategory to be relevant going forward. When the category or subcategory is mentioned, the brand should come to mind. Without the link and the relevance that goes with it, the brand will not be able to influence and manage the new category or subcategory definition. A strong link that allows the brand to dominate the consideration set judgment will provide a significant barrier to competitors.

Ideally the brand should be the exemplar, whereby the category or subcategory is described by evoking the brand name. The degree to which a competitor is relevant to the category or subcategory is then how similar is it to the exemplar. A competitor facing an exemplar brand will be on the defensive because any attempt to differentiate will risk losing relevance.

The right descriptive brand name can be a label for the category or subcategory and thus allow the brand to be the de facto exemplar. In that case, it would be impossible to avoid thinking of the brand link when the category or subcategory is mentioned. Lean Cuisine and Weight Watchers, for instance, are linked to weight control from two perspectives. If the subcategory is weight-control programs, the Weight Watchers brand will be triggered. If, however, low-fat food is the defining characteristic of the subcategory, Lean Cuisine would be predominant. Safeway's O Organics and Eating Right brands provide signals about what categories for which there are relevant.

Of course, a descriptive brand name can also be restrictive. Fiber One would have a hard time going where fiber is not relevant. If Amazon had been Books.com, it would have had a relevance and credibility problem entering the broad range of product categories that it did enter. So there is often a tradeoff between gaining a relevance advantage in a category or subcategory and allowing for future strategic flexibility.

In some cases, of course, there is no brand that steps up to the exemplar role. In that case, the brand needs to be perceived as a credible option for the emerging category or subcategory and create a strong link to it. One way to make the connection is simply by brute force, to use advertising, packaging, or sponsorships to connect the brand and the new category or subcategory. That has been done but can be difficult and expensive because the audience may have inadequate reason to process information and learn connections.

This chapter has discussed examined the four routes to creating barriers to competition. The next chapter will examine the threat of losing relevance for an established brand as new categories or subcategories emerge and the challenge of gaining relevance into an established category.

Key Takeaways

Creating categories or subcategories is expensive, risky, and stressful to the organization. The payoff for those that succeed will depend on the competitive barriers that firms can create. The higher the barrier, the greater the immediate profit flow and market momentum. Among the barriers:

- Creating investment barriers, such as proprietary technology or capabilities, superior execution, scale economies, brand equity, brand networks, and a loyal customer base
- Owning a compelling benefit or benefits by becoming the most authentic brand, by fostering visible credibility, by becoming a moving target, or by branding the innovation with a branded differentiator
- Having a customer relationship going beyond functional benefits that is based on involving the customer with the

brand; energizing the brand; or enriching the brand with shared interests, personality, passion, organization attributes, and social programs

- Developing a strong link to the new category or subcategory, if possible by making the brand an exemplar

For Discussion

1. Examine several major new offerings that are based on substantial or transformational innovations from your firm or others. How long did they enjoy a competitive vacuum or strong edge? What barriers were created? Should some barriers have been made stronger?

2. Identify a brand in your industry and one outside your industry that have created strong barriers. What were those barriers? How were they created? Were there any leveraged firm assets and competencies?

3. Which companies do you admire for building strong customer relationships? For developing branded differentiators that have made a difference? What are the lessons to be learned?

4. Identify brands that are exemplars of their categories or subcategories. How did they achieve that position?

10

GAINING AND MAINTAINING RELEVANCE IN THE FACE OF MARKET DYNAMICS

If you are on the right track, you'll get run over if you just sit there.

—*Will Rodgers*

There is nothing more exhilarating than to be shot at without result.

—*Winston Churchill*

In the face of market dynamics, firms run the risk of losing relevance as the category or subcategory or which they are focused fades or gets redefined and, as a result, the firms' brand becomes relevant to a shrinking number of customers. There are many forces that drive this threat as this chapter will describe, but one is a growing reluctance to buy from a firm that is considered unacceptable in terms of its values or the way it uses its market power. Changing such a reputation is difficult for both internal and external reasons. But Walmart, in one of the most impressive brand stories of the decade, did just that. The case shows both why and how it was done.

A firm that is attempting to become relevant by overcoming customers' reasons not to buy their brand faces the same challenges as a firm addressing threats to the relevance they have already achieved. Hyundai is an example of a brand that needed to overcome four relevance challenges—quality, styling, foreign-made products, and not being premium—in order to obtain a strong market position. Its story is instructive and is presented in the final section of this chapter.

Walmart

In 2005 Walmart was rolling.[1] Its sales were nearly $300 billion—almost three times those of ten years earlier. It had some five thousand stores, up from three thousand a decade before, and the stores on average had bigger footprints. However, there were nagging negative issues, some accompanied by lawsuits or boycotts, that were almost continuously in the press in one form or another.

There were four issues that stood out. First, Walmart had a reputation, fueled by unions, of treating its employees unfairly with inadequate health insurance programs, low wages (described by some as unlivable), and discrimination against female workers—a set of policies that was said to encourage if not force competitors to do the same. Second, the sourcing of goods in China and elsewhere, which affected the U.S. balance of payments, sent jobs overseas, and raised the specter of worker exploitation, was thought to be driven in part by Walmart's focus (an obsession in the eyes of some) on low costs. Third, there was the belief among local politicians and voters that the entry of Walmart into an area caused small retailers to go out of business and created undesirable traffic and sprawl. Fourth, there were stories about how Walmart put so many pricing and brand demands on suppliers who were dependent on Walmart's business that they were forced to compromise their products and brands, source offshore, and even go out of business.

These negative issues not only tended to divert attention from Walmart's messaging but also had a practical impact on its business strategy. More communities were turning down Walmart stores, which affected growth strategies and location decisions. Perhaps more important, a negative image of Walmart among a growing portion of the market, those socially concerned, affected its ability to gain customers and increase loyalty, especially in the face of such competitors as Costco and Target. In one survey,

8 percent of Americans had stopped patronizing Walmart because of its reputation.[2] This was the ultimate relevance challenge. Walmart attempted to counter the negative image by refuting or repositioning the underlying assumptions, but such efforts may have made matters worse because Walmart lacked credibility to address these longstanding criticisms.

Rob Walton, Walmart's chairman and an avid outdoorsman, had been challenged during one of his outdoor adventure trips to get his firm to become a leader in addressing environmental problems, some of which he had seen up close.[3] A light bulb went off. Not only did the argument make sense to a lover of the outdoors but there was the possibility that such a visible effort could change the dialogue around Walmart or at least provide some countervailing information and sentiments that would neutralize the negative press.

In June 2004 Walton brought together the CEO Lee Scott and the environmental consultant who had challenged him in order to discuss next steps, which turned out to be a year-long assessment of Walmart's environmental scorecard. It became clear that Walmart was operating at a low level of environmental sensitivity and, surprisingly, improvement would not only help the environment but would save enormous amounts of money. Just reducing excessive packaging would save $2.4 million in shipping. For its fleet of over seven thousand trucks, the installation of an auxiliary power source to keep the cabs warm or cold during breaks could save $26 million a year. And it went on and on. It looked like a win-win-win proposition.

In August 2005 Scott announced internally that Walmart would indeed become a leader in environmental programs with specific goals in terms of sustainability. The firm developed tangible energy reduction targets for its truck fleet, stores, and products. Organic food and even clothes made from organic cotton became featured items in Walmart stores. Suppliers of environmentally responsive products or packaging, from salmon fishermen in Alaska to Unilever (whose compact detergent uses less space and packaging material than other similar products) were not only favored but supported. Suppliers, some sixty thousand of them around the world, were encouraged to become green. Fourteen networks focusing on sustainability around issues like logistics, packaging, and forest products were formed, consisting of Walmart executives, suppliers, environmental groups, and regulators, with a goal to share information and ideas. Given Walmart's footprint and influence around the world, these programs were poised to make a real difference.

In 2009 the program had proved its worth and was expanded.[4] The corporate effort, termed Sustainability 360, encompassed not only employees but suppliers, communities, and customers. A variety of goals involving programs such as renewable energy sources used for operations and environmentally friendly products ensured greater progress. To get the suppliers motivated, a Beijing Sustainability Summit was held in fall 2009. Who would have thought this level of initiative from Walmart? And the early expectation that the programs would pay for themselves was understated: the savings were more than anticipated, as was the customer response to such offerings as the organic cotton fabrics. Figure 10.1 provides a feel for the scope of the programes.

Figure 10.1 Walmart's Sustainability Message

The programs did affect the dialogue. Out of three thousand U.S. brands tracked by Y&R's Brand Asset Valuator database, Walmart was number twelve on the social responsibility scale in 2008, an incredible achievement.[5] There was one 2010 article titled "Green Project Making It Harder to Hate Walmart," and another titled "Walmart's Environmental Game Changer."[6] The hardcore Walmart critics were still there, but it was clear that their intensity and breadth were visibly lessened. The relevance challenge was not over for Walmart but it was greatly alleviated, and the trajectory was positive, a remarkable change given where the firm started only a few years before.

Avoiding the Loss of Relevance

Creating and managing the perceptions of a new product category or subcategory to make competitors irrelevant is a way to win. But another objective is to avoid losing. A brand loses by failing to maintain relevance, by becoming yesterday's brand. Maintaining relevance not only avoids losing but preserves a platform for future initiatives and successes.

How do you lose relevance? There are two ways.

One route is to lose category or subcategory relevance. Customers simply no longer want to buy what you are making, even though your offering might still be of high quality and the customers who remain love it and your firm as much as ever. If a brand is attached to a category or subcategory that is fading in relation to one that is emerging, the brand's relevance and sales will decline.

The second route is to lose energy relevance, to lose energy and the visibility that goes with it. If brands with energy are available, why consider one that is tired and has nothing new or interesting to offer? Without energy the brand may become locked in the past and suitable for an older generation. Or it may lack the visibility to be considered, it may simply fade into background noise.

This chapter will describe these two dimensions of relevance and will consider active ways to avoid having them emerge as drivers of a relevance decline. These dimensions should be part of every firm's review of brand strategy. Further, understanding how to avoid losing relevance provides additional insights into the relevance concept that will be helpful to all firms engaged in relevance competition.

Product Category or Subcategory Relevance

A brand can lose relevance because the category or subcategory to which it is attached is receding or changing such that it is no longer considered relevant. What is being bought has changed. Losing relevance in this way is insidious in part because it can happen gradually over time. Further, it can happen even if the brand is strong; the customers are loyal; and the offering, benefiting from incremental innovations, has never been better. In the Y&R's Brand Asset Valuator data base, it is clear that relevance is necessary for success; differentiation without relevance is of little value. Losing relevance is crippling and can be fatal.

The all-too-frequent problem is the following. A brand seems very strong because tracking studies show that it retains a high level of trust, esteem, perceived quality, and perhaps even perceived innovation. Customers may still be satisfied and loyal. However, its market share is slipping, perhaps dramatically, and fewer customers, particularly new customers, are considering it. Why? In many cases the brand is in trouble because the product category or subcategory with which it is associated is changing or fading, perhaps being redefined or replaced by another. The brand has become irrelevant to one or maybe more important segments.

If a group of customers wants hybrid sedans instead of SUVs, it simply does not matter how good an SUV people think you have. They might still respect your SUV, believing it has the best quality and value on the market. They may even love it and recommend it to any friend interested in an SUV. If they ever buy another SUV, they will buy yours. However, if they are interested in a hybrid sedan because of their changing sets of needs, then your brand is irrelevant to them if it is too connected to SUVs. That may be true even if your brand also makes hybrid sedans, perhaps under a subbrand, because it might lack credibility in the hybrid arena.

The ultimate tragedy is to achieve brilliance in creating differentiation, winning the preference battle, and expending precious resources behind the brand only to have that effort wasted because of a relevance problem. Consider a pay telephone company that has controlled the very best locations. Or a newspaper with the best editorial staff. Or a brand aiming for a large prestige market in fashion clothing finding that styling has changed.

What has made a brand strong can become a liability when the marketplace changes. Kirin, as noted earlier, was not perceived as a credible choice for dry beer, so when customers changed from lager to dry. Kirin was left out of the consideration set. Its strength in terms of offering the best lager with a rich lager tradition and a loyal, if older, customer base became impediments to adjusting to the new marketplace.

A brand may move into the unacceptable terrain because the bar has risen. Perhaps a competitor has created a new product that highlights a feature or a new performance standard that changes the willingness of customers to consider the brand. Or a customer trend toward healthy eating has made a dimension, such as the fat content of food, more visible and important.

The loss of relevance can also occur after a brand stumbles with respect to a key element of quality or reliability. Audi suffered for decades from a *60 Minutes* segment that suggested that one of its models had a tendency to accelerate on its own, even though that assertion was probably not true. Audi even made a design change that made such an event impossible, but the lingering memory of that publicity made Audi irrelevant for consumers who lacked the motivation to sort through the facts. Toyota, decades later, faced a comparable problem and challenge to regain the trust of the public. Similarly, Perrier once had a water contamination problem that hit at the very basis of its brand equity and affected its distribution and image.

A relatively minor feature might for some become a critical element in their decision to consider a brand. Some customers avoided German cars for years because they did not have cup holders, a quality that German engineers probably rightly felt was a signal that drivers were not serious about a love of driving. A minor attribute thus affected the decision to consider the definition of the category or subcategory. A key question to ask is "What is it about the brand that excludes it from consideration?" The answer can determine a market dynamic that is affecting relevance.

Category or Subcategory
Relevance Strategies

There are four response strategies available to a brand that is or might soon be at risk of losing category or subcategory relevance, as summarized in Figure 10.2. Each will be discussed followed by examination of the disinvest or exist option.

Figure 10.2 Responding to a Category or Subcategory Relevance Threat—Four Strategies

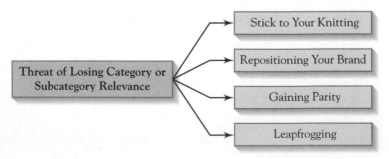

Stick to Your Knitting

The default strategy is to "stick to your knitting." Stop the erosion in sales or even reverse it by making incremental improvements, investing in brand quality, and delivering on the promise. Kirin could have argued to customer that lager was still relevant, perhaps by contemporizing the heritage or finding a way to freshen up the quality story. Perhaps they could have blunted if not reversed the surge toward dry beer.

Think of the safety razor. When electric razors were introduced in the thirties, there was a prediction that the safety razor had seen its day; the advantages of an electric shave—less mess, time, and risk—seemed compelling. However, the exact opposite happened. The safety razor won the battle and enjoyed healthy growth. In part this was due in large part to an incredible flow of innovations from Gillette from Trac II in the early 1970s to the Fusion Power in 2010. The energy and performance these advances represented eclipsed the threat of electric shaving.

Patrick Barwise and Sean Meehan provide a rationale or the "stick-to-your-knitting" strategy in their book, *Simply Better*. They argue that customers, especially of service firms, want to buy the best option, the one that is simply better than the others.[7] The assumption that customers want the unique and the differentiated is overblown according to Barwise and Meehan. Rather, they argue, it is best to just focus on delivering better and better at the core promise instead of attempting to create or join a new subcategory.

The stick-to-your-knitting strategy is certainly employed by several fast-food chains, such as In-N-Out Burger, a chain in the western United States that has developed intense loyalty with a menu of burgers, fries, shakes, and drinks and has made no effort to adjust to the healthy trend. They simply continue to deliver the same menu with uncompromising quality, consistency, and service. One assumption behind its strategy is that the healthy trend will not take over everything; there is a large, stable segment that is more interested in taste and the familiar.

The stick-to-your-knitting strategy involves supporting an effort to win by investing behind the strategy to maintain and improve the existing offering. Rather than being blind to market dynamics, the firm recognizes the emergence of new categories and subcategories and chooses to fight those trends. There is still the risk that the fight is futile and a questions as to whether fighting the new with the old is the best way to invest.

Reposition the Brand

Another route is to modify, reposition, or rebrand the offering so that its value proposition becomes more relevant given the market dynamics. Madonna has had several transformations through the years to maintain her relevance. Barbie has changed with the times, being an astronaut in 1965, a surgeon in 1973, and a presidential candidate in 1992; and in 2007 sponsoring the Web site Barbiegirls.com, on which girls can dress Barbie, furnish a room, buy stuff, and engage with others in a social network using the VIP option.

L.L.Bean, built on the authenticity of the Maine outdoorsman, has transitioned its brand in response to market dynamics. The brand's heritage—hunting, fishing, and camping—was not relevant to the heart of L.L.Bean's current marketplace, hikers, mountain bikers, cross-country skiers, and water-sports enthusiasts. Its challenge was to become germane to the new outdoor generation without abandoning that heritage. The solution was to allow the heritage to evolve in a natural way. The outdoors was treated with the same sense of awe, respect, and adventure but from a different perspective.

Gain Parity

The next option is to gain parity with respect to the competitor innovations disrupting the marketplace. Create enough change so that the customer is denied a reason to classify the brand as not relevant. Consider the fast-food industry, which has seen the development of the healthy subcategory, a shift that has challenged such traditional brands as McDonald's, Wendy's, Burger King, Pizza Hut, and KFC.

One response option for a fast-food brand is to change the menu to make it more acceptable to those seeking healthy fast-food fare, so that if there are three or four in a group selecting a fast-food destination the brand will not get the dreaded veto. McDonald's, for example, developed a way to make their signature fries with dramatically reduced "bad" fat. They also offer grilled chicken sandwiches, a variety of salads, fruit smoothies, and a choice of apples or fries in the kid's Happy Meals. Burger King has wraps plus the Garden Sensations Salads with Marzetti salad dressing that are all natural. This does not make them destinations for the healthy-eating segment, but it can reduce the veto effect.

McDonald's had another relevance problem. The success of Starbucks was a serious threat to its breakfast and other off-hours business. It was also an opportunity. The advent of McCafe in 2007, with a line that included cappuccinos and lattes, changed the competitive landscape. It created for many a point of parity with Starbucks with respect to quality. The result was that a segment of the Starbucks base started to include McDonald's in the consideration set—McDonald's became relevant, a really remarkable achievement that once would have been laughable.

There are three difficulties with this strategy. First, those attempting to gain parity, such as McDonald's in regard to healthy eating, lack brand credibility. McDonald's, for example, is associated with the signature items such as Big Mac, Egg McMuffin, and Happy Meals, which are all designed to delivery eating pleasure rather than healthy eating. Second, it is not easy to create home-run new products, without which gaining parity can be difficult. In fact, a host of McDonald's new products from McPizza to McLean Deluxe to Salad Shakers (whose containers were packed too tight to distribute the dressing) failed to gain acceptance.[8] McDonald's has had few big successes since introducing Chicken McNuggets in 1983.[9] Finally, it is not easy to deliver on the promise. Competitors who have led in a new category or subcategory are real believers, and sometimes that is what it takes.

Leapfrog the Innovation

A fourth potential strategy is to invest to create a superior product, thereby leapfrogging the brand that created and owns the new subcategory. Instead of being satisfied with being relegated to a participant with a parity product, a firm could attempt to take over the subcategory or at least to become a significant player with a substantial or transformational innovation. The payoff from a leapfrog strategy can be huge and it recognizes that a parity strategy may not be successful. An offering matching those of the early market leader of the new category or subcategory with its associated authenticity, may be inadequate to achieving relevance because the task of gaining visibility and acceptance may be too difficult.

Leapfrogging can involve improving performance around common features, adding new features, or reducing or eliminating major limitations. Consider Amazon's blockbuster hit the Kindle, the digital book reader introduced in November 2007 and refined over the years with significant improvements.

Sony and Apple were among the competitors attempting to leapfrog the Kindle. Sony's e-book Reader attempted to surpass the Kindle with touch-screen control of page turning, the option of writing on the page margins directly, a higher contrast screen, and an open source system providing access to millions of books from sources such as some nine thousand bookstores, libraries, and Google, which offers free digital books. Apple, in contrast, created the iPad alternative, which makes book reading only one application out of a much larger set. The hope of Apple is that users will read books on the iPad making the Kindle irrelevant. Kindle is fighting the newcomers with new models and aggressively expanding its Amazon library of Kindle books.

Cisco has again and again turned a parity move into a leapfrog. It looks closely at the market and finds areas in which it has gaps caused by market dynamics. It then closes those gaps through expeditious acquisitions. The acquisition may involve parity products but when combined with the Cisco portfolio and broad systems perspective, it becomes a leapfrog. That was never more true than in 1993 when Cisco, then the first company that offered routes that worked in multiple protocols, made its first acquisition. The customers were starting to signal that switches not offered by Cisco were a key piece in their network systems. Cisco then acquired Crescendo, then a leading switch maker, paying a breathtaking premium that later proved to be a bargain. Once in the Cisco fold the switch business took off and provided the basis for what is today a major part of the Cisco business. The Cisco business strategy is to recognize and capitalize on customer-driven market transitions before they occur and then find a way to become the leaders in an emerging competitive arena.

Disinvest or Exit

If the response options are unattractive or not feasible, the remaining alternative is to disinvest, withhold or withdraw resources for the business, or exit. This strategy involves shifting investments from a declining product market to one that is rising. P&G has exited from most of its food business brands, for example, and invested in cosmetics and skin care, for which the growth and margins are better. GE, whose story is told in the next chapter, has gone into a host of renewable energy businesses and disinvested or exited from others in more mature industries.

Disinvestment from a business is a very painful, unexciting, but vital part of a firm's ability to deal with dynamic markets. One key to business success is to identify what you do not want to do and to be disciplined abut that judgment so that investment is reduced or eliminated toward business areas that are not prioritized.

The disinvest or exit decision is particularly difficult when it represents the heritage of the firm. Objectivity and discipline is needed. Andy Grove famously told about when he and Gordon Moore, the top executives at Intel, imagined what new top management would do with the memory business under attack from Asian companies. With that perspective the painful decision to withdrawal from Intel's legacy business became easy.

Select the Right Response

Which response? The answer will be context specific, but it will involve two questions.

First, What can you do? What is the feasibility of each of the four nondivest response options, given the strengths, weakness, and strategies of the firm? To what extent will one of them result in a long-term success? Which is superior in terms of risk and reward? There should be a realism about the firm's ability to innovate and add capabilities especially considering the difficulty to maintain organizational support for a new approach in the face of other opportunities. There is no point in doing something just to do something. There should be a success prospect that merits the risk and investment.

Second, What do you want or need to do? Do you want to invest to maintain relevance in an emerging category or subcategory? A key step is to evaluate the threat or opportunity and supporting trend that an emerging category or subcategory poses. What is for real? Most trends are complex and intertwined. In the healthy fast-food context, for example, there are chains offering veggie burgers and baked fries; sandwich brands like Subway; fast-casual sandwich shops like Panera Bread; restaurants serving such ethnic food as Japanese and Thai cuisines and on and on. What exactly emerges from this complexity? What are the impact, urgency, and validity of the threat or opportunity?

Energy Relevance

Losing energy relevance is also a threat to established brands, even those that are market leaders with a surplus of trust, perceived quality, and customer loyalty. A brand can lose energy and become tired, old fashioned, and bland. It might still be a great offering and an excellent choice for your father or grandfather, but not contemporary enough for you. It no longer fits. Further, visibility goes down with energy. The brand is no longer among those that come to mind when considering a purchase. It is lost in the noise of the environment. It is no longer relevant.

As noted earlier, the Y&R Brand Asset Valuator database has shown empirically that relevance and differentiation are the bases for a brand's success. But recent studies of the entire database found that another component is needed: energy.[10] An analysis of the total database, including over forty thousand brands and over forty countries from 1993 to 2007, showed that brand equities as measured by trustworthiness, esteem, perceived quality, and awareness have been falling sharply over the years. For example, in the last twelve years trustworthiness dropped nearly 50 percent; esteem fell by 12 percent; brand quality perceptions fell by 24 percent; and, remarkably, even awareness fell by 24 percent. A significant exception were those brands with energy, which remained healthy and retained their ability to drive financial returns.

The energy relevance challenge might be made worse by competitors who introduce new entries or applications or have succeeded in smothering the brand's visibility with heavy advertising or market presence. In any case the brand with inadequate energy, although familiar and trusted, is no longer being thought of at the time of purchase or use.

When a brand lacks energy and visibility, it can move into the "graveyard," a concept introduced in Chapter Two. A graveyard brand is one the customer has heard of and probably is very familiar with but one that is not recalled easily and cannot get into the consideration set. Being a graveyard brand is a substantial handicap because it is hard to generate interest in a brand when the audience assumes that they are already familiar with it. Why pay attention to information about something about which they already know plenty and in which they have little interest?

Energizing a brand may be the most important challenge facing the majority of brands, and for brands with potential energy-driven relevance issues, creating energy may be an imperative.

We turn to two ways to energize the brand—energizing the business or creating a branded energizer.

Energize the Business

The best way to energize a business is by improving the offering through innovation. Apple, Nintendo, Yamaha, Toyota, Virgin, the Memphis Redbirds baseball team, and many others have a continuous flow of innovations that create interest and visibility.

However, that route is not always open. In many cases, successful innovation is elusive even with motivated efforts, talented people, creative processes, and healthy budgets. And innovations that really make a difference, that rise above those that simply maintain a market position, are even more rare. Further, some businesses compete in product categories that are either mature or boring—or both. Whether you make hot dogs or market insurance, it is hard to conceive of new offerings that are going to energize the marketplace. So the need then is to look beyond the offering for ways to make the brand interesting, involving, dynamic, enthusiastic, and even a topic of conversation. Some suggestions follow.

Involve the Customer. Promotions that involve the customer elevate the energy level of the brand and business. Coke Zero, for example, asked basketball fans to upload their most fanatical videos and photos supporting their favorite teams, and winners were shown in a special show before the championship game.

Attaching a social network to the brand is a way to gain involvement. As noted earlier, the Betty Crocker Mixer Web site invites members to talk to experts and connect with others and, on the Harley-Davidson Web site bikers can post pictures of their most recent ride.

Go Retail. A brand can tell its story best if it can control the context. The Apple store is a good part of the success of its products and brand because it presents the Apple line in a way that is completely on-brand. The influence of the Apple store goes beyond the customer experience by making a statement that affects the image. It is not necessary to have a chain to capture substantial sales. Nike and Sony have statement stores that serve to present the brand and offer their stories in compelling and integrative ways.

A brand can also bring the retail experience to the customers. TaylorMade golf equipment representatives travel to golf clubs to demonstrate and sell its equipment, giving customers a more vivid and on-brand way to experience them than they would get in a sporting goods store. Target created the thirty-day Bullseye Bazaar in Chicago to introduce the Tracy Feith Clothing collection, the private-label food line from Archer Farms, and Target furniture as influential.

Hold Publicity Events. Holding publicity events can be a way to gain visibility and even attract conversation. Consider the balloon adventures of Virgin's Richard Branson, the BMW short films created by top directors, or the Snuggie blanket (the blanket you wear) given to media personalities. In each case millions were exposed to the brand in such a way as to emphasize its connection to customers and vitality.

Use Promotions to Attract New Customers. Whereas existing customers may view the brand as old hat, new customers provide not only sales growth but new eyes. It is, of course, difficult to attract new customers, particularly if the brand is already well known. Denny's addressed that problem by giving away more than two million Grand Slam Breakfasts in one day with the help of a Super Bowl commercial and online buzz. Free breakfasts broke through.

Branded Energizer

Another approach, very different from trying to make the brand or business interesting or involving, is to find a branded energizer. A *branded energizer* is a branded product, promotion, sponsorship, symbol, program, or other entity that by association significantly enhances and energizes a target brand. The idea is to find something with energy, attach the brand to it, and then actively manage both the branded energizer and its association with the target brand over an extended time period.

A branded energizer, as the definition and Figure 10.3 suggests, can come from a wide variety of branded entities, some could be sourced outside the firm, but needs to have energy. It should be interesting, youthful, dynamic, contemporary, assertive, and involving.

The branded energizer also needs to be connected to the target brand. This connection task can be difficult and expensive.

Figure 10.3 Branded Energizers

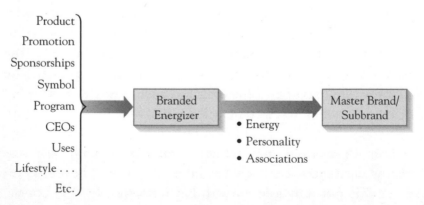

Product
Promotion
Sponsorships
Symbol
Program
CEOs
Uses
Lifestyle . . .
Etc.

Branded Energizer

• Energy
• Personality
• Associations

Master Brand/ Subbrand

Even the Energizer bunny, one of the top icons among U.S. brands, is associated by some with its competitor, Duracell, rather than Eveready despite the exposure over a long time period.

One route to establishing such a connection is to use a sub-brand with the target brand as the master brand, for example Ronald McDonald House, Avon Breast Cancer Crusade, or Adidas Streetball Challenge. All have the target brand in the brand name of the energizer. A second is to select a program or activity that is so on-brand that it makes the link easier to establish. A baby-oriented program, for example, would require little effort to connect to Gerber. Whirlpool and Home Depot have a mutual connection to Habitat for Humanity, a program of building homes for the less fortunate. A third is to simply forge the link by consistently building it over time, as MetLife has done with the *Peanuts* characters.

A branded energizer should significantly enhance as well as energize the target brand and should not detract from or damage the brand by being off-brand or making customers uncomfortable. Offbeat, underdog brands, such as Virgin, Apple, Nike, or Mountain Dew, which are perceived as unpredictable to begin with, have some leeway. "Senior" brands, in contrast, can develop branded energizers edgier than the parent brand but have a lot of options foreclosed; these brands risk offending if they are too edgy.

The problems of finding and managing internal branded energizers lead firms to look outside the organization. The challenge is to find an external energizer brand that is linked into the lifestyle of customers, that will have the needed associations to energize and enhance, that is not tied to competitors, that can be linked to the target brand, and that represents a manageable alliance. This task takes discipline and creativity.

Branded energizers represent a long-term commitment; the brands involved should be expected to have long lives and merit brand-building investments. If the energizers are internally developed, the cost of brand building will have to be amortized over a long enough period to make it worthwhile. If they are externally sourced, the additional cost and effort of linking them to the parent brand will also take time and resources. In either case, they need to be actively managed over time so that they can continue to be successful in their roles.

Two effective branded energizers, sponsorships and programs, illustrate the power of the concept.

Branded Sponsorships. A sponsorship can be an effective energizer. Although Valvoline motor oil is a rather utilitarian product, when it becomes part of the NASCAR scene through sponsorship everything changes. Valvoline leverages its sponsorship with a Web site that is a destination for racing fans. A visitor can access the schedules and results, complete with pictures and interviews. A "Behind Closed Garage Doors" section provides inside information and analyses. There are Valvoline racing greeting cards, a line of racing gear to be ordered, and a weekly newsletter (*TrackTalk*) that provides updates on the racing circuits. Valvoline thus becomes closely associated with the racing experience, much more than simply being a logo on a car. Such a link can pay off. One study found that 60 percent of NASCAR fans said they trusted sponsors' products (as compared to 30 percent of NFL fans), and more than 40 percent switch brands when a company becomes a sponsor.[11]

A sponsorship can provide the ultimate relevance impact, the movement of a brand upward into the acceptable if not leadership position. A software firm trying unsuccessfully to make a dent in the European market became a perceived leader in a few months when it sponsored one of the top three bicycle racing teams in Europe. Part of Samsung's breakthrough from being just another Korean price brand to becoming a real player in the U.S. market was its ongoing sponsorship of the Olympics, which began with the Nagano Winter Games of 1998. Olympic sponsorship says so much about the brand, especially a brand aspiring to a leadership position, so much more than product advertising could ever say.

Tracking data confirms that well-conceived and well-managed sponsorships can make a difference. Visa's lead in perceived credit card superiority went from fifteen percentage points (the percent believing Visa is the best card less the percent attributing superiority to the next closest competitor) prior to the Olympics to thirty points during to twenty points one month after—huge movements in what are normally very stable attitudes.[12]

A significant problem with sponsorship—indeed, with any external branded energizer—is linking it to the brand. DDB Needham's Sponsor-Watch, which measures such linkage, has shown that sponsorship confusion is common.[13] Of the 102 official Olympic sponsors tracked since 1984, only about half have built a link (defined as the percent who believed that a brand was an Olympic sponsor) of at least 15 percent and at least 10 percent higher than that of a competitor who was not a sponsor, hardly demanding criteria. Those successful at creating links, such as Visa and Samsung, surrounded the sponsorships with a host of brand-driven activities and features including promotions, publicity events, relevant Web site content, newsletters, and advertising over an extended time period.

Although most sponsorships are external to the firm, there are cases of internally controlled sponsorships. The Adidas Streetball Challenge is a branded weekend event, started in Germany in the mid-nineties, centered around local three-person basketball tournaments and featuring free-throw competitions, a street dance, graffiti events, and extreme sports demonstrations—all accompanied by live music from bands from the hip-hop and rap scenes. The Challenge hit right on the sweet spot of target customers, for them it does not get any better than a weekend party. And it was connected to Adidas by its brand and supporting signage, and Adidas supplied caps and jackets. It revitalized Adidas at a critical time in its history. Owning a sponsorship means that the future cost is both controllable and predictable and that it can evolve over time adding or deleting features as feedback flows in and the brand changes its products and message.

Branded Social Programs. Branded social programs can pay off by helping establish a customer relationship based on trust and respect. However, they can also provide energy by generating interest, and even passion, tangible results, and opportunities for customer involvement. Consider the energy created by the Avon Breast Cancer Crusade. Its signature Avon Walk for Breast Cancer has raised over $650 million for the fight against breast cancer and involved not only participants but also family members and sponsors. That interest and that energy could never have been created by Avon products, however new and different they might appear to be. And the Walk is branded as Avon complete with a logo.

Creating branded social programs can be effectively costless in that existing philanthropy dollars that are being spent without focus or impact can be diverted into branded social programs. However, such programs are also extremely hard to generate: there are firms that would like to create Avon Walk–type programs but simply can't come up with any. Kellie McElhaney, the director of the Center for Responsible Business at the Haas School at U.C. Berkeley, has suggested several guiding principles for creating a successful program.[14]

Leverage Organizational Assets and Values. The firm should aspire to add value to the program rather than just investing money. It should leverage its values, assets, and competencies. To do so the firm should address very basic questions as to who they are, their strengths and weaknesses, and what they want to stand for.

Be Authentic. There should be a logical fit with the program. Avon's program hits on a key concern of its target market and reflects a relationship with its customers that goes beyond product. The same can be said for Crest's Healthy Smiles (low-cost dental care for poor children), Home Depot's relationship with Habitat for Humanity, and Dove's Real Women. In contrast, many firms have laudable charitable initiatives that lack a logical link to their business and brands and that affects both effectiveness and credibility. For example, Ford's association with the Susan G. Komen for the Cure breast cancer foundation (with Ford donations attached to buying a pink-trimmed Mustang) lacked a logical fit.

Create an Emotional Connection. An emotional connection with customers and potential customers in general communicates much more about a brand than does a set of facts and logic, and enhances the relationship as well. The emotional message is punchier and simpler. So Pedigree's Adoption Drive with its pictures of adorable dogs triggers an emotional response and gives the Pedigree brand a life as something more than a firm that makes pet food. Similarly, the Ronald McDonald House's program that helps children with serious medical conditions and their families presents the emotional side of the kids and the family message of McDonalds.

Involve the Customer. A branded energizer will be more powerful if customers become involved. Involvement is the ultimate way to gain supporters and advocates. Method, a maker of environmentally safe cleaning products, has a brand ambassador program through which customers who sign on will get products and t-shirts and information about why their friends should use the products. Avon's Walk for Breast Cancer perhaps the ultimate involvement energizer, involves hundreds of thousands of participants and supporters each year.

Communicate the Program. There are a host of companies spending real money on programs that are unknown to their customers and potential customers and, often, to their employees. To achieve the objectives of advancing a social cause, energizing the employees, and enhancing the reputation of a corporate brand, the firm needs to communicate its program. That involves accessing the right set of communication tools, including the Web site, social technology, PR, and active employees.

Beware of making the program too complex, too detailed, and too quantitative. Simple, involving stories or metaphors with vivid, understandable messages are best. Brand strategists are discovering the effectiveness of stories to break through the clutter with interesting and memorable messaging.

Gaining Relevance—The Hyundai Case

We have been discussing the threat of losing relevance for a firm that is competing in an established category or subcategory. There is another context in which relevance is a key driver— the case in which a firm wants to become relevant in an established category or subcategory. It turns out that the same two dimensions of relevance apply: the firm needs to establish both category or subcategory relevance and energy relevance. The Hyundai case illustrates.

The Hyundai Challenges

Hyundai entered the U.S. car market in 1986 with the subcompact Excel, which used borrowed technology including a Mitsubishi powertrain. With an enticingly affordable price, the car sold over 100,000 units. Two years later and into the 1990s, however, Hyundai failed to prioritize quality and instead focused on cost reduction to maintain its large sticker-price advantage. The result was disastrous. Many quality problems emerged that had a substantial influence on the reputation and brand image of Hyundai for years, creating a relevance problem. People no longer considered Hyundai a viable option.

Hyundai remarkably overcame this poor reputation and its sales started growing in 1998 from under 100,000 units to 467,000 units in 2007, and nearly that much in 2009 despite a collapsed auto market. How did they achieve this result? The first challenge was to create cars and processes that would deliver quality. In 1999, Chairman Mong-Koo Chung took over the company and switched Hyundai's priority from volume to high quality. He announced the "quality management" program of which he would be in charge. This all-out effort to improve quality was successful in a surprisingly short period of time. In 2001 Hyundai was near the bottom of auto makers in the United States by J. D. Power in their Initial Quality Study (IQS). In 2004, however, Hyundai was among the top three car manufacturers in the same study, even ahead of quality guru Toyota. Hyundai finally was making high-quality cars.

Building high quality was not enough, however. It was also necessary to convince a skeptical and disinterested public. That was not easy. The J. D. Power quality ratings were helpful, but so was an aggressive warranty called the Hyundai Advantage, the industry's first ten-year, 100,000 mile warranty on the powertrain. It was marketed and promoted as "America's Best Warranty," an offer that rather vividly demonstrated Hyundai's willingness to put an enormous amount of money behind its confidence in the quality level. The warranty took the quality risk out of buying a Hyundai. Consumers gradually changed their minds about Hyundai's quality, and as a result Hyundai became relevant to those interested in cars that were economical to buy and operate.

A second challenge was based on a perception that the design of the Hyundai cars, befitting a low-cost entry, was bland. To address the design relevance issue, Hyundai built a North American R&D and design center in 2003. The mid-size sedan Sonata and compact SUV Tucson reflected Hyundai's new design direction, "Fluidic Sculpture." Designed and developed in the United States, these cars appealed to many new consumers who had never considered Hyundai before.

The third challenge was to overcome the resistance of some customers to buy brands made outside the United States. To "Americanize" Hyundai, the firm opened a 1.1-billion-dollar plant in Alabama in 2005 with a capacity of 300,000 cars.

A fourth relevance challenge emerged when Hyundai went after the premium market of Lexus, BMW, and Cadillac with their Genesis sedan, introduced in 2008. People bought premium cars for reasons other than saving money on the price and operation of the cars. They wanted some self-expressive benefits, a feeling that they were driving the best. Telling the Hyundai story with advertisements during prestigious, visible events like the Super Bowl and the FIFA World Cup helped, but the big breakthrough was when the Hyundai Genesis was named the North American Car of the Year at the 2009 Detroit Auto Show by a jury of fifty independent automotive journalists. That event helped Hyundai become a more respectable and modern premium brand for the target market.

Overcoming the four challenges was helped by creative and effective marketing and customer programs as evidenced by *Advertising Age* naming Hyundai as the marketer of the year in 2009. The most visible and successful was its pledge through the "Hyundai Assurance Program" in the early months of 2009 when the United States and world economy was very sick that it would take back a car from anyone who lost a job after the car was purchased. With many hesitant to buy because of employment uncertainty, it was a significant risk reducer. But for many others, it meant that Hyundai actually "got it"; they understood the times, empathized with their customers, and were willing to share the economic risks that people were facing.

Hyundai made significant relevance progress in that the percent of car buyers will to consider its cars rose to over 30 percent in 2009, three times what it was five years earlier. Despite the progress, Hyundai still had a lot of upside with respect to relevance. There were many who were not convinced that Hyundai had "arrived" with respect to quality. Others were skeptical that Hyundai belonged in the premium care subcategory, and there was still a substantial segment for which the brand had little visibility. As a result, in summer 2010 Hyundai introduced the Hyundai "Uncensored" campaign, whereby 125 new customers were given cars to drive, and their uncensored comments would be posted for all to see on the Hyundai Facebook page and incorporated into Hyundai ads. The goal was to increase consideration levels.

Hyundai grew its share from almost nothing in 1998 to over 4.7 percent in 2010 by understanding its market, by having a sound and well-executed strategy, and by successfully overcoming four relevance challenges.

The Challenge of Gaining Relevance

For a firm to gain relevance in an established category or subcategory, it needs to address the two relevance challenges: category or subcategory relevance and energy relevance.

Hyundai actually was faced with four category or subcategory relevance challenges. It gained credibility in the automobile category by making improvements to quality and offering a reassuring warranty. Hyundai also removed or lessened two reasons not to buy by installing a U.S. manufacturing plant and creating a new branded design program, making the cars relevant for a larger group. Gaining credibility with respect to the premium subcategory was an additional challenge. A critical factor was Hyundai's ability to win and then exploit the Car of

Figure 10.4 2009 Car of the Year

the Year award by advertising the recognition and by using it to reassure prospective buyers that they could be proud of a decision to buy the Genesis.

Hyundai also was able to provide energy relevance, an indispensable part of its success. Energy came from prestige sponsorships, from the branded warranty, and from the dramatic offer to accept cars back from those who lost jobs. In each case the energy was not only from the initiative but also from Hyundai's ability to capitalize with marketing and publicity.

Success in achieving relevance is always relative and Hyundai chose to build on the momentum and attempt to expand further the number of customers for whom Hyundai is relevant. The vehicle was the Hyundai Uncensored initiative.

Hyundai's branding strategy has been helpful in climbing these mountains. "America's Best Warranty," "Fluidic Sculpture," the "Hyundai Assurance Program," and Hyundai Uncensored all made more feasible the effort to communicate credibility and to gain visibility. These brands also helped the message stick and thus enhanced the brand equity going forward.

In order to encourage and enable new competitive arenas as well as have timely response to relevance threats and challenges, the right kind of organization needs to be in place and that is not easy to achieve. Three organizational forms that represent inconsistent sets of competencies, cultures, and processes are needed. The next chapter elaborates.

Key Takeaways

Brands can lose relevance even when their offerings are performing exceptionally well and customers are loyal.

One reason for this phenomenon is the loss of category or subcategory relevance due to the firm's failure to make what customers are now buying (for example, they are making SUVs when the customer wants a hybrid sedan). To combat this a firm can stick to its knitting, can reposition the brand, can gain parity, or can leapfrog other firms' innovations. If all fail, then disinvest may be appropriate.

A second reason is the loss of energy and visibility. To ward off this problem, a firm can energize the business or create a branded energizer. A business can be energized by new products, customer involvement, a retail presence, publicity events, and promotions. A branded energizer is something such as a sponsorship, social program, promotion, or product that has energy and is connected to the target brand.

Brands attempting to become relevant in established categories or subcategories need to address the same two relevance challenges.

For Discussion

1. Identify some brands that have ceased to be relevant. Why?

2. What are some brands that lost their relevance and have gained it back? How have they done this?

3. Identify some effective branded energizers.

11

THE INNOVATIVE ORGANIZATION

> In many companies the premium placed on being
> "right" is so high that there is virtually no room for
> speculation and imagination.
>
> —*Gary Hamel, strategy guru*

> We have met the enemy and he is us.
>
> —*Pogo*

Creating substantial or transformational innovation that will drive a new category or subcategory is difficult in any case, but without a supportive organization, the odds against become huge. The right organization does not just happen. It often requires a change initiative, a cohesive set or programs, effective objectives and incentives, and the right people. Only a few have been successful at doing so. That is why the GE story is so instructive and inspirational. GE has taken its innovation heritage going back to Edison and the light bulb and given it a new direction and a new intensity.

GE Story

On September 10, 2001, one day before the infamous 9/11 event, Jeff Immelt took over as CEO of GE from the fabled Jack Welch, who had run GE for two decades.[1] Welch implemented a strategy that involved aggressive cost reduction, systematic efforts to create exceptional managers, forceful performance evaluation of executives, and developing a portfolio of businesses through acquisition and divestiture that were number one or two in their marketplaces. Growing the business from $25 billion to over $100 billion, Welch was one of the most respected CEOs of his time.

Immelt concluded that a change in strategy, dictated by the changed GE and the realities of a dynamic marketplace, was needed. The core GE business units were large and established, and Welch's acquisition and cost containment strategies were no longer going to be a sound basis for growth. Instead, Immelt decided that the focus needed to be on organic growth and needed to be fueled by innovation. To support the strategy, the organization needed to change, and change rather radically.

The signature program, initiated in late 2003, was the internally branded Imagination Breakthrough (IB) initiative, in which each business each year is charged to propose three breakthrough proposals that would realize a $100 million potential in a three- to five-year time frame. To be selected as an IB project by an Immelt-led commercial council, a proposal needed to demonstrate not only the market projection and economic viability but that it had the potential to transform markets. Funding, if needed, was available from an internal "venture capital" source. The central marketing group that led the IB process provided a planning framework that included such dimensions as calibrating the idea, exploring it in the market, creating the offering, organizing to deliver it, and executing in the marketplace. Four years after it was launched, the IB initiative was adding $2 to $3 billion in sales each year and had some forty-five IB projects under way.[2] One was the GE Rail Evolution Locomotive, a fuel-efficient diesel locomotive that meets the aggressive emission standards created in 2005 by the Environmental Protection Agency.

To accentuate the renewed innovation culture, Immelt elevated the innovation thrust of the GE training effort, the centerpiece of which was the John F. Welch Leadership Center in Crotonville, New York, which trains some six thousand employees each year. The center was asked to enhance innovation-oriented content and build growth-oriented programs and objectives. For example, the center created the two-day "Industry 2015" series, such as Healthcare 2015 or Energy 2015, to stretch the minds of executives for whom those topics were central to strategy.

Another change involved the evaluation of people, a key component of the development of GE's envied management team. The existing dimensions around performance were augmented by, innovation- and growth-oriented measures to give incentives to managers to take innovation risks.

There was also a systematic effort to build creativity into the planning process. In part that involved getting executives with innovation agendas into settings outside their normal comfort zone.[3] GE consumer finance executives took a tour of San Francisco, focusing on how people use their money and even how they carry it. When the GE health-care team wanted to research neo-natal equipment, they interviewed not only doctors but others in the specialty facility, such as nurses, receptionists, and even janitors. The top executives of GE's jet engine business talked to pilots and mechanics, and then visited a high-end grocery store and a toy store. The idea is to provide a different perspective on a given industry and its unmet needs. A Star Wars toy, for example, might trigger an insight about the design of a jet engine.

Immelt felt that additional assets and capabilities were needed to support the new innovation strategy and culture. He thus invested in the GE Global Research Center in New York and in other GE research centers around the world as drivers of innovation in specialized areas. For example, the firm's capability in biotechnology was strengthened. Some of these research centers' efforts were funded and controlled by the business units, but close to 30 percent were funded by Immelt and had license to go beyond or between the existing business silos.[4]

The innovation thrust emphasized cross-business fertilizing. Crotonville, by bringing people together from across the firm, had long fostered cross-silo communication and cooperation. One of the Global Research Center's functions is to leverage technology by applying it throughout the firm's business units. To further develop cross-silo cooperation, Immelt encouraged teams from across the company to engage in innovation focused around products and opportunities. As a part of this effort, Immelt started Session T (T stands for technology), through which a marketing team for one business and a technology team from a very different business meet with the center's scientists and talk about a market need. It was in such a meeting that the energy group was able to learn about lightweight materials developed by the aircraft engine business that could be applied to the wind business. The wind business also reached out to rail business experts to improve the gearing systems of the wind products. These improvements and others allowed the wind business, which GE purchased from Enron in 2002 for around $350 million, to grow to some $6 billion in sales six years later.

The new GE innovation culture affected the way the brand was presented to the market as well. The venerable slogan "We bring good things to life" was replaced with "Imagination at work," a concept that resonated with employees as well as customers and reinforced the growth-through-innovation thrust.

As part of the new GE growth strategy to become an innovation leader in the ecology and energy space, Immelt in 2005 launched ecomagination to provide an umbrella brand over all the GE green initiatives, illustrated by the GE ad shown in Figure 11.1. By branding the innovative wind, solar, and other green business units, GE generated a sense of cohesiveness for an important part of its business strategy and provided a vehicle to get marketplace credit for the strategy. The resulting image not only enhanced the perceived innovativeness of the firm but also provided a basis for a relationship with the green segment.

Figure 11.1 GE's Ecomagination

FUEL CONSERVATION. LOWER EMISSIONS. RENEWABLE ENERGY.

SOME OF THE WAYS ECOMAGINATION IS

INCREASING AMERICA'S ENERGY

INDEPENDENCE

NOW.

 imagination at work   **eco**magination

Ecomagination was followed in 2009 with healthymagina-tion, which is positioned to deliver health to the marketplace.[5] The theme is to bring technology and health care together in a way that lowers costs, increases access, and improves the quality of health care for people throughout the world. Like ecomagination, it packages and provides a central strategic theme for many of the health care business lines. One of several initiatives is to help create electronic medical records for all Americans, a program that can save tens of billions of dollars annually.

What is impressive about this story is that GE, a company with a rich tradition of innovation, saw its, innovation capability and priority reenergized with a revised culture, a host of programs, and an organization-wide allocation process, all in the context of a new strategic direction. GE definitely took innovation to a new level. It was opportunistic in terms of finding growth areas in which GE could add value through innovation. At the same time, GE was able to commit to and deliver on these selected growth areas, in part because of its overarching strategy around health care and energy.

The Innovative Organization

Becoming an innovative firm capable of engaging in substantial and transformational innovation that will create new categories or subcategories requires an enabling organization. It sounds straightforward to apply the linear process outlined in this book of conceiving an offering capable of driving a new category or subcategory, evaluating and committing to the offering idea, defining and managing the new category or subcategory, building barriers, and executing it competently. But it is just not easy in the face of organizational realities.

The rude fact is that not all organizations allow ideas to emerge, nurture those ideas, and implement them in the marketplace. It takes a certain type of organization to provide the support needed. Most organizations lack the culture, systems, structure, and people to allow the concept to emerge and then to fund and manage it to success. Sometimes the home-run idea never emerges, and other times the organization is not right or not ready when opportunity knocks, especially when new assets and competencies are required or when the new concepts compete with established businesses for resources.

Figure 11.2 An Innovative Organization

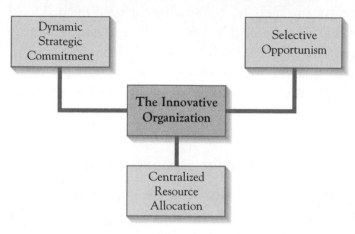

An innovative organization is difficult to create because it really requires three characteristics that are inconsistent with one another. The organization needs simultaneously to be selectively opportunistic, to commit behind a project without being stubborn, and to have an organization-wide resource allocation system. Figure 11.2 summarizes. A weakness in any one of these components can set back success probabilities and, ultimately, cause the firm not only to lose opportunities but also to lose relevance.

Tuchman and O'Reilly, prominent organizational researchers, argue that there is a need to be an ambidextrous organization, to be able to be committed to a set of businesses and still be agile, aggressive, entrepreneurial, innovative, and opportunistic.[6] They believe that organizations facing dynamic markets need to find ways to be both, and they assert that it is difficult but possible and is being done successfully. What is argued here is that an organization needs to be "multidextrous" in that it needs also to be an organization-wide resource allocator, an ambitious but not impossible goal. Firms have found ways to develop supportive cultures, creative structures, flexible systems and processes, and a broad set of people assets to achieve capabilities in all three areas.

What follows is a discussion of the type of organization, its culture, systems, people, and structure, that is needed to succeed in developing each of the three types of organizational characteristics. The challenge is formidable, but the good news is that it is also a challenge for potential competitors, which means those organizations that get it right can have a significant, sustainable advantage.

Selective Opportunism

The organization practicing selective opportunism actively but selectively seeks to identify opportunities by insight or technology development, and then takes advantage of them. An application or unmet need from a customer announces an opening for a new offering. A technological development inside or outside the firm provides a concept that has potential. A shortage of a commodity creates a need. A market trend leads to a new concept.

The idea is that the environment is so dynamic and uncertain that the prudent and profitable route is to detect and capture opportunities when they present themselves. The concept of being selective implies that opportunities need to be screened with respect to their potential and strategic fit. The search for opportunities is not undisciplined or aimless.

Selective opportunism results in economies of scope (synergy due to multiple offerings), with assets and competencies supported by multiple product lines. Nike, for example, applies its brand assets and competencies in product design and customer sensing to a wide variety of product markets. A key part of the Nike strategy is to develop strong emotional ties and relationships with focused segments through its product design and brand-name strengths. The organization is extremely sensitive to emerging segments (such as outdoor basketball) and the need for product refinements and product innovation. Nike's participation in multiple sports and products give it strategic flexibility, a quality that has characterized many successful selectively opportunistic firms.

Entrepreneurial Culture

Success in selective opportunism requires an entrepreneurial culture and the willingness to respond quickly to opportunities as they emerge. The people should be entrepreneurial, sensitive to new opportunities and threats, and fast to react. The organization needs to be decentralized, with people empowered to experiment and invest behind emerging opportunities. The culture needs to support empowered managers, new ventures, and change. The strategy will be dynamic and change the norm. New offerings will be continuously explored or introduced, and others deemphasized or dropped. The firm will enter new markets, and disinvestment from existing ones will always be an option. The organization will be on the lookout for assets and competencies to leverage and new synergies to nurture.

Both insight and action are needed, and people and the organization need to be empowered to deliver both. The insight has to be in place before events overwhelm and opportunities are lost. And action is part of the equation. Xerox, in its remarkable Palo Alto Research Center (PARC) created in 1970, developed the first personal computer, the graphical interface, the mouse, the flat-panel display, the Ethernet standard for local area networks, and the laser printer. They were not able to turn any of these innovations into products—an amazing and instructive story of inaction. The firm was paralyzed by a focus on its successful core business and its business model, and the PARC center, away from the organization's East Coast center of gravity, was perceived to be a think tank and was unable to get the attention of the Xerox executives. The firm lacked most of the qualities of an opportunistic organization.

External Orientation

A selectively opportunistic organization needs to be externally oriented toward the market and surrounding environment rather than being internally oriented. The culture, people, and systems need to encourage the pursuit of current, relevant market information and then facilitate processing and acting on it. Strategy development needs to be outside in and market driven rather than based on leveraging existing assets, competencies, and strategies.

Supported by an externally oriented culture, the management team should be curious about what is going on in the market in regard to not only customers but also competitors and the distribution chain. What is working and what are the problems? The team needs to be talking to customers and others about changing customer tastes, attitudes, and needs. This does not happen automatically, in part because managers tend to focus on and sometimes get overwhelmed by day-to-day crises.

An opportunistic organization, to be close to trends and developments driving opportunities, should have an effective, silo-spanning information system, a system that will not only store and organize information but will facilitate turning it into timely strategic insights. The system, often based on an intranet, can enable the sharing of market information pertaining to customer insights, trends, competitor actions, technological developments, and best practices. Developing a system that avoids information gaps and information overload is very difficult. It depends on the cooperation and support of both information generators and information users. Not easy at all.

Breaking the Silo Trap

A opportunistic firm needs to break out of the silo trap. Managers of silo business units have a bias toward incremental innovation to improve their own offerings. Breakthrough new offerings that will be game changers are more likely to emerge when two other sources of innovation are accessed.

The first is cross-silo innovation whereby a strength or asset of one silo is combined with one of another. The result can be an offering that not only represents an important advance but also will be uniquely owned by the firm. GE is a firm that has cracked the code of cross-silo innovation, and many of their breakthroughs have resulted from their ability to span silos. A key to the ongoing success of the Yamaha Disklavier was the ability of the Yamaha organization to have its electronics groups work intimately with Yamaha Music, an ability that several other Japanese firms notably lack.

The second is between-silo innovation. There may well be innovative offerings that can draw on the organization's assets and competencies that don't fit into an existing silo. To access between-silo space, a central group, such as the GE Global Research Center, can play a key role.

To break down silo barriers, the organization needs to establish systems supported by a culture that values silo communication and cooperation as opposed to the sometimes more natural isolation and competition. Anything that advances the goal works. Bringing people together, as in the Crotonville sessions; rotating people between silos; having central marketing teams act as facilitators and service providers and thereby becoming communication nodes; using cross-silo teams; and having common programs, such as an Olympic sponsorship, can all help to change the silo reality. The book *Spanning Silos*, which reports on a study of over forty CMOs, elaborates.[7]

Reorganizing the firm from being a product-defined business to an organization centered on applications or customer groupings will reduce or eliminate silo barriers to innovation. HP in the early 2000s recognized that it had lost its innovation culture. They termed one route to revive it "inventing at the intersection." Until 2001, HP made stand-alone products and innovations ranging from $20 ink cartridges to $3 million servers. To break down silo barriers in order to gain marketing insight, innovation, and improved customer service, the firm established three "cross-company initiatives"—wireless services, digital imaging, and commercial printing. The result was a renewed focus on what customers are buying and an increased ability to detect unmet needs. The concept was good but hard to implement because there is such a high level of comfort with the autonomy of the silo world, and because change is threatening.

Strategic Drift

A significant risk is that the selective opportunism model creates strategic drift. Investment decisions are made incrementally in response to opportunities rather than directed by a vision. As a result, a firm can wake up one morning and find that it is in a set of businesses that lack the needed assets and competencies and that provide few synergies. A related problem is that an organization well suited to finding and pursuing opportunities can generate more projects than can be adequately funded, and at the extreme the lack of resources can doom all of them.

At least three phenomena can turn opportunism into strategic drift. First, a short-lived, transitory force may be mistaken for one with enough staying power to make a strategic move worthwhile. Second, opportunities to create immediate profits, perhaps from specialized customer applications, may be rationalized as strategic when in fact they are not. For example, a firm making instruments such as oscilloscopes might receive many requests from some of its customers for special-purpose instruments that could conceivably be used by other customers but that have little strategic value for the company. Third, expected synergies across existing and new business areas may fail to materialize owing to implementation problems, perhaps due to culture clashes, or because the synergies were only illusions in the first place.

The *selective* aspect of selective opportunities helps reduce the risk of drift and also the excessive numbers of projects. The opportunistic firm needs to screen opportunities in two ways. One screen involves eliminating those opportunities that lack the potential to create new categories and subcategories that the firm can dominate and leverage. The ability to screen out the mediocre and the losers will help reduce destructive drift. Evaluation needs to be ongoing. Some projects may cling to life even when their success probability fades, making the resource constraint worse.

A second screen is strategic. There should be an overarching strategy, as there was at GE, to make sure that each opportunity fits into the emerging sets of assets and competencies of the firm. The strategy need not be set in stone. It can evolve and allow for new platforms of growth. But those new platforms should represent substantial potential with acceptable risk to get resources.

Dynamic Strategic Commitment

At some point a new concept and its associated new category or subcategory may have enough promise to gain strategic commitment, and the organization needs to be willing to make that commitment. Nearly all successful new brands that changed the marketplace have earned organizational commitment even when there were developmental, competitive, and market uncertainties still lingering. Certainly a commitment to a clearly defined business strategy was behind the success of Google, the Walmart environmental initiatives, and many others. And the willingness to bet the farm by expanding capacity was crucial to the success of Asahi Super Dry, the Chrysler minivan, Starbucks, and so on. There are many firms that lost the opportunity of a generation because they were willing to put their toes in the water but could not take the plunge.

Strategic commitment needs to be dynamic, which means that it should not be locked in stone. The portfolio of projects should always be subject to change, because some have prospects that fade and others emerge that are more promising. So there is a yin and yang around commitment. True commitment is needed, but it is not forever without qualification.

Strategic commitment, a passionate, disciplined loyalty to a clearly defined and resourced business strategy and a new category or subcategory, involves a long-term perspective. In investment decisions and strategy development, the focus is on the future. There is a commitment to the success of the business and an organization willing to supply the needed resources to build assets and competencies and to execute the strategy. The planning horizon may extend two, five, or more than ten years into the future depending on the type of business.

Google established its position with a commitment to building and operating the best search engine when its competitors, such as Yahoo and Microsoft, were expanding their services in order to drive traffic and exploit customer visits. Google had a single-minded focus on the search engine guided by a ten-point philosophy that includes several core values such as the following: [8]

> "It's best do one thing really, really well. We do Search."
>
> "Focus on the user (and user experience) and all else will follow."
>
> "Fast is better than slow."
>
> "Great is good enough, it's a starting point."

The result was a leadership position with a product that featured a simple interface, fast loading, placement of search outputs based on popularity rather than bribes, and advertising that appears to be relevant to the user's search.

Leadership

To successfully execute a commitment strategy, leadership is required at several levels. There needs to be an internal offering champion with passion, a clear strategic vision, and an ability to communicate to his or her team an understanding of and enthusiasm for what the strategy is and why it is persuasive, achievable, and worthwhile. In particular, the team should know and believe in the components of the strategy, the value proposition, the target market, the functional strategies, and the role of assets and competencies. The business rationale should be about more than achieving financial objectives; there should be a purpose that is valued if not inspirational.

Also critical is the support of the CEO. It is rather amazing how frequently a branded offering that successfully established a new category or subcategory is supported by a CEO that has a strong strategic vision, a commitment to the strategy, and, a willingness to fund the development and execution of the offering. In many cases, such as with the Apple products, Segway, the Chrysler minivan, Asahi Super Dry, Muji, Whole Foods Market, Prius, Saturn, and Enterprise, the CEO was also the offering champion or a close partner. There have been countless efforts to disrupt the marketplace, and perhaps existing businesses, that failed or got killed because the CEO never supported the strategy. Recall the efforts to create a minivan winner at Ford that were frustrated by a CEO who did not climb aboard the minivan initiative.

Obsession with Execution

Most new offerings fail, often because a good concept was simply not executed well. The organization needs to be set up to excel in a host of tasks, which means that competent, motivated people need to be in place, the right resources need to be made available, and the systems and culture need support the effort. Among the key tasks are:

Designing the Offering. The offering starts with the functional and aesthetic design. If the offering is not well designed, it does not matter how flawlessly it is produced and serviced. The Chrysler minivan, the Prius, the iPod—all had designs that worked. If there were problems these were easily corrected by tweaking the designs.

Introducing the Offering into the Marketplace. The introduction of a new offering is no longer about spending money and turning the crank. The fragmented media, information overload, the clutter, and the reality of social technology mean that the introduction of even the most impressive and novel offering needs to be in the hands of talented and creative professionals who are willing to think outside the box and then execute.

Managing by Customer-Driven Objectives and Metrics. The culture and systems of the organization need to support a commitment to deliver on the promise and, when possible, to provide an offering that exceeds expectations. Toward that end a key element is to determine what customer-driven metrics, including visibility, understanding, and loyalty measures, are needed to reflect the new category or subcategory.

Continuous Improvement

In addition to execution, a commitment strategy needs to be supported by incremental innovation, continually improving (rather than changing) the offering, reducing the cost, improving efficiency, enhancing the value proposition, increasing customer satisfaction, and strengthening the assets and competencies that underlie the new offering. The offering and the category and subcategory should be a moving target, evolving and improving over time. Each year should see an enhancement of the offering and its profitability. Japanese firms such as Shiseido or Canon call this continuous improvement *kaizen* and have built successful companies around it.

Creating Substantial and Transformational Innovation from the Core

Strategic commitment and opportunism can live together when a core business in a decentralized firm actively looks to create subcategories. The business looks to substantial and transformational innovation, but within the category. The resulting offerings would draw on existing assets, including brand assets; competencies; and market knowledge, and are likely to have less market and organizational risk than offerings that venture away from core businesses. The fact that a core business is close to the market and to the technology of the offering means that the business has a big advantage in both identifying and responding to opportunities.

A good example is P&G's Tide, which has had an average of one incremental innovation a year for some sixty years but has also aggressively developed substantial and transformational offerings that have served to define clear subcategories for which Tide has enjoyed significant price premiums, loyalty, and barriers to competitors. There was liquid Tide in 1984, Tide with Bleach in 1989, Tide High Efficiency (HE) in 1997, Tide with Febreze in 1998, Tide with a Touch of Downey and Tide Coldwater in 2004, plus several others that might also be classified as transformational. Tide Coldwater, for example, during its first few years, was used as an energy-saving product in seven million American households.[9] Tide increased its share of the detergent market from around 20 percent in the early 1980s to over 40 percent with a series of new offerings, each of which created a new subcategory.

The Tide effort was in large part due to the Innovation Leadership Team that was formed within Tide to create new momentum.[10] Spanning functions, it included people from sales, brand management, operations, finance, and more. The charge was to identify some ten new Tide ideas each quarter, ones that would potentially transform the marketplace.

Strategic Stubbornness

There is the risk that strategic commitment will turn into strategic stubbornness. A lot can go wrong. The vision surrounding the commitment may become obsolete or faulty, and its pursuit may be a wasteful exercise. There may be implementation barriers in design or in execution. The new offering may be undercut by another paradigm shift, perhaps brought about by a competitor's innovation. If the strategic commitment is pushed by the top executives it can result in overinvestment and premature market entry, which may be difficult to reverse.

That happened with Apple's Newton, mentioned earlier, the PDA that was ahead of its time when launched in 1993 with handwriting recognition that did not work. One of the biggest failures in consumer electronics, its impact on Apple was larger than it should have been because of a huge commitment that not only had resulted in up-front investment but also kept the product alive for five full years until Steve Jobs arrived and killed it.

The term *dynamic strategic commitment* implies that the commitment is not forever. Is the new business meeting the target goals? Is the mature business experiencing any changes in the marketplace that shift the assumptions underlying the commitment? If so, the commitment strategy might be changed to using resources less aggressively or even exercising a milk or exit option.

Dynamic strategic commitment is self-contradictory in that a true commitment would not have a dynamic element to it. The fact that a commitment is reviewable means that it is not firm and raises logical and organizational complications. The solution, in part, is a credible organization-wide resource allocation system, a topic to which we now turn.

Organization-Wide Resource Allocation

An innovative organization needs to have a third characteristic in addition to being selectively opportunistic and having dynamic strategic commitment. It must be capable of allocating resources through a process that is disciplined, objective, and organization-wide and that actually precipitates hard decisions that will get implemented. Resource allocation is indispensable to a viable innovative organization because it provides a way to make sure that the best options are funded. There are limited resources in any organization, and funding low-yield offerings, be they existing or proposed, will suck resources away from offerings that could mean the future.

However, inserting hard-nosed resource allocation into an organization is not easy. Managers are used to having proposals evaluated in a limited context and can be threatened by a broader competitive set in which the power of their silo units is muted. Even the basic elements, such as common criteria and processes discussed in Chapter Seven, are not easy to accept.

An effective allocation process should have several characteristics. It should be both clear so that managers know when and how to access it and it should be supported by a team with credibility so that decisions will be respected. It should have an organization-wide scope; a proposed new offering should compete with others across the organization. If the evaluation lacks a broad scope, then inevitably some inferior options will be funded at the expense of better choices that lacked the right context or political backing. Finally, it should compare new offerings with existing ones. The key can be to stop or slow down resources going to tired businesses that have limited growth potential or, worse, are realistically only able to reduce an inevitable decline.

Bias Against the New Business

There is nearly always a significant bias toward funding existing businesses. Chapter Seven discussed the personal and professional reasons to cling to a business that is fading and has little chance of recovering. However, even successful core businesses can stand in the way of a new offering with the potential to transform a market getting adequate funding. There will be biases against the risky new venture that go beyond economic analysis. The organization will often reject a proposed new offering just as a body will reject a transmitted organ: it recognizes that it is foreign, that it does not belong. This reaction will often occur even in the face of an expressed need for the organization to develop new growth platforms that will be the lifeblood of the future. There are several organizational issues or "curses" that champions of innovative new offerings need to recognize and counter in some way.

One issue might be called the "stick-to-your-knitting curse" or the curse of commitment to a core business. Successful incumbent firms focus on their core businesses, investing vigorously in incremental innovation to reduce costs, improve the offering, and satisfy their loyal customers. As a result:

- They are so focused that they fail to see opportunities even when they are obvious.

- If there is any chance that the new business will cannibalize the core business, the new business will have a natural, powerful enemy. Why invest in an offering that may kill the golden goose?

- The capabilities of the core business tend to be applied to whatever new business comes along, even if that is a recipe for failure. Intel's Craig Barrett called its microprocessor business the creosote bush, after a desert plant that poisons the ground around it to prevent other plants from growing, because of this phenomenon. Out of some fourteen ventures started during the 1990s at Intel, the only one that really paid off, Intel Capital, involved investments but no operating responsibility which means that Intel was unable to move beyond its basic business model.[11]

Then there is the "curse of success." When times are good and the business is doing well, resources should be available to take risks and create new business areas. Curiously, however, complacency usually wins the day. Why change if the current business is generating growth and profits? Why not instead invest in a sure thing to make the costs even lower and the profits even higher? It is much easier to change when there is a crisis, although in a crisis both resources and time may be in short supply. Crisis conditions enabled the Chrysler minivan to live and the Walmart environmental initiative to happen. In the absence of a real crisis, an artificial one can sometimes be created, as the CEO of Toyota did when he mandated that the Prius be designed in two years.

Another is the "competing story curse." Nearly every executive in the organization will have a list of investments that are worthwhile, even indispensable, for his or her silo business. Many if not most will represent incremental innovations. A proposed new offering, particularly a game changer, will compete for those resources. An array of political forces can line up against commitment to a project that would draw resources away from the alternatives especially if the new offering involves a different culture, market, or operations.

These three curses just described are all magnified by the pressure to create short-term growth and margins, in part driven by the desire for stock returns and in part driven by managers with short job tenures. Short-term results can best be obtained by diverting R&D funds to supporting strategic growth to efforts to enhance the core businesses by improving the attractiveness and performance of the offering and increasing efficiency and productivity. Creating a new business platform is risky and expensive and likely to result in a short-term financial pain.

Venture Capital

To determine support for innovation in a firm, follow the money. In most cases, existing core businesses have the power, are generating the current profits, and get to use those profits to support their incremental innovation agenda even while starving the potential businesses of the future. To counter this bias, firms create internal venture capital funds.

A venture capital fund with a screening process to select offerings to finance can not only provide secure funding but also help elevate the innovation proposals. Champions can be encouraged by the screening process and by guidance from senior executives to have more professional and complete plans. Further, a firm-spanning screening group can make suggestions as to how a proposal can be linked to capabilities in the organization.

P&G has the Corporate Innovation Fund (CIF), which resembles a venture capital firm and specializes in high-risk, high-reward ideas.[12] Lead by the CIO and CFO, the fund is in place to provide seed money for projects with the potential to create major disruptive innovations. Completely separate from business units, it is free to focus on innovations that span business units or find white space between business units. Crest Whitestrips, introduced in 2001, for example, combined the film technology from corporate R&D with the bleach technology from the laundry group to provide a teeth-whitening treatment for the oral-care group. None of these groups would have sponsored the innovation effort on their own.

Another unit at P&G, Future Works, consists of multidisciplinary teams that instead of reacting to proposals seek out innovation opportunities inside and outside P&G unconstrained by existing categories.[13] The unit is free to explore radical ideas to create new categories or subcategories. For example, Future Works, stimulated a P&G joint venture with Swiss Precision Diagnostics or at-home health-monitoring devices, a venture that never would have been championed by an existing business unit. Each initiative has a sponsor with the P&G organization so it will not get too far afield and will have a link into at least one existing P&G business.

A major business group within HP created the Innovation Program Office (IPO) in order to support the development of innovative new products that were significant departures from existing ones.[14] One output was the Blackbird computer for high-end gaming. A key question used to screen proposals is whether this product has the potential to fundamentally change the competitive landscape or create new consumer demand. The program's target is to develop two new products each year. Achieving that goal means that many more have to enter the pipeline. The IPO review board spent about $100 thousand on each of twenty products to get them to the point of getting customer feedback. Seven of eight proposals will pass to the prototype stage, four will go from prototype to limited launch, and two will be commercialized.

Skunk Works

Another tactic is to create or allow a separate organization to develop a concept. Termed a *skunk works*, it is a development program that operates outside the firm, perhaps in a different location, in order to protect it from a culture and processes that may inhibit its progress. A skunk works is helpful when a project has potential, at least in the eyes of some, but cannot get official support and funding, perhaps because it is off-strategy, it is perceived as technologically deficient, or the market is considered inadequate. The firm may tolerate a skunk works with a modest or no budget.

Tide was developed in a skunk works that operated under the radar for years. The flash memory product, developed at Intel in the early 1980s with little management support, was also created in a skunk works. Intel at the time was focused on funding a different, established memory product and microprocessors, and they did not believe that flash memory had as much potential, a belief that turned out to be wrong.

The skunk works model has a role to play but should be used sparingly and when other options are precluded. A skunk works will often find it difficult to access the knowledge, capabilities, and assets that are spread throughout the organization. Also, it necessarily will be operating on a reduced budget and may, as a result, make progress slower than would a more resourced effort. Too many skunk works will negate the strengths embodied in the whole organization.

Centralized Resource Allocation

Because of its broad scope, an effective resource allocation process needs to have highly centralized control over budgeting. Such control stresses the organization. Organizational silos used to having life-and-death funding decisions under their control will resist seeing some or all of that control move to a central entity, no matter how logical the change might be. Personal careers are tied up in businesses. Those in charge of the silo units will argue that their success depends on maintaining independence and the ability to use the profits generated for their own purposes. They also observe that decentralization with autonomous business units provides the firm with accountability; vitality; intimacy with the offerings and customers; and the ability to manage a large, diverse organization. There is a reason why it is the modal organizational form.

But centralized control of funding is indispensible to the firm's ability to fund and support innovations that are not within the purview of an existing business or are too ambitious to be funded by a current core business. There needs to be an objective process and executives with the authority, the credibility, and the wisdom to make the hard decisions, including the tough defunding and no-go decisions. There should be a venue in which champions can argue their cases for business proposals, but also a time for people to commit and work toward the success of the selected proposals.[15]

Strategic Stifling of Ideas

Centralization of resource allocation is theoretically healthy in that it can lead to optimal allocation, which is practically impossible in an organization with autonomous decision making. The criteria used to evaluate proposals will be guided by an overall firm strategy, as in the GE case, with a specific strategic direction. A centralized process will also have well-defined financial hurdles that will apply to all potential initiatives.

However, centralized resource allocation has its own risks. Some initiatives may not fit into the firm's overall strategy or may not have pessimistic sales and profit expectations because they are unfamiliar or a needed innovation may seem unlikely. Because the central decision body is not intimate with the area, it may be hard to recognize potential success.

This book started by observing that brand relevance has the potential to both drive and explain market dynamics, the emergence and fading of categories and subcategories and the associated fortunes of brands connected to them. It went on to note that brands that can create and manage new categories or subcategories making competitors irrelevant will prosper while others will be mired in debilitating marketplace battles or will lose relevance and market positions.

These observations should now have more meaning as during the course of the book, the links between market dynamics and brand relevance have been shown, often dramatically. Dozens of case studies have illustrated how new categories and subcategories have been formed and how brands as a result have prospered or, sometimes, failed to realize the potential. A systematic approach toward creating new categories or subcategories involved finding a concept, evaluation, defining and managing the category or subcategory, and creating barriers to competition has been introduced. The concept of fighting a slide to irrelevance by connecting to emerging categories and subcategories and by energizing the brand was discussed.

The challenge is to do it. To innovate. To create and connect to new categories and subcategories. And to reap the benefits of reduced competition.

Of course, it is not easy. The Epilogue summarizes why by putting the opportunity and challenges into perspective.

Key Takeaways

To generate innovation, there needs to be a supporting organization with three rather contradictory qualities. The organization needs:

- Selective opportunism: good, ongoing, external intelligence; the ability to detect and understand trends; the willingness to engage in substantial and transformational innovation; and the agility to pounce on opportunities when they arise but to do so selectively. Evaluation processes and strategic guidance inhibit drift.
- Dynamic strategic commitment: the willingness to focus on, to fund, and to execute behind an opportunity and to engage in incremental innovation. The commitment needs to be dynamic in that it allows for withdrawing from disappointing ventures rather than being stubborn.
- Organization-wide resource allocation so that initiatives that do not fit into powerful business units can receive resources. This depends on having an evaluation tool that is applied to all businesses within the organization, including those that have already received commitment.

For Discussion

1. Consider GE's innovation initiatives. What is the downside?
2. Identify organizations that are very opportunistic. Identify those that are committed.

3. What is the difference between opportunism and commitment? How can both reside in the same organization?

4. Organization-wide resource allocation involves centralizing that function. Do both opportunism and commitment work best in a decentralized organization? If so, what are the problems associated with implementing organization-wide resource allocation?

Epilogue

THE YIN AND YANG OF THE RELEVANCE BATTLE

It ain't over till it's over.
—*Yogi Berra*

The market dynamics and strategic options discussed in this book need to be placed in perspective. There is a yin and yang connected to the battle to create or maintain brand relevance and to make competitors irrelevant. The downside as well as the upside of a relevance driven strategy should be on the table.

It is true that creating new categories and subcategories often involves a huge payoff. Competition without competitors or with reduced or weakened competitors is a lot more profitable than fighting a brand preference war and, in addition, is a lot more pleasant. Even if the period of enjoying a hospitable competitive arena is limited, it may still create a profit flow, market momentum, and customer base that will pay off as the competitors become relevant.

It is true that the incidence of firms succeeding in creating market spaces with little or no competition is high. There are dozens of such cases explored in this book, but these represent a small fraction of those that exist. A set of cases similar to the Chrysler minivan, Enterprise Rent-A-Car, Yoplait's Go-Gurt, SoBe, Muji, Zara, the iPod, and Asahi Super Dry can be found in most industries. Further, the incidence of new categories and subcategories emerging is increasing as markets become more dynamic.

It is true that avoiding or missing an opportunity to engage in a disruptive innovation often means not only a loss of profits and market position but also that competitors will likely seize that opportunity. As a result, disruption of the existing market will still occur, and that will necessitate either an expensive effort to catch up or a decline or demise of a business. It is very possible, as a result of such a failure to act, to wake up one morning not relevant because customers are no longer buying what you are making or are perceived to be making. It is much better to be the trend driver than the trend responder or the firm that ignores trends.

Creating an organization that will support innovation and invest in new concepts that involve risk and uncertain prospects will be worthwhile.

However, some perspective is needed.

Creating new categories or subcategories is not easy. For a given firm, the opportunity does not arise on a regular basis.

It is difficult to find a concept that has the potential to create a new category or subcategory. It can take insight that is not natural for a firm focused on improving the current strategy by increasing the value proposition or decreasing the cost.

Evaluation is difficult. Concepts evolve over time, and it is easy to terminate one prematurely just before a key breakthrough occurs. Changing customer needs and preferences, technological advances, or competitor actions are hard to predict and can change basic assumptions.

Even with a winning concept, it is not easy to gain organizational commitment to a new concept in the face of uncertainties and alternative investments. One appealing option, to foster incremental innovation in the current business areas, will have more certain returns. Further, there are political barriers that go beyond the objective analysis as silo business units resist initiatives that potentially deprive them of resources. The timing can be off. A firm can promote an initiative that is premature, acting before the market or the technology is ready. Or the firm can react to an opportunity too late. If there is one generalization from this whole book, it is that timing is crucial. Even being a bit early or a bit late can be fatal. And it is not easy to be there and ready at exactly the right time.

Implementation is difficult, especially when it involves programs and capabilities unfamiliar to the organization that then have to be acquired or learned.

Market acceptance is uncertain. Even the best concepts with sound logic around demand potential can disappoint. The market response can be less than expected, or the response can be good but the market too small.

Even when an offering is successful, the firm could have failed to create barriers, in which case the success will be short-lived and the advantage in creating the new category or subcategory will be modest and perhaps too small to justify the investment.

In summary, the effort to develop an offering that will create a new category or subcategory can be uncertain and risky. If it should fail, significant investment in resources and time that could have been spent elsewhere could be wasted. Even worse, the initiative may have been important enough to distort the strategic direction of the firm.

Because engaging in innovation is uncertain, risky, and expensive does not mean that a firm should not be aggressively innovative and invest in organizational change to become more supportive of innovation. The fact is that it is also risky to be a trend responder and an even greater risk to be a trend-unaware firm, one with such tunnel vision that the firm does not sense or chooses to ignore market dynamics.

The message is to be aggressively innovative but with recognition of the challenges and investment required in both individual projects and organizational changes. The successful organization will actively manage the difficulties and uncertainties of innovation, which will allow it to seize opportunities to make competitors irrelevant or less relevant and avoid seeing a healthy business drift into irrelevance.

Notes

Chapter One

1. From a talk given by Ken Olsen at the 1977 World Future Organization in Boston. He actually was referring to the computerization of a home, which only recently is becoming possible, but it has been widely interpreted to mean the PC.
2. Steve Jobs in a talk introducing the Macintosh in January of 1984.
3. David Halthaus, "P&G Chief: Have a Purpose in Life." November 18, 2009, http://news.cincinnati.com.
4. Sun Tzu, *The Art of War* (Simon & Brown, 2010), Chapter Six, point 30.
5. Peter N. Golder and Gerard J. Tellis, "Pioneer Advantage: Marketing Logic or Marketing Legend?" *Journal of Marketing Research*, 1993, 30(2), 158–170.
6. Dan P. Lovallo and Lenny T. Mendonca, "Strategy's Strategist: An Interview with Richard Rumelt," *McKinsey Quarterly*, 2007, 4, 58.
7. Richard Foster and Sarah Kaplan, *Creative Destruction* (New York: Doubleday, 2001), 158–170.
8. Chris Zook with James Allen, *Profit from the Core: Growth Strategy in an Era of Turbulence* (Boston: Harvard Business School Press, 2001), 11.
9. Ibid, 8.
10. W. Chan Kim and Renee Mauborgne, *Blue Ocean Strategy* (Boston: Harvard Business School Press, 2005).

11. Ashish Sood and Gerard J. Tellis, "Do Innovations Really Pay off? Total Stock Market Returns to Innovation" *Marketing Science*, 2009, *28*(3), 442–458.

12. Carl Schramm, Robert Litan, and Dane Strangler, "New Business, Not Small Business, Is What Creates Jobs," *Wall Street Journal*, November 6, 2009.

13. Susan Nelson, "Who's Really Innovative," *Marketing Daily*, September 2, 2008, www.mediapost.com/publications.

14. W. Chan Kim and Renee Mauborgne, *Blue Ocean Strategy* (Boston: Harvard Business School Press, 2005); Andrew Campbell and Robert Park, *The Growth Gamble* (London: Nicholas Brealey, 2005); Gary Hamel, *Leading the Revolution* (Boston: Harvard Business School Press, 2002); Chris Zook, *Beyond the Core* (Boston: Harvard Business School Press, 2004); Michael L. Tushman and Charles A. O'Reilly III, *Winning Through Innovation* (Boston: Harvard Business School Press, 2002).

Chapter Two

1. Joel B. Cohen and Kunal Basu, "Alternative Models of Categorization: Toward a Contingent Processing Framework," *Journal of Consumer Research*, March 1987, *14*, 455–472.

2. Mita Sujan, "Consumer Knowledge: Effects on Evaluation Strategies Mediating Consumer Judgments." *Journal of Consumer Research*, June 1985, *12*, 31–46.

3. Eleanor Rosch, "Principles of Categorization." In Eleanor Rosch and Barbara B. Lloyd (eds.), *Cognition and Categorization* (Hillsdale, NJ: Lawrence Erlbaum, 1978), 27–48.

4. C. Page Moreau, Arthur B. Markman, and Donald R. Lehmann, "'What Is It?' Categorization Flexibility and Consumers' Response to Really New Products," *Journal of Consumer Research*, March 2000, *26*, 489–498.

5. S. Ratneshwar, Cornelia Pechmann, and Allan D. Shocker, "Goal-Derived Categories and the Antecedents of

Across-Category Consideration," *Journal of Consumer Research*, December 1996, *23*, 240–250.

6. George Lakoff, *Don't Think of An Elephant!* (White River Junction, VT: Chelsea Green, 2004).

7. Lakoff, *Don't Think of An Elephant!* xvii.

8. I. P. Levin and G. J. Gaeth, "Framing of Attribute Information Before and After Consuming the Product," *Journal of Consumer Research*, March 1988, *15*, 374–378.

9. Jennifer Aaker, Kathleen Vohs, and Cassie Mogilner, "Non-Profits Are Seen as Warm and For-Profits as Competent: Firm Stereotypes Matter," *Journal of Consumer Research*, 2010.

10. Dan Ariely, George Lowenstein, and Drazen Prelec, "Coherent Arbitrariness: Stable Demand Curves Without Stable Preferences," *Quarterly Journal of Economics*, 2003, *118*(1), 73–105.

11. Dan Ariely, *Predictably Irrational* (New York: Harper Books, 2008), 162–163.

12. Ibid.

13. David Aaker and Douglas Stayman, "A Micro Approach to Studying Feeling Responses to Advertising: The Case of Warmth." In Julie A. Edell and Tony M. Dubitsky (eds.), *Emotion in Advertising* (New York: Quorum Books, 1990), 54–68.

14. Brian Wansink, *Mindless Eating* (New York: Bantam Books, 2006), 19–23.

15. Itamar Simonson and Amos Tversky, "Choice in Context: Tradeoff Contrast and Extremeness Aversion," *Journal of Marketing Research*, August 1992, *29*, 281–295.

16. Susan M Steiner and Rayna Bailey, "Its Not Delivery, It's DiGiorno," *Kraft Foods, Inc.* Retrieved May 9, 2010, from www.jiffynotes.com.

17. Amos Tversky, "Utility Theory and Additive Analysis of Risky Choices," *Journal of Experimental Psychology*, 1967, *75*(1), 27–36.

18. James R. Bettman, Mary Frances Luce, & John W. Payne, "Constructive Consumer Choice Processes," *Journal of Consumer Research*, December 1998, 187–217.

19. Herbert Simon, "A Behavioral Model of Rational Choice," *Quarterly Journal of Economics*, 1995, 6, 99–118.

20. Joel Huber and Norren M. Klein, "Adapting Cut-offs to the Choice Environment: The Effects of Attribute Correlation and Reliability," *Journal of Consumer Research*, December 1991, 346–357.

Chapter Three

1. Caroline Roux, "The Reign of Spain," *Guardian*, October 28, 2003.

2. Jackie Crosby, "Entrepreneur Turned Geek Squad into a Geek Army," *Los Angeles Times*, April 1, 2010, www.Latimes.com.

3. Jackie Crosby, "Geek Squad a Killer App for Best Buy," *The Seattle Times*, April 5, 2010, www.seattletimes.nwsource.com.

4. Matthew Boyle, "Best Buy's Giant Gamble," *Fortune*, April 3, 2006, 69–75.

5. Marc Gunther, "Best Buy Wants Your Junk," *Fortune*, December 7, 2009, 96–100.

6. Subway Web site, July 2010, www.subway.com, retrieved July 2010.

7. Duane Swierczynski, "Stupid Diets . . . That Work!" *Men's Health*, November 1999, *14*(9), 94–98.

8. Subway Web site, November 2009, www.subway.com, retrieved July 2010.

Chapter Four

1. "GM, Toyota Bet Hybrid Green," *Wall Street Journal*, December 12, 2006.

2. Chris Isidore, "GM: Hybrid Cars Make No Sense," *CNN Money*, January 5, 2004. See www.money.cnn.com/2004.

3. "Lexus 400," Toyota50th.com/history.htm, 2009, 1.

4. "2010 Toyota Prius Hybrid Car," www.SoulTek.com, August 30, 2009.

5. Micheline Maynard, "Say 'Hybrid' and Many People Will Hear 'Prius,'" *New York Times*, July 4, 2007.

6. David Welch, "Honda's Prius-Fighter Is Stuck in First," *BusinessWeek*, December 28, 2009, 94.

7. Roger B. Smith, statement at Saturn news conference, January 8, 1985.

8. Chrysler Minivan Sales Slump Forces Job Cuts," March 5, 2009, www.asiaone.com/motoring/news.

9. J. D. Power and Associates, *Sales Report*, August 2009.

10. Paul Ingrassia and Joseph B. White, *Comeback: The Fall and Rise of the American Automobile Industry* (New York: Simon & Schuster, 1995).

11. Paul G. McLaughlin, *Ford Station Wagons* (Hudson, Wisc.: Iconografix, 2003).

12. Jason Vuic, *The Yugo: The Rise and Fall of the Worst Car in History* (New York: Hill and Wang, 2010).

13. Carol J. Loomis, "The Big Surprise Is Enterprise," *Fortune*, July 24, 2006, 142. See http://ow.ly/2mLJ8.

14. Ibid.

15. "Green Benefits, Zipcan.com," April 24, 2010. www.zipcar.com/is-it/greenbenefits.

16. Scott Griffith, "Zipcar," *Advertising Age*, November 16, 2009, 16.

17. Brendan Conway, "Car Sharing Attracts Large Rental Agencies," *Wall Street Journal*, March 24, 2010.

Chapter Five

1. Nathan Pritikin and Patrick M. McGrady, *The Pritikin Program of Diet and Exercise* (New York: Bantam Books, 1979).

2. *Dr. Dean Ornish's Program for Reversing Heart Disease* (New York: Ballantine Books, 1990).

3. Ancel Keys, "Coronary Heart Disease in Seven Countries," *Circulation*, April 1970, *4*, 381–395.

4. U.S. Senate Select Committee on Nutrition and Human Needs, *Dietary Goals for the United States* (2nd ed.) (Washington D.C.: U. S. Government Printing Office, 1977).

5. Gary Taubes, "The Soft Science of Dietary Fat," *Science*, March 2001, *291*, 2536–2545.

6. Nabisco has been a part of Kraft since 2002.

7. "Dreyer's Develops Revolutionary 'Slow Churned' Technology That Makes Light Ice Cream Taste as Good as the Full-Fat Variety," *Business Wire*, January 22, 2004.

8. See, for example, Paris Reidhead, "How About Some Genetically Engineered Fish Proteins in Your Breyer's Ice Cream?" *Milkweed* (Wisconsin Dairy Farmer Magazine), December 2006, www.organicsconsumers.org.

9. Eric C. Westman, Stephen D. Phinney, and Jeff S. Volek, *A New Atkins, A New You* (New York: Touchstone/Fireside, 2010).

10. Arthur Agatston and Marie Almon, *The South Beach Diet* (New York: St. Martin's Press, 2003).

11. General Mills, *Annual Report*, 2005.

12. Karlene Lukovitz, "IRI Ranks '09 Top Product Launches," *Marketing Daily*, March 23, 2010, www.mediapost.com/publications.

Chapter Six

1. An excellent reference for the iPod story is Steven Levy, *The Perfect Thing* (New York: Simon & Schuster, 2007).

2. Erik Sherman, "Inside the Apple iPod Design Triumph" (cover story), *DesignChain*, Summer, 2002, www.designchain.com/coverstory.asp?issue=summer02.

3. Sea-Jin Chang, *Sony vs. Samsung* (Singapore: Wiley, 2008).

4. Daniel Lyons, "Think Really Different," *Newsweek*, March 26, 2010, www.newsweek.com/2010/03/25.

5. Tom Kelly, *The Art of Innovation* (New York: Doubleday, 2001), 55–62.

6. Eric von Hippel, "Lead Users: A Source of Novel Product Concepts," *Management Science*, July 1986, *32*(7), 791–805.

7. Richard J. Harrington and Anthony K. Tjan, "Transforming Strategy One Customer at a Time," *Harvard Business Review*, March 2008, 86, 62–72.

8. Spencer E. Ante, "The Science of Desire," *BusinessWeek*, June 5, 2006, 99–106.

9. G. Lafley and Ram Charan, *The Game Changer* (New York: Crown Business, 2008), 47–49.

10. Grant McCracken, *Chief Culture Officer* (New York: Basic Books, 2006), 120–131.

11. Kelly, *The Art of Innovation*, 30.

12. Catherine Clarke Fox, "Drinking Water: Bottled or from the Tap?" February 14, 2008, http://kids.nationalgeographic.com/kids/stories/spacescience/water-bottle-pollution/.

13. Lafley and Charan, *The Game Changer*, 43–44.

14. Ram Charan, "Sharpening Your Business Acumen," *Strategy & Business*, Spring 2006, *44*, 49–57.

15. "First Break All the Rules," *Economist*, April 17, 2010, 7.

16. "The Power to Disrupt," *Economist*, April 17, 2010, 17.

17. Jeffrey R. Immelt, Vijay Govendarajan, and Chris Trimble, "How GE Is Disrupting Itself," *Harvard Business Review*, October 2009, 63.

18. Lafley and Charan, *The Game Changer*, 131–137.

19. Lafley and Charan, *The Game Changer*, 134.

20. Andrew Razeghi, *The Riddle* (San Francisco: Jossey-Bass, 2008), 21.

21. Robert I. Sutton, *Weird Ideas That Work* (New York: Free Press, 2002), 26.

22. Ibid, 28.

23. Jeroen Molenaar, "Unilever R&D Chief Seeks a Swiffer Repeat of Polman," Bloomberg.com, November 16, 2009, http://ow.ly/2mV5O.

Chapter Seven

1. John Heilemann, "Reinventing the Wheel," *Time*, December 2, 2001, 85–86.
2. Heilemann, "Reinventing the Wheel," 86.
3. Gary Rivlin, "Segway's Breakdown," *Wired*, March 2003, http://ow.ly/2mWwR.
4. Wil Schroter "When to Dump That Great Idea," *Forbes*, July 6, 2007, http://ow.ly/2mWGa.
5. Nicole Perlroth, "Who Knew?" *Forbes*, August 24, 2009, 34, http://ow.ly/2mX8D.
6. Andrew Campbell and Robert Park, *The Growth Gamble* (London: Nicholas Brealey, 2005), 43.
7. A. G. Lafley and Ram Charan, *The Game Changer* (New York: Crown Business, 2008), 67.
8. Peter S. Cohan, *You Can't Order Change* (New York: Portfolio, 2008), 83–88.
9. Irma Zandl, "How to Separate Trends from Fads," *Brandweek*, October 23, 2000, 30–35.
10. Faith Popcorn and Lys Marigold, *Clicking* (New York: HarperCollins, 1997), 11–12.
11. Ben Casselman, "Trends Don't Favor Crocs," *Wall Street Journal*, March 19, 2009.
12. James Daly, "Sage Advice—Interview with Peter Drucker," *Business 2.0*, August 22, 2000, 134–143.
13. Steven P. Schnaars and Conrad Berenson, "Growth Market Forecasting Revisited: A Look Back at a Look Forward," *California Management Review*, Summer 1986, 28(4), 71–88.
14. Robert A. Burgelman, *Strategy Is Destiny* (New York: Free Press, 2002), 64.
15. Clark G. Gilbert and Matthew J. Eyring, "Beating the Odds When You Launch a New Venture, *Harvard Business Review*, May 2010, 87, 93–98.
16. Jacob Goldenberg and others, "Innovation: The Case of the Fosbury Flop," *MSI Working Paper Series*, no. 04–001 (2004).
17. "Our Company," www.mint.com/company/.

18. Andrew S. Grove, Keynote speech to the Academy of Management, San Diego, August 1998. http://ow.ly/2mYdj. The concept of the inflection point is also discussed in Andrew S. Grove, *Only the Paranoid Survive* (New York: Crown Business, 1996).

19. Andrew S. Grove, *Only the Paranoid Survive*, 32.

Chapter Eight

1. The material for the salesforce.com story is taken largely from the book by the founder, Marc Benioff, *Behind the Cloud* (San Francisco: Jossey-Bass, 2009).

2. Steve Hamm, "An eBay for Business Software," *Business Week*, September 19, 2005, http://ow.ly/2hell.

3. Steve Jobs, "Apple's One-Dollar-a-Year Man," *Fortune*, January 24, 2000, http://ow.ly/2hn7U.

4. James C. Anderson and James A. Narus, "Selectively Pursuing More of Your Customer's Business," *MIT Sloan Management Review*, Spring 2003, 43–49.

5. Rita Gunther McGrath and Ian C. MacMillan, "Market Busting," *Harvard Business Review*, March 2005, 83, 81–89.

6. Clayton M. Christensen, *The Innovator's Dilemma* (Boston: Harvard Business School Press, 1997); Clayton M. Christensen and Michael E. Raynor, *The Innovator's Solution* (Boston: Harvard Business School Press, 2003); Clayton M. Christensen, Scott D. Anthony, and Erik A. Roth, *Seeing What's Next* (Boston: Harvard Business School Press, 2004).

7. Aaron Baar, "Attraction to 'Do Good' Brands Is Escalating," *Marketing Daily*, October 21, 2009, www.mediapost.com/publications.

Chapter Nine

1. Much of the Yamaha story comes from a personal interview with Terry Lewis in May 2010.

2. Mark Walsh, "Study: Amazon Most Trusted Brand in U.S.," *Marketing Daily*, February 23, 2010, www.mediapost .com/publications.

3. Christopher Rosica, *The Authentic Brand* (South Paramus, NJ: Noble Press, 2007).

4. "Drivers of Authenticity," Authenticbrandindex.com, December 3, 2009, http://authenticbrandindex.com/what2 .htm.

5. Kariene Lukovitz, "EarthGrains Plots to Save the Earth," *Marketing Daily*, February 5, 2010, www.mediapost.com/ publications.

6. Gregory S. Carpenter, Rashi Glazer, and Kent Nakamoto, "Meaningful Brands from Meaningless Differentiation: The Dependence on Irrelevant Attributes," *Journal of Marketing Research*, August 1994, *31*, 339–350.

7. See Douglas Atken, "In Building Communities, Marketers Can Learn from Cults," Forbes.com, February 21, 2001, http://ow.ly/2mZyn.

Chapter Ten

1. Wal-Mart, *Annual Report*, 2005.

2. Marc Gunther, "The Green Machine," *Fortune*, August 7, 2006, 46.

3. Ibid. This article contains the 2005 part of the how sustainability came to Walmart, 44–48.

4. Walmart, *Annual Report*, 2009.

5. Susan Nelson, "Beyond Green," *Marketing Daily*, August 31, 2009, www.mediapost.com/publications.

6. Andrew S. Ross, "Green Project Making It Harder to Hate Walmart," SFGate.com, February 28, 2010, http://ow.ly/ 2n0LX; Rosabeth Moss Kanter, "Walmart's Environmental Game-Changer," March 22, 2010, http://ow.ly/2n0Cm.

7. Patrick Barwise and Sean Meehan, *Simply Better* (Boston: Harvard Business School Press, 2004).

8. Pallavi Gogoi and Michael Arndt, "Hamburger Hell," *BusinessWeek*, March 3, 2003,104–108.

9. Grainger David, "Can McDonald's Cook Again?" *Fortune*, April 14, 2003, 120–129.

10. John Gerzema and Ed Lebar, *The Brand Bubble* (San Francisco, Jossey-Bass, 2008), 16.

11. Kevin Lane Keller, *Strategic Brand Management* (3rd ed.) (Saddle River, NJ: Prentice-Hall, 2004), 317.

12. James Crimmins and Martin Horn, "Sponsorship: From Management Ego Trip to Marketing Success," *Journal of Advertising Research*, July–August 1996, 36, 11–21.

13. Ibid.

14. Kellie A. McElhaney, *Just Good Business* (San Francisco, Berrett-Koehler, 2008), Part II.

Chapter Eleven

1. An excellent picture of Jeff Immelt's early years at GE can be found in David Magee, *Jeff Immelt and the New GE Way* (New York: McGraw-Hill, 2009).

2. Shahira Raineri, "GE Imagination Breakthroughs," innovate1st-str.com, November 2007, http://ow.ly/2n18b.

3. *Jonah Bloom*, "GE: The Marketing Giant Lights Up with Imagination," *Creativity*, October 2005, 63.

4. Magee, *Jeff Immelt and the New GE Way*, 103.

5. Aaron Baar, "GE Launches 'healthymagination' Program," *Marketing Daily*, May 7, 2009, www.mediapost.com/publications.

6. Michael L. Tushman and Charles A. O'Reilly III, *Winning Through Innovation* (Boston: Harvard Business School Press, 2002).

7. David Aaker, *Spanning Silos* (Boston: Harvard Business School Press, 2009).

8. "Our Philosophy," Google.com, June 2010, www.google.com/corporate/tenthings.html.

9. A. G. Lafley and Ram Charan, *The Game Changer* (New York: Crown Business, 2008), 82–83.

10. Ibid, 82–83.

11. Andrew Campbell and Robert Park, *The Growth Gamble* (London: Nicholas Brealey, 2005), 44.

12. Lafley and Charan, *The Game Changer*, 122–123.

13. Ibid, 124–127.

14. Ibid, 123–124.

15. Robert A. Burgelman, *Strategy Is Destiny* (New York: Free Press, 2002), 103.

INDEX